Discovering t...
APPALACHIAN TRAIL

HELP US KEEP THIS GUIDE UP TO DATE

Every effort has been made by the authors and editors to make this guide as accurate and useful as possible. However, many things can change after a guide is published—trails are rerouted, regulations change, facilities come under new management, and so forth.

We would love to hear from you concerning your experiences with this guide and how you feel it could be improved and kept up to date. While we may not be able to respond to all comments and suggestions, we'll take them to heart, and we'll also make certain to share them with the author. Please send your comments and suggestions to the following address:

FalconGuides
Reader Response/Editorial Department
246 Goose Lane, Suite 200
Guilford, CT 06437

Or you may email us at:

editorial@GlobePequot.com

Thanks for your input, and happy trails!

Discovering the
APPALACHIAN TRAIL

A Guide to the Trail's Greatest Hikes

JOSHUA NIVEN and
AMBER ADAMS NIVEN

FALCON ®

Guilford, Connecticut

FALCON®

An imprint of Globe Pequot, the trade division of The Rowman & Littlefield
Publishing Group, Inc.
4501 Forbes Blvd., Ste. 200
Lanham, MD 20706
www.rowman.com

Falcon and FalconGuides are registered trademarks and Make Adventure Your Story
is a trademark of The Rowman & Littlefield Publishing Group, Inc.
Distributed by NATIONAL BOOK NETWORK

British Library Cataloguing in Publication Information available

Library of Congress Cataloging-in-Publication Data available
ISBN 978-1-4930-6070-2 (paper : alk. paper)
ISBN 978-1-4930-6071-9 (electronic)

∞™ The paper used in this publication meets the minimum requirements of American National Standard for Information Sciences—Permanence of Paper for Printed
Library Materials, ANSI/NISO Z39.48-1992.

The authors and The Rowman & Littlefield Publishing Group, Inc., assume no
liability for accidents happening to, or injuries sustained by, readers who engage
in the activities described in this book.

For
River Axel and Indie Oaks

Contents

Acknowledgments

This dream project was huge, and we have so many people to thank. We worked on the book for two years; however, many more hours and miles were clocked before we began "the work." How does one even begin to express seas of gratitude? I guess we would like to start by saying thanks in advance to you. You keep the wheels turning, the lights on, and make all of this matter. And if you are reading book acknowledgments, you're probably a pretty cool, curious, and caring individual—so thanks.

OK, then.

Thank you, to our families, for everything, always. Parents, grandparents, sisters, brothers, cousins—you make up the foundation that every artist dreams of having. Like a small army, you all come to our aid whenever we need you. We are so lucky to have a big, loving, hilarious, supportive family like you.

To Jay and Kyra, thanks for taking such good care of our spirited toddler and sweet baby girl. We are so lucky to have you in the cove. Giving birth during a snowstorm while writing a book is intense. Thanks for helping us navigate it all.

Thank you, Ryan Klinger, for the connection with Falcon Guides and for letting us use your beautiful elevation profiles. This wouldn't have happened without you.

Thanks to Falcon Guides and David Legere for believing in us and for answering our many "first-time author" questions.

Thank you, David Miller, for making the best technical guidebook on the Appalachian Trail and to AntiGravityGear for allowing us to publish snippets.

Thank you to our contributors who also happen to be our friends: Nick Brown, Jarred Douglas, Kevin Burk, Jamie Gault, Jen Toledo, Gary Sizer, Sarah Jones Decker, Rebecca Harnish, Sean Kamp, Michael Begansky, Danny Reed, and Evans Prater. Thanks for helping us create a book with a range of voices. We love you.

A very special thank-you to Mark Hylas for letting us use the Native Lands map and for jumping on board and delivering five more brilliant, artistic overview maps. So glad our trails crossed!

Thank you, Dan Webb, for your geology expertise and honest critique. I will never think of an exclamation point the same way again. Lillie, for all the things.

To the following people who were generous with their time and wisdom of the trail: Brian King at the Appalachian Trail Conservancy, Sanne Bagby at Earl Shaffer Foundation, Paige MacGregor at the ATC, Wendy K. Probst at the ATC, Pete Buak at Georgia Appalachian Trail Club, Daniel Chazin at New York–New Jersey Trail Conference, Joe Roman at AMC, Cosmo Catalano Jr. at AMC Western Mass Chapter,

Christopher R. Tripoli, Bew Davis, Greg Hoover, Warren Doyle, Leslie Stoltz, Debra Irwin, and Todd Elliott. And to Elise and Cori for proofing very early work. Thank you for helping us get things right. Any errors that remain are ours, not yours.

To the kindhearted Trail Angels and dedicated volunteers of the AT for restoring our faith in humanity and reminding us that there is so much goodness in the world. You are an inspiration to us. These people, in particular, helped us in significant ways during our hikes and beyond: Bill and Bobbie Jean Thomas, Miss Janet, Colleen King, and Regina and Rohun Anderson.

To Osprey Packs for making a fantastic baby carrier. (No, we aren't sponsored by them, and we don't receive anything by mentioning them. We are just really grateful for a product that allowed us to hike with our kids!)

Thank you to all The Thru Project supporters, donors, and hikers who contributed to supporting Josh on his thru-hike in 2013, helping him successfully create the backbone of what would eventually become *Discovering the Appalachian Trail*.

Lastly, thank you, Damascus, for putting on the Appalachian Trail Days festival and hosting such a special homecoming for us hikers. This is where Josh and I met, and it is a homecoming for our love every year.

See y'all on the trail!

Land Acknowledgment

When we walk on the Appalachian Trail, we are walking on Native Land, places where our nation's ancestors lived, worshipped, gave birth, built homes, hunted, and foraged. The AT travels through twenty-two Native Nations' traditional territories. These indigenous communities were the original stewards of the Appalachians before they were brutally forced to leave, separating them from the land, one another, and their culture.

The map below highlights the traditional territories of Native Nations along the Appalachian Trail, including the current boundary line of the Eastern Band of Cherokee Indians in western North Carolina. It was created by Mark Hylas using spatial data from native-land.ca, a website run by the nonprofit Native Land Digital.

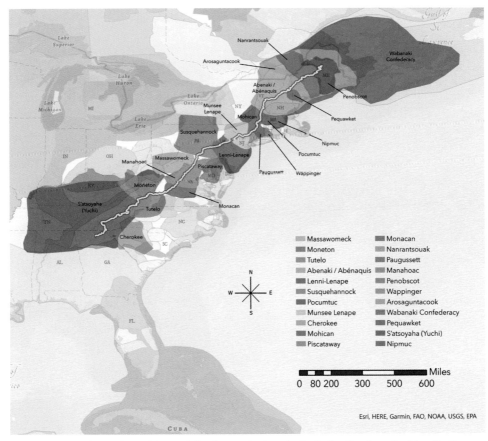

AT Native Lands Territory Map originally created exclusively for the Appalachian Trail Conservancy by Mark Hylas

The land is the real teacher. All we need as students is mindfulness.

—Robin Wall Kimmerer, *Braiding Sweetgrass*

Meet Your Guides

Hi, I'm Amber. I'll be your guide throughout this book journey, along with my husband, Joshua, who gets the credit for your visual experience.

The Appalachian Trail brought us together in 2015 when we met in Damascus, Virginia, at the annual Appalachian Trail Days festival. We were both pursuing creative ventures inspired by the AT. I was fresh off the trail kick-starting The Wander Trees, a small artist collective, and Joshua was there selling art from his 2013 thru-hike production, *The Thru Project*. Now we're married with two kids, living in an old cabin with a view of Firescald Knob, one of the most cherished pieces of the AT in Madison County, North Carolina. We both grew up hiking throughout the Appalachian Mountain region and are delighted to share our passion for this trail with you.

We guide you through the entire Appalachian Trail, starting in the south and ending in the north. Each chapter features popular hikes, campsites, maps, elevation profiles, and more bits

Amber, Josh, and Mundo at their homestead

of information you may find helpful or amusing. In addition, we give a brief introduction for each featured hike, at-a-glance specs, a detailed description with miles and directional cues, and a difficulty rating.

We took stories from our most treasured moments, including a few from our friends, and used everything we discovered while hiking the Appalachian Trail to create this inspirational guidebook for you. Enjoy the book from cover to cover, or flip to any page for stunning landscapes, breathtaking heights, deep wilderness, and stories that highlight the spirit of the AT.

Before You Hit the (Literary) Trail

Here are some "good to know" things to take note of before setting out on your adventure from the comforts of your armchair.

THE PHOTOGRAPHS

The photographs in this book are in sequential order from south to north, allowing you to experience the AT end to end in the most visceral way possible from a book. Joshua selected them from a catalog of 20,000 photographs he created over his fourteen years of hiking on the AT. The majority came from his 2013 thru-hike while creating a photographic book titled *The Thru Project*.

THE HIKES

All the hikes in this book are presented in sequential order from south to north on the Appalachian Trail. However, a particular hike may be outlined as a southbound hike. For example, Blood Mountain, the second hike in the book, is in the Georgia section, where it belongs, in between the Springer hike and the hike to Clingmans Dome. Yet the actual hike travels southbound, beginning at Mountain Crossings and going south to Blood Mountain. So, although not all hikes are northbound hikes, they are in correct order as far as the book as a whole goes.

MILEAGE AND ELEVATION PROFILES

The trail data, mileage, and maps are sourced from the 2021 edition of *The A. T. Guide* by David Miller. Thanks to David and AntiGravityGear for allowing us to borrow from their guide for this book.

RATINGS

We have rated each hike as easy, moderate, or strenuous. Easy hikes are primarily level, maybe slightly inclined, and are generally suited for anyone who enjoys a walk in the woods. Moderate hikes are great for novice hikers and will likely have terrain that involves inclines and steeper sections. Strenuous hikes will challenge most hikers with steep elevation gains, long distances, or technical terrains, such as rock scrambling or river crossings. Keep in mind that mileage is nebulous on hiking trails. A mile on the

AT is not the same as a mile on the street, and the same distance can feel very different depending on a range of conditions. So just because we have labeled something as difficult does not necessarily mean big miles. For example, the hike through Mahoosuc Notch is only a mile long, but we rated it as strenuous because you have to navigate through, around, up, and over so many boulders. We do our best to explain our reasoning for difficulty ratings.

FURTHER READING

This guidebook's aim is more inspirational than technical. For more technical information, reach out to your local trail club. They are super helpful and highly knowledgeable when it comes to trails in their area. They can help with questions about routes, parking, and current trail status. Of course we can't recommend *The A.T. Guide* by David Miller enough. It is a wealth of resources and incredibly useful, especially while backpacking on the AT.

A NOTE ABOUT "DISCOVERY"

The act of discovery means finding something unexpected or becoming aware of something. *How you discover the Appalachian Trail is your own journey.*

You can find the AT at any age, whether you are five or fifty-five. You can discover it over the course of a day, a week, or a lifetime. If this book is your first time learning about the Appalachian Trail, we urge you to lace up your boots to see what you can find. Nothing compares to placing your own two feet on the roots of ancient oak trees and sleeping on a bed of pine needles. The AT has so much for you to discover, and we've learned firsthand that even when you are not "on the Trail," it still leads you to unexpected places after you return home.

Introduction to the Appalachian Trail

The Appalachian Scenic Trail, commonly known as the AT, is the longest hiking-only footpath globally. More than 2,100 miles long, it roams across woodlands, ridgetops, pastures, and culturally rich towns as it travels through fourteen states, traverses eight national forests, and passes through six other units of the National Park System. Millions of people visit the AT every year, and thousands set out to hike its entire length from the southern terminus in Georgia to the northern terminus in Maine. The Appalachian Trail Conservancy (ATC), whose mission is to "protect, manage and advocate for the trail," is responsible for maintaining the AT. The vision of the ATC is that "the Appalachian Trail and its surrounding landscape are protected forever for all to enjoy."

A footpath for those who seek fellowship with the wilderness

There is something about the Appalachian Trail that stays with you. It becomes a part of you. Or at least, that's how it feels for us and our friends, whose stories we are honored to share throughout this book. Many hikers will agree that you gain far more than what you set out to get when hiking the Appalachian Trail. You gain more than an adventure or a check off your bucket list. You gain perspective, community, newfound hope in humanity, a sense of belonging, and deep respect for the natural world.

The AT remains with me even though seven years have passed since I took my first steps on the trail. The experience confirmed to me the necessity of living life outdoors and how amazing it is to be surrounded by like-minded people who challenge you every day. When I completed my southbound thru-hike I vowed that my hiking days were done, yet the pull of the trail and nature never really left. This led me to a career in the wilderness leading hiking tours and teaching kids the power of a life lived outside. It is easy to trace many of my life decisions back to lessons learned on the AT. If that doesn't tell you the power of the trail, then nothing will.

—Jamie Gault ("Strider," Maine-Georgia, 2014)

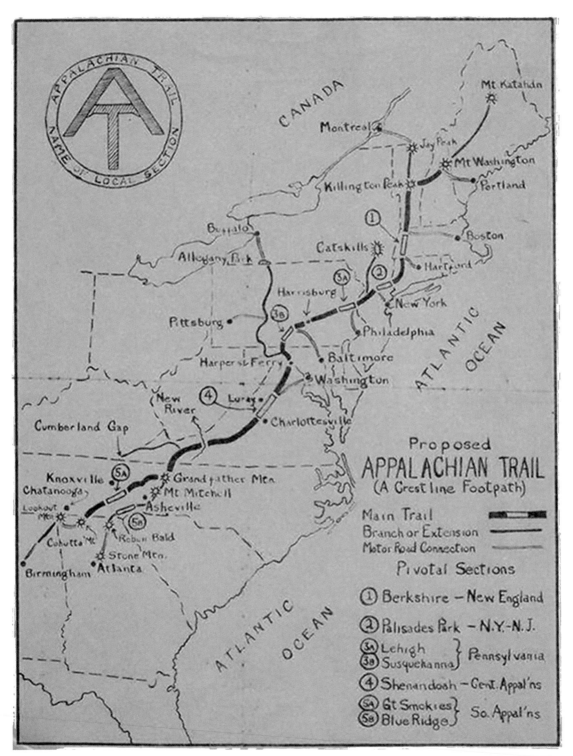

Proposed map of the AT hand-drawn by Benton MacKaye, 1925

BLAZING THE PEOPLE'S PATH

The history of the Appalachian Trail, famously known as "the people's path," is an enthralling story. This long-distance footpath endured so much while going from dream to reality. It was an idea that survived through wars, economic fallout, and political quarrels. But, just as the Appalachian Mountains themselves were born of tremendous upheaval, the trail and the people behind it would push forward to see it through, despite the political or socioeconomic climate.

The origin story began in the 1920s, when America was going through a rough patch. World War I was ending, and the Great Depression and World War II were looming on the horizon, both with their impending hardships. War, capitalism, and industrial exploitation of the environment resulted in a divisive time immersed in doom and gloom—especially for those living in cities along the eastern seaboard, apart from nature. Luckily, Benton MacKaye (rhymes with *sky*), a policy analyst and former forester from New England, presented a possible solution to the "problem of living" so many Americans were facing. His grand idea, in short, was to create "forest camps" in the Appalachian Mountains, connected by a long-distance trail that extended from the highest mountains in New England to the highest in the South.

The story goes that while MacKaye was sitting in a tree on Stratton Mountain during a post-college bushwhacking trip in the summer of 1900, he gazed out over the Green Mountains and imagined a trail. Years later, after his wife took her own life in April 1921, MacKaye retreated to longtime colleague Charles Whitaker's farm in New Jersey. Whitaker was editor of the *Journal of the American Institute of Architects* (AAI) at the time and urged him to start putting his Appalachian Trail–specific ideas on paper. Whitaker then introduced him to Clarence Stein, chairman of the AAI's Committee on Community Planning, and both helped MacKaye refine his proposal. In October 1921, the American Institute of Architects published MacKaye's groundbreaking essay, "An Appalachian Trail, A Project in Regional Planning." In it he expresses his ideas about the healing powers of nature:

> *The oxygen in the mountain air along the Appalachian skyline is a natural resource (and a national resource) that radiates to the heavens its enormous health-giving powers with only a fraction of a percent utilized for human rehabilitation. Here is a resource that could save thousands of lives. The sufferers from tuberculosis, anemia, and insanity go through the whole strata of human society. Most of them are helpless, even those economically well off. They occur in the cities and right in the skyline belt. For the farmers, and especially the wives of farmers, are by no means escaping the grinding-down process of our modern life.*

MacKaye was adamant about his idea and spent many years working toward his vision. More than a decade after his proposal essay, he stated at the Appalachian Trail Conference in 1935: "The physical path is no end in itself; it is a means of sojourning in the primeval or wilderness environment whose preservation and nurture is your particular care. The Appalachian Trail, as originally conceived, is not merely a footpath through the wilderness but a foot of the wilderness."

He hoped to create a wilderness path that would serve more than just recreational purposes. He wanted the trail to be as much about getting back to the land as possible—"a retreat from profit." Unlike others who helped him build the footpath, whose primary focus was creating a connected path no matter the route, MacKaye was primarily concerned with making sure it was a wilderness trail. In a letter to Myron Avery in 1935, he wrote: "Here then is the first issue between us. You are for a connected trail—whether or not wilderness. I am for a wilderness trail—whether or not connected."

MacKaye's plan included a series of "shelter camps," building on what was already in place in the White Mountains at the time. From the shelter camps, he hoped that smaller "community camps" would naturally form, followed by "farm and food camps." These communities would be located on or near the trail and be centered on "nonindustrial" purposes, things like nature schools or, perhaps, retreat centers. Thus people could have fun and find meaning and satisfaction within outdoor camping life. A connected footpath was simply one part of his grand vision; the camps along the AT would be a significant piece of the puzzle. MacKaye writes in detail about them in his 1921 essay. He believed that once people visited the trail and the camps, they would be inclined to live off the land permanently. The dense population of cities would decrease as urban dwellers spread out into the country.

It has been a century since Benton MacKaye's dream was simply a dream. We can now look back and be grateful for everything that happened to enable MacKaye's original idea to materialize and grow into the Appalachian Trail we know and love today. Countless hours went into promoting the AT to trail clubs and consulting with national forest and park services. This proposed hiking trail was HUGE! We are talking about miles and miles of routing; mapping; brush cutting; creating steps, boardwalks, handholds; and marking the trail. It was going to take years of hard work from willing souls—and lots of them. Luckily, others shared his passion and rallied behind him to make it happen.

Any good visionary needs the support of trailblazers—people who can bring the vision to life. Enter Myron Avery. Avery had the skills and connections to execute the plan. MacKaye receives a lot of well-deserved praise and recognition, but Avery's efforts also deserve notice. He worked tirelessly to build and shape the trail from MacKaye's original vision. Avery served as the chairman for the ATC from 1930 until a month before he died in 1952. The two outdoors advocates may have had a rocky history, with opposing personalities and viewpoints; however, their passion for the AT never wavered. Both were instrumental in the trail's creation, as were many others who devoted their life's work to the design, protection, and ongoing maintenance of the Appalachian Trail.

The AT was complete in 1937, thirty-six years after Benton's proposal went public; however a hurricane came through the following year, destroying and damaging large sections. After World War II and years of repairing the damage, the AT was officially reopened in 1951. Of course the trail would not be what it is today without the ATC, created in 1925, and the National Trails System Act, signed in 1968. The ATC was and continues to be responsible for maintaining the AT by acting as a parent organization for the many trail clubs and their members. In addition, without the National Trails System Act, there would be no federal protection for the AT. Innumerable hands played a part in the creation of the AT and still do today, as many individuals continue to work toward fulfilling MacKaye's full vision of a back-to-nature utopian society.

This only scratches the surface of the Appalachian Trail's history. If you want to learn more, we recommend Thomas R. Johnson's book *From Dream to Reality*. Johnson was a historian, hiker, and trail maintainer and highly knowledgeable about the AT. You can also tour the AT Museum in Pine Grove Furnace State Park in Pennsylvania and visit the Appalachian Trail Conservancy's website (appalachiantrail.org). And if you are intrigued by Benton MacKaye, the man who envisioned the AT, check out *Peculiar Work* by Larry Anderson.

Dragon's Tooth, Virginia, Mile 702.1 northbound; 2013 thru-hike

THE BIRTH OF THE APPALACHIAN MOUNTAINS

The faulted and folded beds of sedimentary, igneous, and basement rocks found in exposed cliffs throughout the Appalachian Mountains serve as stark reminders of the mountain range's deep and complex geological history. Studies of these outcrops and their lithology suggest that the oldest sections of the Appalachians began forming some 480 million years ago during the Ordovician period, the second stage of the Paleozoic era. This point in time marks the beginning of a long series of orogenic events.

Ancient beds of rock were uplifted and folded under the immense pressure along the plate boundary over the course of multiple mountain-building episodes, forming the mountains we know today. Weathering throughout this process wore the peaks down, and streams incised deep valleys filled with eroded minerals moving downslope as sediment.

> The mountains are the soul of a region. To understand the mountains is to know ourselves.
> —Sandra H. B. Clark

Ice and water have helped to carve gorges, steep ravines, caverns, and narrows throughout the ages. Some of the rivers that flow through them are older than the mountains themselves. The ceaseless water action has also resulted in smooth-sided domes such as Looking Glass Rock in western North Carolina. Climate also has played a part. Glaciers have influenced the landscape by distributing boulders and polishing the peaks in the north while driving plants and animals farther south so they could survive.

Whether you choose to visit dramatic rock formations like the Dragon's Tooth monolith, glacial valleys like Franconia Notch, the Mahoosuc Notch boulder pit, or the iconic outcropping at McAfee Knob, one thing is for sure: Geological sightseeing abounds on the Appalachian Trail. There is so much to discover—from tiny minerals like shimmery mica and milky quartz beneath your feet to giant metamorphosed rock like the marble slabs at the Cobbles in Massachusetts or the greenstone of Shenandoah National Park.

DID YOU KNOW?

Plants have been valuable allies to the people of the Appalachians for a long time. Herbal remedies made from the roots and seeds of flowers, fungi, and herbs can be traced back to native uses and knowledge. Early settlers could not have survived without the healing remedies adopted from the indigenous tribes like the Cherokee. We have included some folk uses for historical curiosity only, not as a guide for use. Please do not pick, harvest, or ingest any flora while hiking the Appalachian Trail. Take only photographs. Let's all do our part in helping to protect the plants for future generations to enjoy.

The geology of the Appalachian Mountains is layered and lengthy. We recommend diving deeper with a more detailed account of its natural history. Scott Weidensaul's book *Mountains of the Heart* is an excellent place to start if you want to learn more about the geology, ecology, climate, and evolution of the Appalachian Mountains.

PLANTS OF APPALACHIA

The flora of the Appalachian Trail is a wonderment year-round. Showy flowers paint the meadows in the spring. Vines of fragrant honeysuckle cover the hillsides in the summer. Deciduous trees blanket the mountains in warm hues during the fall. Evergreens contrast beautifully with the winter snowfalls. The AT is lined with myriad ferns, old stumps adorned with bright green mosses, juicy wild berries, and vibrant wildflowers that sprawl down mountain slopes.

Known as the "green tunnel" since most of it travels through dense tree coverage, the Appalachian Trail traverses a mountain region that was once covered entirely by forest. Evergreen trees such as pine, cedar, red spruce, and balsam fir grow in the lofty elevations. Common throughout the north are paper birch, sugar maple, and other hardwoods such as red oak, elm, and beech. Farther south you will find hickory, poplar, walnut, hemlock, and more. Before being destroyed by a disastrous fungal blight, the American chestnut tree dominated the eastern forests. Their towering height and large diameter included them among the northern giants like the redwood and sequoia.

However, American chestnuts had far more to offer than their good looks. They were stain-resistant, rot-resistant, strong, lightweight, and produced a nut that was once a high cash crop of rural communities. People called them the "cradle to the grave" trees for their variety of uses.

Redbud, hawthorn, dogwood, locust, and sourwood trees all produce beautiful blooms during different seasons. Adding to the botanical splendor are flowering and fruit-bearing shrubs like mountain laurel, flame azalea, and serviceberry.

Closer to the forest floor lie bloodroot, pink lady's slipper, Dutchman's breeches, mayapple, jack-in-the-pulpit, and many species of trillium. Mushrooms and mosses flourish in moist and

Wild blackberry flower

shaded areas created by the leafy canopy of the southern mountains. Loftier elevations nurture alpine plants such as mountain cranberry and diapensia.

We've only scratched the surface of the vegetation you may experience while hiking the AT, as the plant life from Maine to Georgia is highly complex and extensive. There are thousands of wildflowers alone in this ecologically diverse region. Pick up a recently updated field guide on trees, flowers, or fungi so that when something catches your eye, you're able to learn more.

WILDLIFE OF APPALACHIA

The mountains and rivers of Appalachia support a wide variety of animal life. Black bear, white-tailed deer, fox, raccoon, and many other small creatures are common throughout the region. You are likely to see mice in the shelters at night and squirrels doing their thing during the day. Some animals you may not see but will undoubtedly hear, such as owls or coyotes in the distant woods. Spruce grouse and the elusive Maine moose roam the northern woods, where pesky blackflies are common. You may catch sight of an otter playing in the many bodies of water throughout Maine. The Appalachian region is home to numerous species of birds, fish, amphibians, and insects. Hundreds of birds patrol the trail from the canopy above while filling the air with cheerful melodies.

We've spotlighted creatures throughout the book so that you can learn more about the well-loved and some commonly feared wildlife you might discover on the Appalachian Trail.

Red-spotted newt

By Kevin Burke, Tour Guide, Ventures Birding Tours

Part of the allure of the Appalachian Trail is the deep meaningful connection with the natural world you get while being immersed in it for the duration of your journey. A new tree that you have never noticed, spring wildflowers, and the dawn chorus of birds urging you on your way are all treasured parts of the AT experience. Starting from the Springer or Katahdin terminus, birdlife on the trail is inevitable. The great spectacle of migration starts from the southern terminus and runs up the spine of the Appalachians following your own AT migration. Warblers start to sing in the southern reaches of the trail in the early spring. The Hooded Warbler's loud and musical song is commonly heard throughout the South. Black-throated Green Warblers are denizens of the deep woods throughout the trail. The magical flutelike song of the wood thrush will carry you on your way. One cannot forget about the owls along the way too. The Barred, Eastern Screech, and Great-horned Owls are all sure to be heard as you drift off in your shelter at night. The Northeast brings some new sounds to the trail. The sought-after Bicknell's Thrush reaches the high elevations as you cross the White and Green Mountains. Magnolia and Blackpoll Warblers greet you there as well. There is a lot of birdlife to experience on the Appalachian Trail, and there are many apps you can get for your phone that will help you along the way. Try the Sibley Guide to Birds app for bird identification. To identify a song or call you may not be familiar with, try the BirdNET app. It will record what you are hearing and tell you what bird is singing to you. You may even want to bring a compact set of binoculars with you. A smaller magnification to save weight is recommended, such as 8×32 or even 8×25.

Barred owl PHOTO BY KEVIN BURKE

Top 10 Birds on the AT

Hooded Warbler
Wood Thrush
Eastern Screech-Owl
Black-throated Green Warbler
Ruffed Grouse
Bicknell's Thrush
Barred Owl
Golden-crowned Kinglet
Blue Jay
Scarlet Tanager

Scarlet tanager PHOTO BY KEVIN BURKE

ICONS AND SYMBOLS

BLAZES

White paint strips 2 inches wide and 6 inches long mark the Appalachian Trail in both directions. We call them "blazes." Most commonly painted on trees, rocks, and posts, they also can be found on guardrails, streetlights—and the deck of the ferryboat in Maine. Blue blazes mark side trails that lead to water sources, shelters, camping, and views.

Check out the glossary in the back of the book for more descriptions of blazing, such as aqua-blazing and yellow-blazing.

DOUBLE BLAZES

If you see two blazes painted on top of the other, this signals an upcoming obscure turn or a change in direction. Sometimes the upper blaze will be offset, indicating the change in direction. Watch for a turn in the direction of the upper blaze whenever you see these "kick-over" blazes.

CAIRNS

When the trail is above tree line, a pile of rocks called a cairn is used to identify the route.

If you have gone a few hundred yards without seeing a trail marker, stop and retrace your steps until you locate one. Distance between blazes varies, so be sure you haven't missed a turn. When your map or guidebook indicates one route and the blazes show another, the ATC recommends that you follow the blazes.

AT blaze on Firescald Knob hike; 2021

Double blaze on the AT, the Firescald Knob hike; 2021

Cairn on the AT, Mount Moosilauke; 2013 thru-hike

DID YOU KNOW?

According to the National Park Service, there are approximately 165,000 blazes along the Appalachian Trail.

AT Culture

You will hear it over and over, you will see it in trail registers, and you might even catch yourself saying it to others: "Hike your own hike" (sometimes abbreviated as "HYOH"). The old trail adage has become our collective outdoors oath. It simply means to do what's best for you and try not to tell other hikers how to hike. It doesn't matter how fast or slow you walk, what direction you go, what gear you take, or even who you hike with—as long as you are hiking your way and being kind in the process, that's what matters. If safety is our number-one criterion in the outdoors, then kindness must be our second. There are norms and proper ways of doing things in the backcountry. Being respectful is at the very core of our trail etiquette system. So, hike your own hike, but don't forget to be kind and considerate. Don't overindulge in Trail Magic. Clean your dishes downstream. Be quiet after dark. Think of your comrades.

Michael "Dumptruck" Wilson and Kit "Clever" McCann on Mount Moosilauke; 2013 thru-hike

Some use guidebooks and maps; some depend on the Data Book; others just follow the white blazes to wherever they might lead. Some carry stoves; some use fires; others content themselves with cold foods. Some sport the most advanced and expensive backpacking gear available; some make do with Army Surplus. Some go the distance in less than 90 days; others take twice that long. In other words, there is no common denominator for success. What you must learn, and hopefully you will learn it before being washed out, is what works for you.

—Darel Maret answers the question, "What's the best way to hike the AT" in his book *The Philosopher's Guide to the AT*, published in 1983.

HIKERS

The term "thru-hiker" describes anyone who has hiked the entire Appalachian Trail in a continuous journey or within a single year. Thru-hikers represent a large portion of hikers who set out to experience the AT. Each year, more than 3,000 thru-hikers register with the ATC, but only a quarter finish. "Section-hikers" take their time and piece together the entire trail over the years. "Flip-floppers" are hikers who walk the trail in discontinuous sections. Many choose this approach to avoid crowds or extreme

Trail Angel Miss Janet preparing bacon, peanut butter, and jelly sandwiches for hikers, roadside in Massachusetts; 2013 thru-hike

weather and, in some cases, for logistical planning purposes. "Day hikers" are anyone who goes out for a single day, usually with a small pack for food, water, and rain gear.

TRAIL MAGIC AND TRAIL ANGELS

Yes, the Appalachian Trail is so enchanting that chances are high that you'll encounter magic and angels. Trail Magic is food, drinks, and other unexpected acts of service AT hikers experience while on the trail. Often, Trail Magic occurs in divine timing, such as a cooler full of ice-cold beverages left at a road crossing on a sweltering hot day when water is scarce. I received my first Trail Magic in the 100-Mile Wilderness when I was nearly out of food with two more days to hike. Someone had walked in a bag of rice and beans that I was beyond grateful to have for dinner. Sometimes Trail Magic is a ride into town or the opportunity to camp on a lawn.

The individuals that perform these random, selfless acts of kindness are called Trail Angels. Every single AT hiker has a Trail Magic story and Trail Angel to thank. The generosity surrounding the Appalachian Trail is proof that there is so much goodness in humanity.

Bryan Anderson hitchhiking to Trail Days; 2013 thru-hike

TRAIL TALK

Some language used by long-distance hikers may cause confusion to non-walkers. You might wonder what on earth these hikers are talking about when you hear words like "aqua-blazing," "nero," or "tramily." Popular sayings like "Hike your own hike" or "The Trail provides" are easy to grasp. Still, they carry weight and meaning to us hikers. Our language is creative and meaningful to us. It doesn't take long to learn trail lingo once you are in the woods. (In the meantime, you can visit the glossary in the back of the book for some commonly used terms and phrases.)

Next time you find yourself sitting around the campfire bonding with fellow hikers, listen for new words and phrases. Our language is constantly growing!

> Thru-hiker language is interesting and, like all aspects of culture, is always evolving. Sooner or later, you may find yourself platinum-blazing a flip-flop with an aqua-blaze in the middle.
>
> —Liz "Snorkel" Thomas, *Backpacker* magazine

CREATIVE CUISINE

Have you ever tried peanut butter and jelly with Marshmallow Fluff and Snickers rolled into a tortilla? That was my brother's go-to lunch for a few hundred miles. How

Tucker Adams enjoying lunch on top of Moxie Bald Mountain, 2014

about brownie mix stirred into instant oatmeal? That was a hiker named Fish Flakes's secret to take in more calories, also addictively delicious. On the Appalachian Trail, you may see curious versions of chili-mac and hikers using hot-sauce in new ways you never dreamed of. Hiker-hunger is real!

Hikers prioritize foods that are packable, nutrient-dense, ready-to-eat, and lightweight. Popular foods include instant rice and beans, lentils, instant pasta, instant mashed potatoes, nuts, nut butter, hard cheeses, dried fruit, tortillas, jerky, tuna, energy bars, oatmeal, and freeze-dried meals. And let's not forget about Snickers— good for breakfast, lunch, dinner, and snack time.

We need a lot of food to get up and down the steep mountains. Did you know that thru-hikers can easily burn upwards of 6,000 calories a day! That's equivalent to burning off 300 Clif Bars!

Every hiker enjoys cooking outdoors over an open flame and feasting by firelight after a long day of walking in the woods. But during a thru-hike, freeze-dried meals and plain instant mashed potatoes get boring. Luckily, there is plenty of time to figure out how to spice up Pasta Sides. While trudging along during the last mile of the day, the conversation is typically centered on food. It's a powerful motivator. We might be limited to a single pot and few ingredients, but that doesn't thwart our creativity. It fuels it. Next time you are on a long-distance hike, don't forget to bring your spices.

Jack "Cinnamon" Dickinson in Harpers Ferry, West Virginia, during his 2013 thru-hike

HIKER STYLE: FUNCTION OVER FASHION

Fashion plays a huge role in many subcultures. However, it's not so much about how fashionable your clothes are in the woods as it is about how functional they are. Sure, some folks want to look good in the backcountry, but most of us want to *feel* good. We want our clothes to be comfortable, breathable, warm, moisture-wicking, and light. What you wear outdoors seriously affects your experience. Bad clothing choices can make a hiker downright miserable. Soaking wet blue jeans, unbreathable shirts, or improper shoes are no fun. So if you are a beginner hiker, pay attention to materials, fit, and comfortableness when choosing what to wear in the backcountry. Don't worry; you can still be on-trend if that's your thing. Plenty of outdoor companies make great-looking hiking clothes. Or you can follow in the footsteps of the many thru-hikers who scour thrift stores for a more affordable way to express themselves.

All you need to get to heaven is a good pair of boots.

—Shelton Johnson, *Gloryland*

Even if you are going out for a day, remember, you never know what can happen in the woods; it's always best to be prepared. *So what does that look like?* Glad you asked! We've come up with some simple guidelines and tips for choosing optimal hiking clothes. However, as always, we recommend visiting your local outfitters for more personalized advice.

Shirts, pants, and base layers. Popular fabric choices among hikers include wool, fleece, polyester, nylon, and silk. Depending on the time of year you are hiking will determine what material will best fit your needs. Typically, when hiking on the AT you will want lightweight base layers that have wicking capabilities and fit so that they don't cause chaffing. Mid layers need to be insulating; your outermost layer needs to be both windproof and waterproof, or water resistant at the very least. Pants should be durable enough to sustain bramble snags but allow for good range of motion.

Rain gear. Get yourself a good jacket and rain pants, and, while we're at it, don't forget a pack cover. Think water resistant or waterproof, but breathable! There's nothing more unpleasant than hiking in the middle of a summer thunderstorm with a jacket that doesn't let the sweat out! Trust us, we've been there.

Shoes and socks. Pay special attention to what you put on your feet. You want to be sure that you have the right support, protection, and traction. It doesn't really matter if you opt for traditional boots or trail runners, just make your feet comfortable and make sure there is extra room to allow for mild swelling. Socks can be thick, thin, low, or tall depending on the weather. Just be sure they are breathable and able to wick moisture away from your skin. Also make certain that they are high enough to avoid blisters on your heel. Always bring extra socks! Always!

Warm jacket. We recommend a puffy insulated jacket that is filled with down or a synthetic blend. A fleece jacket works great too. Just make sure you have some sort of mid-layer option every time you go into the woods.

Accessories. Other things you might need to complete your hiker ensemble include a bug net (especially handy in Maine during blackfly season), gaiters, gloves, a large-brimmed hat, sunglasses, and a bandana or buff.

Joshua Niven's pack; 2013 thru-hike

Backpacking Basics

EQUIPMENT: THE ESSENTIALS

Proper equipment is paramount in the outdoors. You never know what could happen, so it's always best to be prepared. Get in the habit of packing these essentials to ensure that you are prepared for the unexpected. Of course, the longer your hike, the more equipment you will need. Seasonality also plays a role in determining what kind of gear and how much is necessary. For example, if you are hiking in the winter, microspikes might be an essential piece of gear. If you are hiking somewhere buggy in the summer, you might consider a bug net. If you are new to hiking, stop in your local outfitters to talk more about the gear that will fit your personal needs.

Here are the essentials we recommend for overnighting in the backcountry:

1. Food and water
2. Clothing
3. First-aid kit
4. Knife
5. Fire—matches, lighter, tinder
6. Headlamp or flashlight
7. Navigation—map, compass, or GPS unit
8. Tent, tarp, or some other form of shelter
9. Sleeping bag
10. Cooking system

WEATHER AND SAFETY

Backcountry weather conditions change constantly. It's your responsibility to be prepared, especially for the unexpected. Always be aware of weather forecasts and research trail closures. Some places on the AT require you to ford rivers that can be waist-high. Take extra precaution after heavy rainfall. Trail updates such as road closures, shelter closures, special regulations, bear activity, and more can be found on the Appalachian Trail Conservancy's website.

> **DID YOU KNOW?**
>
> You can get hypothermia in the summer. The weather doesn't have to be extremely cold for a person to be at risk of hypothermia. It can take just one slip into a cold river, pack and all, with no way to get warm for things to turn dangerous. Do some research to learn more about how you can be proactive in preventing, recognizing, and treating hypothermia in the backcountry.

Nick Browne and Mellow Johnny fording a river in Maine; 2013 thru-hike

WILDERNESS PERMITS

The Appalachian Trail is free for everyone to enjoy. There are no fees or permits to simply walk on the trail. However, a few places along the AT require permits to stay overnight in shelters or campsites, such as Great Smoky Mountains National Park, Baxter State Park, and parts of the White Mountain National Forest. You can obtain any necessary permits or learn more about where you need to register by visiting NPS.org.

TRANSPORTATION

There are numerous shuttle and taxi services along the Appalachian Trail. We recommend referencing the most recent version of David Miller's *The A.T. Guide* for transportation services in the area you will be hiking.

DOGS

You can bring your canine companion with you as you hike the Appalachian Trail except for when you are visiting Great Smoky Mountains National Park and Baxter State Park in Maine, where dogs are prohibited. Be sure to keep your dog on a leash, and don't forget to bring sufficient water!

Outdoor Ethics

The seven principles outlined below are part of the Leave No Trace initiative (© 1999 by the Leave No Trace Center for Outdoor Ethics: www.LNT.org). These simple practices help preserve natural environments like the Appalachian Trail. While the steps are easy to learn, it takes a devoted hiker to adhere to them. However, if we all do our part to minimize our impact, the AT will remain beautiful and protected for future generations to enjoy.

PLAN AHEAD AND PREPARE

1. Know the regulations and special concerns for the area you'll visit.
2. Prepare for extreme weather, hazards, and emergencies.
3. Schedule your trip to avoid times of high use.
4. Visit in small groups when possible. Consider splitting larger groups into smaller ones.
5. Repackage food to minimize waste.
6. Use a map and compass to eliminate the use of marking paint, rock cairns, or flagging.

TRAVEL AND CAMP ON DURABLE SURFACES

1. Durable surfaces include established trails and campsites, rock, gravel, dry grasses, or snow.
2. Protect riparian areas by camping at least 200 feet from lakes and streams.
3. Good campsites are found, not made. Altering a site is not necessary.

DISPOSE OF WASTE PROPERLY

1. Pack it in, pack it out. Inspect your campsite and rest areas for trash or spilled foods. Pack out all trash, leftover food, and litter.
2. Deposit solid human waste in catholes dug 6 to 8 inches deep at least 200 feet from water, camp, and trails. Cover and disguise the cathole when finished.
3. Pack out toilet paper and hygiene products.
4. To wash yourself or your dishes, carry water 200 feet away from streams or lakes and use small amounts of biodegradable soap. Scatter strained dishwater.

LEAVE WHAT YOU FIND

1. Preserve the past: Examine, but do not touch, cultural or historic structures and artifacts.
2. Leave rocks, plants, and other natural objects as you find them.
3. Avoid introducing or transporting non-native species.
4. Do not build structures, furniture, or dig trenches.

MINIMIZE CAMPFIRE IMPACTS

1. Campfires can cause lasting impacts to the backcountry. Use a lightweight stove for cooking, and enjoy a candle lantern for light.
2. Where fires are permitted, use established fire rings, fire pans, or mound fires.
3. Keep fires small. Only use sticks from the ground that can be broken by hand.
4. Burn all wood and coals to ash, put out campfires completely, then scatter cool ashes.

RESPECT WILDLIFE

1. Observe wildlife from a distance. Do not follow or approach them.
2. Never feed animals. Feeding wildlife damages their health, alters natural behaviors, and exposes them to predators and other dangers.
3. Protect wildlife and your food by storing rations and trash securely.
4. Control pets at all times, or leave them at home.
5. Avoid wildlife during sensitive times: mating, nesting, raising young, or winter.

BE CONSIDERATE OF OTHER VISITORS

1. Respect other visitors and protect the quality of their experience.
2. Be courteous. Yield to other users on the trail.
3. Step to the downhill side of the trail when encountering pack stock.
4. Take breaks and camp away from trails and other visitors.
5. Let nature's sounds prevail. Avoid loud voices and noises.

Illustration by Aaron Warner

Trail Finder

Note: Hikes are listed, by hike number, from south to north.

For Summit Seekers

- 2   Blood Mountain, Georgia
- 4   Newfound Gap to Charlies Bunion, North Carolina/Tennessee
- 6   Big Firescald Knob, North Carolina/Tennessee
- 24   Mount Moosilauke, New Hampshire
- 26   Presidential Range, New Hampshire
- 28   Bigelow Mountain Range, New Hampshire
- 30   Mount Katahdin, Maine

For Fall Foliage

- 4   Newfound Gap to Charlies Bunion, North Carolina/Tennessee
- 5   Max Patch, North Carolina/Tennessee
- 7   Roan Highlands, North Carolina/Tennessee
- 12   Milam Gap to Big Meadows, Virginia
- 19   Lions Head and Bear Mountain, Connecticut
- 21   Mount Greylock, Massachusetts

For Rock Scramblers and the Geology-Minded

- 9   Dragons Tooth, Virginia
- 14   Annapolis Rocks and Black Rock Cliffs, Maryland
- 15   Chimney Rocks, Pennsylvania
- 18   Lemon Squeezer to Hessian Lake, New York
- 20   The Cobbles, Massachusetts
- 27   Mahoosuc Notch, Maine
- 30   Mount Katahdin, Maine

For History Lovers

- 2   Blood Mountain, Georgia
- 11   Brown Mountain Community, Virginia
- 13   Harpers Ferry Historical Hike, West Virginia
- 22   Stratton Mountain, Vermont

For Iconic Photo-ops

  1   Springer Mountain, Georgia
  8   Grayson Highlands, Virginia
10   McAfee Knob, Virginia
13   Harpers Ferry Historical Hike, West Virginia
16   Boiling Springs to Center Point Knob, Pennsylvania
30   Mount Katahdin, Maine

For Swimming, Falls, and other Water Features

  1   Springer Mountain, Georgia
  3   Fontana Dam to Clingmans Dome, North Carolina/Tennessee
16   Boiling Springs to Center Point Knob, Pennsylvania
18   Lemon Squeezer to Hessian Lake, New York
23   Clarendon Gorge to Bromley Mountain, Vermont
25   Franconia Notch to Crawford Notch, New Hampshire
29   100 Mile Wilderness, Maine

Stroller and Wheelchair Friendly*

  1   Springer Mountain, Georgia
12   Milam Gap to Big Meadows, Virginia
13   Harpers Ferry Historical Hike, West Virginia
17   Pochuck Valley Boardwalk and Stairway to Heaven, New Jersey
18   Lemon Squeezer to Hessian Lake
26   Presidential Range, New Hampshire

Note: Only sections of these hikes are stroller and wheelchair accessible.

Bryan Anderson and Jarred Douglas setting up camp at Wolf Laurel Top, Georgia, during 2013 thru-hike, Mile 34.9

Roan Highlands at Round Knob, Mile 381.2, 2016 northbound

PART I

THE SOUTHERN MOUNTAINS

Georgia | North Carolina | Tennessee

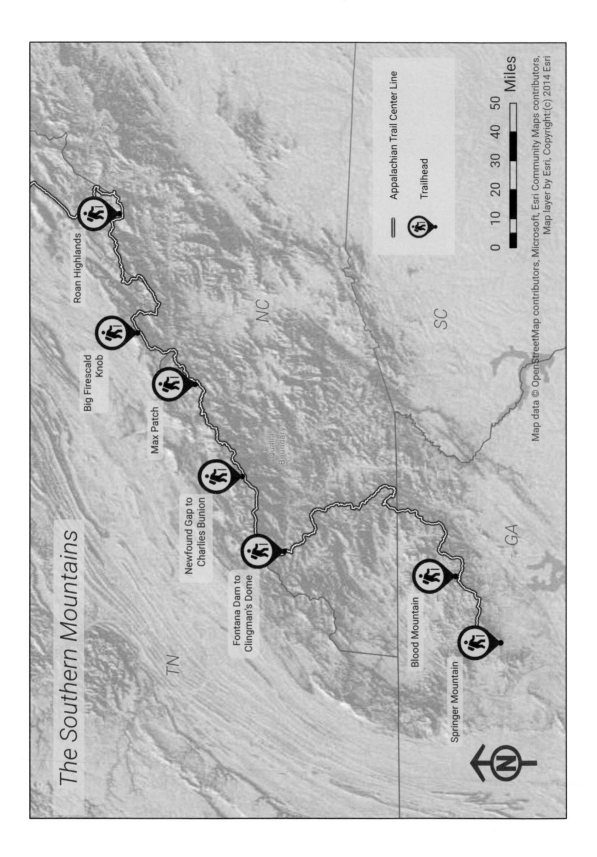

The Southern Mountains

Roan Highlands

Big Firescald Knob

Max Patch

Newfound Gap to Charlies Bunion

Fontana Dam to Clingman's Dome

Blood Mountain

Springer Mountain

Qualla Boundary

TN

NC

SC

GA

Appalachian Trail Center Line

Trailhead

Miles

0   10   20   30   40   50

Map data © OpenStreetMap contributors, Microsoft, Esri Community Maps contributors,
Map layer by Esri, Copyright (c) 2014 Esri

N

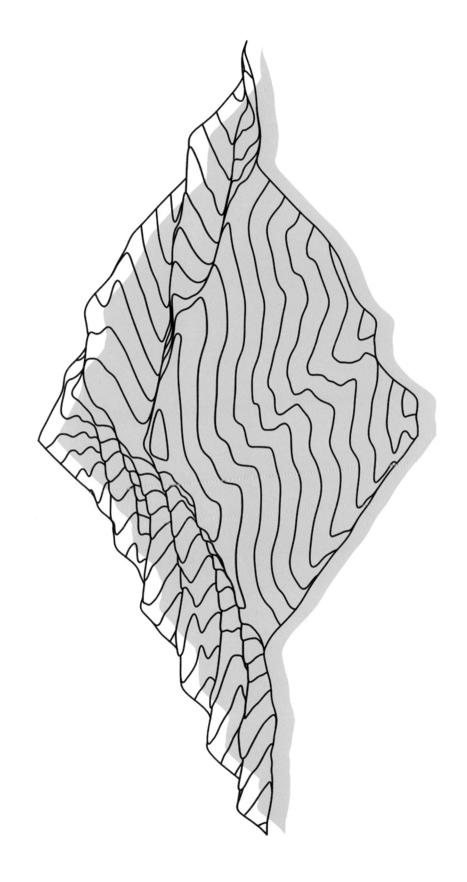

6,643'

CLINGMANS DOME, NC/TN

Topographic illustrations by Ryan Klinger

Springer Mountain, Mile 0.0; 2016

Georgia

WELCOME TO GEORGIA!

Georgia may be well known for producing some of the world's best pecans and peaches, but the state is also known in the hiking community as the place that molds some persistent backpackers. The mountains of northern Georgia are far different from its flat farmland. The Appalachian Trail travels over 75 miles through the Chattahoochee National Forest in Georgia, which is enough time for northbound thru-hikers to develop a strong pace and steadfast attitude to take them all the way to Maine. For hikers going south, Georgia marks their last hurrah and the place to celebrate their long journey and perseverance. Similar to the Maine's North Woods, this section is always bittersweet for thru-hikers, as it marks the beginning or end of their journey. Throughout this chapter we will cover iconic landmarks and popular hikes and talk about discovering a sense of strength.

> That day, I discovered that my favorite sound in the world is women laughing up and down the trail.
>
> —Anna Huthmaker reflecting on her hike to Springer in 2007 with twenty other "Trail Dames," *AT Journeys,* 2018.

DID YOU KNOW?

In early March, hikers from around the world flock to Amicalola Falls State Park to attend the thru-hiker kickoff before they begin their trek to Mount Katahdin. We call these hikers Northbounders, or NOBOs for short. Most hikers choose to travel from Georgia to Maine, even though the AT was designed from "Maine to Georgia." Hikers who start in Maine and complete their journey in Georgia are called, you guessed it, Southbounders, or SOBOs.

1

AMICALOLA FALLS STATE PARK TO SPRINGER MOUNTAIN VIA THE AT APPROACH TRAIL

Springer Mountain in northern Georgia has the distinction of marking the southern terminus for the Appalachian Trail as well as being one of the most popular hiking destinations in the state. This is where thousands of hikers set out each year to actualize their dream of walking the complete length of the Appalachian Trail. While northbound thru-hikers start here, Southbounders rejoice here, as it is the end of their journey. Springer Mountain is also well loved by day hikers and section hikers for its accessibility and many offerings. Amicalola Falls, only a short walk from the trailhead, attracts many waterfall enthusiasts with its seven cascades. At 729 feet, Amicalola is the highest waterfall in Georgia. At the peak of Springer Mountain, you will find the first white blaze (or the last, depending on your point of view), two iconic plaques, a trail register, and a pleasant view on clear days.

The hike to Springer Mountain via the AT Approach Trail is marked with blue blazes and begins at the visitor center of Amicalola Falls State Park under the stone archway, an iconic AT threshold. Although these 8.5 miles aren't technically on the

Start of the approach trail at Amicalola Falls, Georgia, Mile 0; 2021

Appalachian Trail, we felt they were important enough to include in this guidebook. The scenic approach trail has become popular among the AT community, since it is the more traditional way to start a northbound thru-hike. This hike is a great option for a moderately strenuous day hike or a perfect overnight trip for beginners who aren't ready to do many miles in a single day. Be careful, though, this trail will stoke your inner fire—you may find yourself dreaming of thru-hiking once you return home!

DISTANCE: 17.6 miles out and back
DIFFICULTY: Moderate due to elevation gain and A LOT of steps
TRAILHEAD GPS: 34.5576892 / -84.2489898
NEARBY TOWN: Dahlonega, Georgia
HIGHLIGHTS: Gorgeous waterfall and iconic landmarks, such as the AT's southern terminus

TIPS

- Amicalola Falls State Park charges a nominal parking fee.
- This trail is pet friendly! Just make sure dogs are on-leash.
- Springer Mountain is well-known and well-loved, so be prepared to pass plenty of fellow hikers. If you are staying overnight, bring a tent in case the shelter is full.
- There is a water source 0.25 mile past the top of the falls.
- West Ridge Falls Access Trail (0.3 mile one way) is a wheelchair-accessible trail to the bottom of Amicalola Falls. Great views.

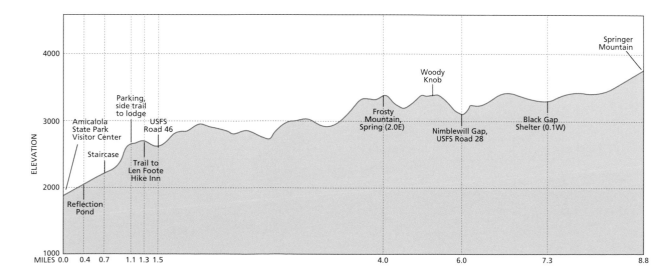

Amicalola Falls view, 8.0 miles from the AT

MILEAGE MARKERS (SOUTH TO NORTH)

SECTION	MILES FROM SPRINGER	LANDMARK	ELEVATION (IN FEET)
0.0	8.8	Amicalola Falls State Park Visitor Center	1,800
0.4	8.4	Reflection Pond at base of falls	2,003
0.7	8.1	Staircase—604 stairs to the falls	2,216
1.1	7.7	Parking, side trail to lodge	2,639
1.3	7.5	Trail to Len Foote Hike Inn (5.0 miles east), blazed lime green	2,656
1.5	7.3	USFS Road 46	2,584
4.0	4.8	Frosty Mountain; spring (2.0 miles east) is unreliable	3,384
5.7	3.1	Woody Knob	3,406
6.0	2.8	Nimblewill Gap, USFS Road 28	3,100
7.3	1.5	Black Gap Shelter (0.1 mile west)	3,300
8.8	0.0	Springer Mountain	3,782

THE HIKE

This hike begins at the famous stone archway, located behind the Amicalola Falls State Park Visitor Center. From here, walk about 1 mile to a beautiful reflection pond, where you may see people fishing or kids playing in the water. It's a gradual incline, but it gets your blood pumping. After the trail skirts the pond, you continue to gain in elevation as you make your way to the bottom of Amicalola Falls. Trilliums, wild geranium, bloodroot, and many other wildflowers line the path during spring. A towering poplar tree can be seen on your left before you get to the falls. Snap a photo and take a breather from the base of Amicalola Falls before climbing up the grueling 604-step staircase.

Once you crest the top of the enormous waterfall, your heart will be racing, but you will be rewarded with awe-inspiring views. The terrain roller-coasters for another 7 miles through the dense forest before reaching the iconic, albeit somewhat anticlimactic, 3,782-foot peak. On a clear day, you can see a view of the Blue Ridge Mountains.

A plaque on Springer Mountain reads: "Appalachian Trail, Maine to Georgia, A footpath for those who seek fellowship with the wilderness," Mile 0.0

Southern terminus plaque and trail log container, Mile 0.0

However, the view isn't what makes Springer significant—it's the fact that this is the official starting point (or ending point) of the Appalachian Trail. You will find two plaques as well as a trail register (located inside a metal box) where you can sign your name and become part of the AT community. There are plenty of campsites and a shelter near the top.

To return, retrace your steps to Amicalola. Or continue northbound to discover more on the Appalachian Trail!

DID YOU KNOW?

Mount Oglethorpe, the southernmost peak in the Blue Ridge Mountains, was the original southern terminus of the Appalachian Trail. The trail was relocated to Springer Mountain in 1958 due to increased development at Oglethorpe.

2

BLOOD MOUNTAIN: TALLEST PEAK IN GEORGIA

NEEL GAP TO BLOOD MOUNTAIN SUMMIT

Blood Mountain—the name itself can rattle some nerves. One may pause to wonder what happened here to deserve such an ominous label. The climb to the top is intense, but not as harrowing as the name makes it sound. Blood Mountain is said to be named for a gruesome battle between the Creek and Cherokee Indians, causing the land to turn red from the bloodbath. Although steeped in bloody history, this mountain is more than just a marker of conflict. It has the honor of being Georgia's highest peak on the Appalachian Trail and is also the location of the AT's oldest shelter. The

Blood Mountain summit, Mile 28.9 northbound; 2013 thru-hike

hike is strenuous but rewarding with spectacular views, especially in the fall, when the hardwood trees display their vibrant colors.

DISTANCE: 4.8 miles out and back
DIFFICULTY: Strenuous due to steep terrain
TRAILHEAD GPS: 34.741433 / -83.922850
NEARBY TOWN: Dahlonega, Georgia
HIGHLIGHTS: Iconic AT landmark and incredible views

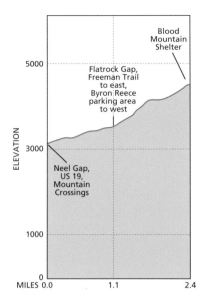

TIPS

- Great views year-round, but note that thru-hiking season begins in March, so the trail will be extremely crowded with eager hikers during early spring.
- Parking is free and located 0.25 mile from Mountain Crossings. The lot is heavily trafficked, so be sure to get there early. Park only in designated spots; do not park along US 19/129. Ask the outfitter about shuttles.

MILEAGE MARKERS (NORTH TO SOUTH)

SECTION	MILES FROM SPRINGER	LANDMARK	ELEVATION (IN FEET)
0.0	31.3	Neel Gap; US 19, Mountain Crossings	3,125
1.1	30.2	Flatrock Gap; Freeman Trail to the east, Byron Reece parking area to the west	3,487
2.4	28.9	Blood Mountain Shelter	4,457

THE HIKE

The hike to Blood Mountain begins in the heart of the Chattahoochee National Forest at Neel Gap. Located here is the historic Mountain Crossings at Walasi-Yi. If you need a new backpack, water bottle, trekking poles, or any other equipment before the hike, we highly recommend stopping in to check out the vast selection of gear Mountain Crossings has to offer. Once you finish perusing the enormous collection of gear, make your way to the store's breezeway, which serves as this hikes' trailhead. Look up and see the many worn-out boots hanging in the trees.

Mountain Crossings, Mile 31.3 northbound; 2021

From the breezeway at Mountain Crossings, hike southbound through lush, dense forest as the trail ascends quickly to Flatrock Gap, where the AT intersects the Freeman Trail, which leads east. A parking area for the Byron Reece Trailhead is to the west, an excellent alternate access point for this hike. Once you reach Flatrock Gap, the trail continues to climb steeply to the summit of Blood Mountain. It's a quick but grueling hike. From the 4,457-foot peak you can enjoy far-reaching views of the Chattahoochee National Forest and check out Blood Mountain Shelter, the oldest shelter on the Appalachian Trail. Depart the summit by retracing the route back to Neel Gap.

Mountain Crossings famous hiking boot tree, Mile 31.3 northbound; 2013 thru-hike

Mountain Crossings breezeway, where the AT goes through the building, Mile 31.3 northbound; 2021

MOUNTAIN CROSSINGS AT WALASI-YI

At roughly 30 miles from Springer, the Appalachian Trail passes directly through the stone breezeway of Mountain Crossings at Walasi-Yi. The Civilian Conservation Corps (CCC) completed construction of the historic building in 1937. During the 1960s, it served as a dining hall and inn, but it is well-known today as one of the most popular outfitters and hostels along the AT, with expert staff who help thousands of hikers each year.

Long before there was even a building here, however, there were the Cherokee. The Cherokee lived in the town they called Walasi-Yi, meaning "Home of the Great Frog" or "Frog Town," until they were forced on the Trail of Tears in 1838.

Mountain Crossings is famous for Northbounder shakedowns, as it's the first place to ditch some unnecessary gear in an attempt to make heavy packs more manageable. It's become a tradition for hikers to lighten their load at Mountain Crossings, both physically and mentally. The experienced staff comb through gear piece by piece while

Blood Mountain Shelter, Mile 28.9 northbound; 2013 thru-hike

answering any lingering questions, putting hikers at ease, and sending them on their way with more confidence and pep in their step to finish their journey, whether it be 9 miles or 900.

Many northbound thru-hikers consider this landmark the "make-it or break-it" point. At this first checkpoint, with convenient opportunities to hitch a ride home, northbound hikers ask themselves: *Do I keep going, or is this where my journey ends?* Southbounders rest here in the fall to prepare for the last leg of their thru-hike.

TALES FROM THE TRAIL: THE END

by Jamie Gault ("Strider," Maine–Georgie, 2014)

Sometime around 4 p.m. during the fall of 2014, my weary legs brought my excited body along the final reaches of the Appalachian Trail. Finally, I stood on the summit of Mount Springer. Its plaque is not as dramatic as the one on top of Mount Katahdin, yet its meaning is equally important to all the other Southbounders and me. It was the end, yet the beginning of the discovery into just how much the trail had changed me.

Our final night had beer, music, and cards, with the rain pouring down on the tin-roofed shelter, our last shelter after some 150 nights on the trail. In the morning we woke to the same pitter-patter. Our last day would be rain-soaked. But we still packed our bags with vigor and predictability, having done this so many times before. First to leave were Nun and Sarge, then Lone Stride. We yelled out congratulations, raising our hands in some victory pose. It caused me to knock over an unopened can of Budweiser I had saved just for the summit. I was eager to get going, eager to complete the hike just like I had started: with a rush of adrenalin. Yet time had made me stronger. I could never have hoped to finish the final 15 miles in a 5-hour waltz along ridgelines and rivers. I will miss being Strider.

As I walked away from the Gooch Gap Shelter, Smilie, Church, Big Bird, and Wookie all looked on, cheering, and I could feel my sense of where home was fade. Yet I still had the biggest grin as I turned the corner and followed the white blazes. There are some 80,000 white blazes that mark the Appalachian Trail, yet I was down to the final few. I never had to think about my direction; I just looked up and followed like a well-trained monkey. It made me wonder how I would go back to the so-called "real world" with no marked trees to guide me. The rain fluctuated in strength yet still managed to soak through my long-defunct rain jacket. In the cold, I could feel the sweat begin to make its way into my base layers. I knew if I kept moving, it would be OK, but a moment's break would release the shivers. In the end, hunger won out; hunger always won. So I took a break at the nearest shelter—7.5 miles done, a meager 8 more to go. Just 0.36 percent left on one of the longest continually marked trails in the world. I was emotionally numb.

Church and Smilie appeared at the shelter as suddenly the cold front changed to icy winds. The temperature continued to plummet. The trail had taught me the value of action, the rewards of effort. In the wilderness, sometimes the best reward is simply warmth. So there it was; somewhat fed, I was on my feet again, striding toward the southern terminus.

The trail began to share its path with the Benton MacKaye Trail, named for the man who came up with the absurd idea to make a 2,000 mile dirt path from the top of the East Coast to almost the bottom. As I walked, I thought about him and his crazy goal and how it was just as crazy to go along and attempt it myself. Yet he did something extraordinary, and I wanted to know what that felt like. So I upped the pace. Soon enough, I was within a mile—1 mile left; 5,280 feet to walk. Fifteen minutes remained before I switched from prospect to proven, thru-hiker to thru-hiked. Present to past tense. It was then it hit me that this was going to be a quick ending. I could stand atop Springer for an entire week and it would still feel quick, still pale in comparison to the larger body of work. I was sad, exhilarated, proud, confident, and hesitant all at the same time.

I almost wanted to stay in this moment forever, knowing that as soon as I crossed the finish line, I could never go back. I could never return to the feeling I had; all I could do was remember it. I stopped a fifth of a mile away from the summit and walked to the Springer Mountain Shelter, the last shelter. Alongside Lone Stride, I whipped out my sleeping bag to stay warm and grabbed the shelter logbook. It was bare of southbound entries. I imagined everyone was too eager to stop so near the summit. But we had chosen to wait for everyone, at least to prolong the special feeling we all shared being out here. It was a flame about to be extinguished. We were holding onto the sight of it with all we had. I wanted to summit, but I didn't. I didn't know what I wanted. The trail felt like home, yet I was Strider, a 2014 thru-hiker, not a homeless man. Church and Smilie arrived, so now only three were still making their way along.

Lone Stride, however, couldn't wait; his ride home was parked down the approach trail. We hugged, and I watched him walk away. The bond that formed so instantly with fellow hikers was whisked away to a faraway place. I didn't know when or if I would see him again.

Jamie Gault on his 2014 thru-hike

Where in the "real world" could one lose such a connection so swiftly? But I knew it was a part of the magic of the trail. We had come from different parts of the world, different lifestyles and worldviews, yet once placed in the AT melting pot, the camaraderie developed at the drop of a hat. I read the logbook and found northbound entries from way back in March. All these hikers had been experiencing their first day on the trail. I wondered how many of them made it all the way. Only one in four would. I remembered my first entry; I didn't have a trail name yet, so I called myself "The Aussie" for lack of creative genius. And then it struck me; today wasn't the most important day. Summiting was no more important than the Blood Mountain climb the previous day, no more important than the muddy canopies of Vermont. It just felt major because it was the last day.

As I reflected, I began to feel more comfortable about being so close. That if today was no more important and special than all the 152 days previous, then it would be the culmination of all the miles and memories I would cherish rather than the final few steps. With that in mind, I hiked to the top of Springer, a journey of approximately 5 million steps coming to a close. I stood at the top, speechless, as the rain on the leaves froze around me. My phone turned on and off due to the cold. I was content. Because although it was terrible weather to summit in, I wouldn't have had it any other way.

As the wind blasted past me, I thought about the beautiful summer day on top of Avery Peak. I remembered the sun-soaked and snowcapped peaks of the Smokies and the people I shared it all with.

Although the summit marks the end, only now can I sit and truly appreciate all the amazing things that occurred. As nine of us squished into a five-seater Jeep, our final dose of Trail Magic, we placed the final memories into our Appalachian Trail catalog. We knew well that everything we had attained, learnt, and experienced would remain with us for the rest of our lives.

FEATURED SHELTER:
BLOOD MOUNTAIN SHELTER

Blood Mountain Shelter, the oldest shelter on the Appalachian Trail, sits at 4,440 feet. The shelter is located on the summit of Blood Mountain, 28.9 miles from Springer Mountain and 2,163.1 miles from Mount Katahdin. It has a sleeping capacity of eight and a privy nearby. Built in 1937 by the Civilian Conservation Corps, the stone building was originally constructed for the Georgia State Park System, but in 1956 it was transferred to the USDA Forest Service. It was restored in the 1980s by the Georgia Appalachian Trail Club and is maintained by them today.

Blood Mountain Shelter facade, Mile 28.9 northbound; 2013 thru-hike

CREATURE FEATURE: WHITE-TAILED DEER

You are very likely to see white-tailed deer, as they roam in abundance the entire length of the Appalachian Trail. They are often spotted munching on plants during the early morning but can be seen any time of day. During the spring you may come across a newborn fawn nestled in woodland areas. The white of their tails acts as a flag for young deer to easily follow their mothers when they feel threatened. Deer are extremely fast and excellent leapers. They can run at speeds up to 35 miles per hour.

White-tailed deer, Shenandoah National Park, during 2013 thru-hike

FLORA FEATURE: MAYAPPLE

Mayapple can be found on the forest floor near the Reflection Pond on the AT Approach Trail. It typically blooms mid-April through early May. The white flower, with eight petals and bright yellow stamens, can be found beneath large, light green umbrellalike leaves.

Detail of a mayapple flower

Mayapple patch

The flowers bloom, the songbirds sing,
And though it sun or rain,
I walk the mountain tops with spring
From Georgia north to Maine.

—Earl V. Shaffer, written during his 1948 thru-hike,
with a sketch he made of Pinnacles of Dan

If you're a newcomer to the AT, you won't pass many campfires (if any) before you hear the name Earl Shaffer. The Appalachian Trail legend is the first person to complete the trail in a continuous journey. In 1948, Shaffer hiked from Mount Oglethorpe in Georgia to Mount Katahdin in Maine, only eleven years after the trail's completion. During his hike he sketched Pinnacles of Dan in Virginia and wrote a short poem (the one above) on a folded piece of paper, which he sent to the ATC meeting, letting them know he was determined to go all the way. Inside, Shaffer had recorded his departure date from Oglethorpe and his ETA at Katahdin. Some people were skeptical and wondered how he could do it. Others wondered why he wanted to. Shaffer dubbed himself "Crazy One," and yet, crazy as it seemed, people ended up seeing Shaffer in a new light. After close examination of his photos, notes, and personal journal, he became regarded as a person with high integrity and determination. Later, he penned *Walking with Spring* and finally answered the "why" behind his hike. His story has and will continue to inspire thousands to ignore the doubters and skeptics by chasing the dream of thru-hiking the Appalachian Trail with a trailblazing can-do attitude. Not only is Shaffer the first individual to complete a thru-hike, he is also the first one to hike the AT in both directions and the first to have completed thru-hikes incorporating each of the trail's southern termini. Both his 1965 and 1998 hikes included Springer Mountain.

Earl Shaffer self-portrait, 1948

The above photo is a self-portrait that he captured with a trigger wire. The story goes that it was too foggy on his first ascent to get a clear shot, so he hiked the mountain a second time to get this photo, most likely taken the day after he first summited Katahdin. Actually, Shaffer went back all along the trail, intending to get good images of various spots he'd not captured at all or that hadn't turned out well due to not having film, his camera not functioning, poor weather, etc.

On the AT in Georgia, location unknown; 2013 thru-hike

DISCOVERING STRENGTH

There is something uniquely special about the Appalachian Trail in Georgia, as it is where some thru-hikers discover the strength they didn't know they had. We aren't just talking about physical strength. Sure, hiking requires strong legs and a powerful core, but it also takes strength of heart and mind. Georgia is the first and last place thru-hikers experience a need to dig deep for inner strength, whether it's mental fortitude to go farther or courage to follow the inner wisdom that is whispering to cut the trip short. Sometimes it takes more guts to leave the woods and return to the life we left behind in pursuit of a grand adventure than it does to continue onward.

Tree canopy on the AT in Georgia; 2013 thru-hike

Hiker blues can set in early for all sorts of unforeseen reasons. However grand and fulfilling a hike may be, it doesn't take long for sore feet, cold nights, and relentless rainy days to dampen our spirit. The aches and pains start to drum up a discomfort that many can't handle. So it's no wonder that "embrace the suck" is such a famous saying on the trail. Embracing the suck is about finding joy even on days full of suffering and accepting that it's all a part of the journey.

The stretch of AT in Georgia may be the testing ground for thru-hikers traveling north, but it's the final, glorious push for Southbounders—another reason this state is so special. It has the honor of marking the most transformation among hikers.

Georgia–North Carolina border, Mile 78.1 northbound; 2013 thru-hike

Hikers will never forget the place as the beginning (or the completion) of an adventurous journey.

Many thru-hikers spend months, years, and decades preparing for the long 2,000-plus-mile journey. Time and effort go into acquiring gear, planning logistics, and saving money for the hike. However, once the boots hit the trail, it doesn't take long for hikers to feel the surreal sense of "I'm doing it." With everything we need on our back, limited contact with the outside world, and limitless time to reflect, we discover early on just how much this dream will require from us.

Grassy Ridge, Mile 382.6 northbound; 2021

North Carolina and Tennessee

The Appalachian Trail meanders its way back and forth across the North Carolina and Tennessee border for more than 350 miles, which is why the two states are typically bundled together as one section in other guidebooks. The AT traverses stretches of the Pisgah, Cherokee, and Nantahala National Forests. It also travels 70 miles through Great Smoky Mountains National Park, where the biological diversity, rich human history, and abundant scenic views attract visitors worldwide. It's home to the tallest point on the Appalachian Trail and the "Salamander Capital of the World." Although we are honored to share our knowledge and love for all of the Appalachian Trail, this chapter reigns supreme in our humble opinion, since it's also the place we call home.

> It is one of the many blessings of wilderness life that shows us how few things we need in order to be perfectly happy.
>
> —Horace Kephart

THE GREAT SMOKY MOUNTAINS

Seventy miles of the Appalachian Trail lie within the border of Great Smoky Mountains National Park, a 522,427-acre natural wonderland that has a little something for everyone to enjoy. Millions of visitors travel to the Smokies each year to explore more than 850 miles of hiking trails and the vast display of biological diversity. The Great Smoky Mountains are home to wildlife, wildflowers, and people with a rich history. It's here that President Franklin D. Roosevelt stood at Newfound Gap with one foot in North Carolina and one foot in Tennessee to formally dedicate the national park as a sanctuary for the world to enjoy. Before it was a park, the land belonged to the Cherokee, local farmers, timber companies, and families. The Appalachian Trail crosses the parking lot of the Rockefeller Memorial

Jarred Douglas atop the Albert Mountain Fire Tower, Mile 99.7 northbound; 2013 thru-hike

Hiking through a North Carolina rhododendron tunnel; 2013 thru-hike

AT blaze in North Carolina; 2013 thru-hike

Siler Bald Shelter facade, Mile 113.6 northbound; 2013 thru-hike

Abby "Mowgli" Self spending an evening inside Siler Bald Shelter, Mile 113.6 northbound; 2013 thru-hike

Wesser Bald observation tower, Mile 130.2 northbound; 2013 thru-hike

View from Rocky Top, Mile 184.8 northbound; 2013 thru-hike

dedication site, which pays homage to the thousands who donated their land and money to help create the park that now so many lovingly enjoy.

If northbound thru-hikers didn't gain their "hiker legs" in Georgia, they are bound to get them after finishing the section of AT in the Smokies. It's tough terrain with lots of ups and downs, but the trail stays interesting, with far-reaching views, diverse plant life, and scenic water features. There is absolutely no shortage of inspiration or beauty here!

The Blue Ridge Parkway is a fantastic way to experience the southern mountains for those who are not physically able to hike the steep slopes. The Parkway extends from Great Smoky Mountains National Park near Cherokee,

DID YOU KNOW?

The Great Smoky Mountains are known as the "Salamander Capital of the World." An abundance of salamanders inhabit the Smokies, and many different species have been identified. Keep your eyes peeled for a hellbender, the region's largest by far!

There are trees here that stood before our forefathers came to this continent; there are brooks that will run as clear as on the day the first pioneer cupped his hand and drank from them. In this park, we shall conserve the pine, the redwood, the dogwood, the azalea, the rhododendron, the trout and the thrush for the happiness of the American people.

The old frontier that put the hard fibre in the American spirit, and the long muscles on the American back, lives and will live in these untamed mountains to give future generations a sense of the land from which their forefathers hewed their homes.

—President Franklin D. Roosevelt, 1940 address at the dedication of Great Smoky Mountains National Park

North Carolina, to the southern terminus of Shenandoah National Park's Skyline Drive in Virginia.

BEST TIME TO VISIT
The Great Smoky Mountains are great to visit year-round; however, you will get a special treat during spring, when wildflowers blanket the valley in beautiful blooms, and in the fall, when the leaves turn the mountains vibrant hues of orange, yellow, and red.

Bryan Anderson ascending from Fontana Dam in Great Smoky Mountains National Park during a 2013 thru-hike

3

FONTANA DAM TO CLINGMANS DOME

This long-distance hike begins at the threshold of Great Smoky Mountains National Park at a small parking lot near Fontana Village in North Carolina and extends to Newfound Gap at the border of Tennessee. You will pass many iconic landmarks, including the mountain that inspired Tennessee's state anthem, "Rocky Top," and the highest peak along the Appalachian Trail, Clingmans Dome. This trip can be done in two to three days, depending on your pace. If you have the time to explore beyond

Clingmans Dome tower, Mile 200.1 northbound; 2021

Newfound Gap, we recommend traveling farther north to visit Charlies Bunion and the Mount Cammerer lookout tower.

DISTANCE: 35.4 miles one way
DIFFICULTY: Moderate due to steep ascents and descents
TRAILHEAD GPS: 35.4414 / -83.7968
NEARBY TOWN: Fontana Village, North Carolina
HIGHLIGHTS: Incredible views, a high-elevation spruce-fir forest, and a historical landmark

TIPS

- The visitor center at Fontana Dam is open early May to late October.
- Except for the Gatlinburg and Oconaluftee River Trails, dogs are not allowed on hiking trails in Great Smoky Mountains National Park.
- Overnight permits are required.
- The road that leads to the parking lot at Clingmans Dome is closed in winter.
- Fontana Dam Shelter, often referred to as the "Fontana Hilton" for its impressive design and creature comforts, is 0.4 mile north of the visitor center. If you are getting a late start, enjoy the night here to start out in the morning refreshed.

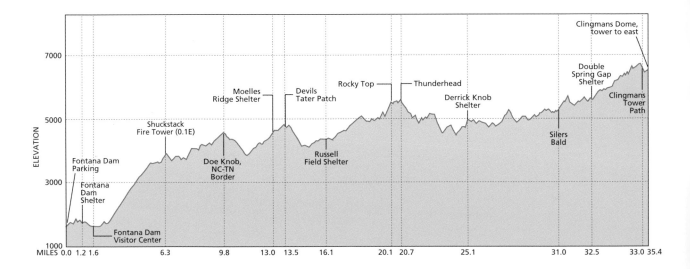

MILEAGE MARKERS (NORTH TO SOUTH)

SECTION	MILES FROM SPRINGER MOUNTAIN	LANDMARK	ELEVATION (IN FEET)
0.0	164.7	Fontana Dam parking	1,756
1.2	165.9	Fontana Dam Shelter ("Fontana Hilton")	1,853
1.6	166.3	Fontana Dam Visitor Center	1,700
6.3	171.0	Shuckstack Fire Tower (0.1 mile east)	3,889
7.6	172.3	Birch Spring Gap; campsite (100 yards west); unreliable spring	3,736
9.6	174.3	Side trail (0.3 mile west) to Gregory Bald	4,443
9.8	174.5	Doe Knob, North Carolina–Tennessee border	4,520
11.3	176	Ekaneetlee Gap	3,842
13.0	177.7	Mollies Ridge Shelter; unreliable spring	4,585
13.5	178.2	Devils Tater Patch	4,775
14.6	179.3	Little Abrams Gap	4,120
16.1	180.8	Russell Field Shelter; spring (0.1 mile west)	4,247
19.0	183.7	Spence Field Shelter (0.2 mile east) on Eagle Creek Trail	4,914
20.1	184.8	Rocky Top	5,440
20.7	185.4	Thunderhead Mountain	5,527
23.3	188.0	Starkey Gap	4,552
25.1	189.8	Derrick Knob Shelter	4,884
27.8	192.5	Buckeye Gap	4,817
30.8	195.5	Silers Bald Shelter; spring	5,452
31.0	195.7	Silers Bald	5,607
32.5	197.2	Double Spring Gap Shelter	5,509
33.0	197.7	Clingmans Tower Path; paved path between parking area and observation tower	6,553
35.4	200.1	Clingmans Dome; tower to the east	6,643

View from Fontana Dam, Mile 164.7 northbound; 2013 thru-hike

Jarred Douglas on Fontana Dam, Mile 164.7 northbound; 2013 thru-hike

THE HIKE

Locate the trailhead near the Fontana Dam Visitor Center and begin hiking north on the AT. Cross the southern boundary of Great Smoky Mountains National Park, traverse through the boulder jumble, and ascend the mountain to take in the views on Shuckstack. Once you reach the top, you can take a quick side trail (0.1 mile east) to

Interior of Shuckstack Fire Tower, Mile 171.0 northbound; 2013 thru-hike

View from Shuckstack Fire Tower, Mile 171.0 northbound; 2013 thru-hike

Spence Field Shelter, Mile 183.7 northbound; 2013 thru-hike

Trail leading to Spence Field Shelter, Mile 183.7 northbound; 2013 thru-hike

View of Spence Field Shelter from the ridge (shelter is the square in the center of the image); 2013 thru-hike

The Appalachian Trail and Mountains-to-Sea Trail sign below Clingmans Dome, Mile 200.1 northbound; 2021

View from Clingmans Dome, Mile 200.1 northbound; 2021

View of paved path to Clingmans Dome parking lot, Mile 200.1 northbound

Sign for Mount Collins Shelter and Sugarland Mountain Trail, Mile 202.8 northbound; 2013 thru-hike

Privy at Mount Collins Shelter, Mile 202.8 northbound; 2013 thru-hike

check out the fire tower. There is a campsite at Birch Spring Gap with tent pads, bear cables, and a spring located just over 1 mile from Shuckstack. Or you can hike a bit farther to stay at Mollies Ridge Shelter.

Hike up to Devils Tater Patch and then descend 660 feet to Little Abrams Gap. From here you will begin to climb in elevation once again as you pass the Russell Field Shelter and Spence Field Shelter. Both are great camping options to rest before climbing Thunderhead.

Begin a steep climb of more than 500 feet before reaching the summit of Rocky Top, the place that inspired Tennessee's official state song. Enjoy spectacular views of the Smokies before hiking to Thunderhead Mountain, descending into Starkey Gap, and through Sugar Tree Gap. The trail skirts past Derrick Knob Shelter, where there is a reliable spring.

Cross Cold Spring Knob at 5,204 feet and descend rapidly to Buckeye Gap. Then hike roughly 3 miles to Silers Bald, a mountaintop meadow with lovely views of the Smokies. In the summer, you might find an extra treat of delicious wild blackberries. Beyond the bald is the Double Spring Gap Shelter, a great place to camp before climbing to Clingmans Dome.

From the shelter, climb steadily for roughly 3 miles, crossing over Mount Buckley and past a side trail that leads to parking for Clingmans Dome, gaining more than 1,000 feet in elevation. Finally, reach Clingmans Dome, the highest peak on the Appalachian Trail. A short side trail will take you to the top of the summit's observation tower. From the tower you can see 360-degree views of the Great Smoky Mountains (unless the peak is surrounded by clouds, which happens often).

Once you are ready to leave the observation tower, take a short walk down the paved path to a small gift shop. The walkway continues onward to restrooms and a parking lot. Be sure to arrange for a shuttle beforehand if you won't have a car waiting for you. There is also a short trail to Andrews Bald, a lovely hike to spot flame azalea and rhododendron in bloom during late spring and early summer.

Another option to consider is to continue hiking southbound roughly 7.5 miles on the AT toward Newfound Gap, where our next featured hike picks up. You will cross Mount Collins, pass the shelter, and traverse Mingus Ridge before descending to Newfound Gap.

DID YOU KNOW?

The Appalachian Trail runs across the top of Fontana Dam, the tallest dam on the eastern seaboard. At nearly 500 feet tall and 2,365 feet long, this modern marvel creates Fontana Lake, the largest lake in western North Carolina. It offers 240 feet of shoreline for recreation activities such as fishing and camping. Fontana Dam was constructed in the 1940s by the Tennessee Valley Authority for a waterpower source and flood control.

by Ricky J. Adams ("Chief Badweather")

My first solo hike on the Appalachian Trail came years ago when I was in my twenties. It was late August, just before sunrise, when my girlfriend (I call her wife now) dropped me off in the Cosby section of the Great Smoky Mountains. I planned to stay out on the AT for four nights, walking south to Newfound Gap and hitchhiking back to Gatlinburg, home.

My trusty pack I had at the time was an external frame Jansport, and it was WAY TOO HEAVY once I loaded it down. My infantry days should have taught me better (they did, I just overpacked!). Equipment back then wasn't near as low weight as it is these days. And if I remember correctly, I was wearing a good old-fashioned pair of Levi blue jean shorts with my old combat boots and cotton socks. My sleeping bag was a US Army surplus (mountain bag). It was considered a smaller, lighter bag back then, and I was happy to have it. I don't know why I had a hatchet, but for some reason it seemed like a good thing to have with me at the time. Not to mention all the extra food I had, probably enough to feed a local Boy Scout troop.

So there I was. My shirt, drenched in sweat already, and the sun hadn't even come up yet. *Whew, easy on that water bottle*, I tell myself as I wipe my forehead. I catch myself looking down at the trail a lot as I hike. I try to look up, but it seems a lot easier to breathe and walk as I look down. Wow! I thought I was in shape. For goodness' sake, I had just gotten out of the police academy a few months earlier. *I think it's time for me to take my first break of the day. But wait, it's still dark.* I check my watch and realize that I've only been hiking for 20 minutes. I can still smell the coffee brewing at the Cosby campground! Jeez . . .

Finally, I was at the intersection of Low Gap and the Appalachian Trail. A cool breeze was blowing, and the smell of the evergreens was in the wind. As I walk into the Cosby Shelter, I find that I have the place to myself. It's as quiet as a mouse. Ironically, the only sound I heard was the pitter-patter of a mouse scurrying off as I came in the door. (Back then, the Park Service used chain-link fences to keep bears away from hikers.) With plenty of daylight left, I decided to hike on to the Tri-Corner Knob Shelter. *Somewhere around 8 miles south shouldn't be a problem.*

After a couple of miles, I'm feeling it and sucking down my water like a thirsty hunting dog. I catch myself chugging my water and stop a few swigs before I'm totally empty. I don't want to be dry of water because your mind goes into a panic when it knows it can't quench a quick thirst. I hike on and hope the next spring is close. Just a short time later, a sign of water appears. Wow, the trail really does provide! A wooden sign reads, "Mt. Guyot Spring 100 feet." I finish off the last of my water as I head toward the spring. As I get closer, I can see another sign that reads, "Mt. Guyot Spring," but the spring is as dry as dust! All a person can do is hike on. So that's what I do. Before long, I'm at the Tri-Corner Knob Shelter with cool, clean, plentiful water.

It's early afternoon, and the place is quiet as a mouse—not even a mouse in sight this time. There is still lots of daylight left and nobody here to talk with; in fact, I've not seen anyone all day long. So I decided to hike on once again. *Look out Pecks Corner Shelter! Just a little over 5 miles away, I should be fine.*

Once the sun started to set, I found a place to camp out for the night. I hung my hammock, enjoyed a meal, and found a tree to hang my food bag. *Now I know why I brought that hatchet. I'll use my trusty hatchet as a weight to hang my food bag.*

I tie my rope (an old clothesline) to the bottom of my hatchet and do a couple of warm-up motions before I attempt to toss it over a tree limb. Then, just like Daniel Boone, I throw the hatchet as I hold the other end of the clothesline (I mean rope) to keep from losing it. But my plan backfires. My hatchet hits the limb instead of going over it, unintentionally inviting the tree to play a game of catch. I duck down while letting out a little-girl scream as the tree tosses the hatchet back at a high rate of speed.

Finally, after a few rounds of this dangerous game of catch, I am successful. My bag is out of the bear's reach, and I've successfully climbed into my hammock. All is good! Until . . . *BAM! BAM! BANG!*—a thunder and lightning storm from out of NOWHERE! The lightning strikes—CLOSE! TOO CLOSE! ABORT! ABORT! I've got to get to the lower ground! Where is that shelter? It's got to be close! I packed up in record time, and with my poncho on, I ran down the trail looking like Batman. I think my clothesline is still hanging in that tree to this day (not really). FEET, DON'T FAIL ME NOW!

As I approach Pecks Corner Shelter, I can smell food cooking and hear people talking; I hope for enough room to lie down for the night. Only seven people were inside, and they all looked surprised to see me coming in so late. However, everyone was friendly and welcomed me with a place to sleep near the wall of the top bunk. As I rolled out my sleeping bag, another hiker leaned back against the chain-link fence, reading a book. He said, "Well, looky here, folks." As I turned to look, a black bear walked up to the fence from the other side. Everyone reached for their cameras, while the book-reading hiker held his spot up against the fence. As the bear came closer, he talked to the bear, saying "How ya doin' buddy?" Evidently, the bear couldn't speak English and took offense to what the book-reader said, because he slapped the fence just inches away from the reader's head and gave out a loud grunt! (I speak a little black bear; the bear said, "SHUT UP!") The book reader said, "JESUS!" as did the others in the shelter (I think I peed just a little); jeez . . .

Gosh. I love the AT. That night, I slept like a baby with the rain coming down on the tin roof after a 15-plus-mile day. The wooden bunk felt great. I was woken up once or twice by someone below me snoring, but that's part of shelter life. The following morning, while I was packing up, I overheard an older man vent to another hiker about "that kid" that kept him awake snoring. As I stepped around the corner, the two stopped talking once they saw me. I didn't think anything of it as I saddled up and told everyone, "See ya down the trail."

It wasn't long before the older hiker caught up to me, wanting to apologize for the snoring comment. Evidently, he thought I was "THE KID." He was in his late 60s and could hike like a mountain goat. I was amazed at the pace he kept. While we hiked out to Charlies Bunion, we swapped many stories of our lives. I stayed at Charlies Bunion while he hiked on. I couldn't hold his pace.

My four-night hike turned into a one-night walk, but with the same miles under my boots. As I come out of the woods at Newfound Gap, the tourists are everywhere. I stick out my thumb for a ride, and the first van that comes by stops and tells me to get in. As I start to load up, I look over and see my older hiking buddy lying in the grass in the middle of the parking lot. Looking at me, he raises his hand to tell me goodbye with a long pause. I returned the raised hand to him; we both nod to each other as if to say, "See you down the trail."

Since that time, I've had many campfires on the AT, and with the good Lord's help, I hope to have many more. I'm my old buddy's age now, approaching 60, and still love the trail life on the Appalachian Trail.

FEATURED SHELTER: THE "FONTANA HILTON"

Hikers dubbed this shelter the "Fontana Hilton" for its unconventional amenities. The shelter sleeps over twenty people and has warm showers, bathrooms, and even a solar-powered charging station. Some folks are worried about shelters becoming overdeveloped, ultimately taking hikers away from the wonder of sleeping outdoors by promoting modern amenities over the natural environment. A valid concern, but with its close proximity to the visitor center and Fontana Village, the Fontana Hilton might as well be a primitive hostel. Relax, take a shower, and enjoy the view.

"Fontana Hilton," Mile 165.9 northbound; 2021
PHOTOGRAPH BY SARA JONES DECKER

Gateway to the Smokies

Once you get to Newfound Gap, consider catching a ride into Gatlinburg, Tennessee. Gatlinburg, the gateway to the Smokies, is often used as a base camp since it sits on the edge of the 522,427-acre national park. It's a popular travel destination for those seeking to explore the national park's numerous offerings: trails roaming to cascading waterfalls, spectacular places to see wildlife, and remnants of old settlements that give glimpses into the history and culture of the people of Appalachia and more. Over the years, Gatlinburg has become highly touristy, yet beauty remains beyond the crowded sidewalks. Here are some of our recommendations if you decide to visit:

- Check out the **Sugarlands Visitor Center** for expert hiking and park information. They can point you in the direction of some fascinating history hikes.
- Stop in the **Nantahala Outdoor Center** for any necessary gear.
- Visit the famed **Donut Friar** for a French cruller, and be sure to get a second to eat on the trail!
- Ride the trolley through the **Great Smoky Arts and Crafts Community** after visiting the nationally renowned **Arrowmont School of Arts and Crafts.**
- Taste some mountain-made moonshine at **Ole Smoky Distillery,** the first federally licensed distillery in the history of east Tennessee.

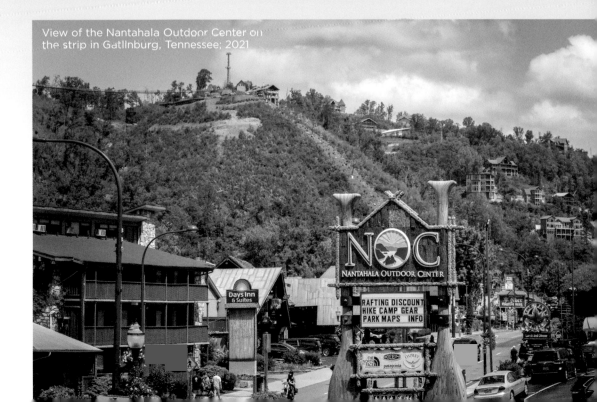

View of the Nantahala Outdoor Center on the strip in Gatlinburg, Tennessee; 2021

4

NEWFOUND GAP TO CHARLIES BUNION

This 8.0-mile hike is perfect for avid day hikers who are seeking an excellent view of the Great Smoky Mountains. Fall is the perfect time to experience this craggy vista. Leaf-lookers, this one's for you!

DISTANCE: 8.0 miles out and back
DIFFICULTY: Moderate due to elevation gain
TRAILHEAD GPS: 35.6112 / -83.4257
NEARBY TOWN: Gatlinburg, Tennessee (15 miles west)
HIGHLIGHTS: Incredible panoramic views, history

View from Newfound Gap, Mile 207.7 northbound; 2021

TIPS

- Except for the Gatlinburg and Oconaluftee River Trails, dogs are not allowed on hiking trails in Great Smoky Mountains National Park.
- Overnight permits are required for backcountry camping.
- There are restrooms at the Newfound Gap parking area.
- Newfound Gap receives a lot of snow during the winter. Be sure to check for road closures if you plan on hiking during the cold season.
- You can view a "Fall Color Report" at smokiesinformation.org.

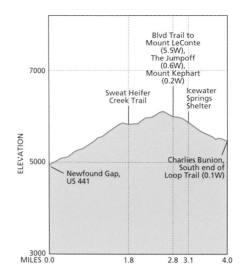

Trailhead at Newfound Gap, Mile 207.7 northbound; 2021

MILEAGE MARKERS (SOUTH TO NORTH)

SECTION	MILES FROM SPRINGER	LANDMARK	ELEVATION (IN FEET)
0.0	207.7	Newfound Gap, US 441	5,045
1.8	209.5	Sweat Heifer Creek Trail (to the east)	5,834
2.8	210.5	Boulevard Trail to Mount LeConte (5.5 miles west); The Jumpoff (0.6 mile west); Mount Kephart (0.2 mile west)	6,035
3.1	210.8	Icewater Springs Shelter	5,935
4.0	211.7	Charlies Bunion, south end of loop trail (0.1 mile west)	5,521

THE HIKE

Locate the trailhead, near the Rockefeller Monument, and begin hiking north. Following the white blazes, you will travel through dense forest as you walk gently uphill. In roughly 3 miles you will top out at 6,035 feet at an intersection of trails that lead to other great views, including Mount Kephart (0.2 mile west), The Jumpoff (0.6 mile west), and Mount LeConte (5.5 miles west), the crown jewel of the Smokies. Three-tenths of a mile from the intersection, the AT passes Icewater Spring Shelter, a comfortable spot to enjoy a snack. Then the trail starts to descend to Charlies Bunion.

Yes, we know what you are thinking, and we agree: It's a strange name for such a beautiful overlook. The legend is that a group of hikers, including Horace Kephart and Charlie Conner, went out to survey the area, and when they came upon the craggy outcrop, one hiker exclaimed, "That sticks out like Charlie's Bunion," and the name stuck (without the apostrophe). The panoramic views from "the bunion" are extraordinary. You can take the Charlies Bunion Loop Trail (0.1 mile west) for more views before you leave.

To return, retrace your steps by hiking south on the AT back to the parking lot.

DID YOU KNOW?

As hikers, we know that air is typically cooler at higher elevations than at lower elevations. However, under certain atmospheric circumstances an unusual weather phenomenon called "thermal inversion" can happen. When cool air rapidly sinks into the valleys as the sun goes down and mixes with moisture, it creates a layer of fog, with mountain peaks resembling islands rising from a misty sea. Thermal inversion can happen in many places along the AT, although the Southern Appalachians, with their favorable topography of deep valleys and many ridgelines, offer the most stunning vistas to experience floating above an undulating sea of clouds.

Bryan Anderson on Charlies Bunion, Mile 212.0 northbound; 2013 thru-hike

Trail leaving Charlies Bunion, Mile 212.0 northbound; 2013 thru-hike

Why should this last stand of splendid, irreplaceable trees be sacrificed to the greedy maw of the sawmill? Why should future generations be robbed of all chances to see with their own eyes what a real forest, a real wildwood, a real unimproved work of God is like.

—Horace Kephart

As a prolific writer and advocate for the Smokies, Kephart was instrumental in creating Great Smoky Mountains National Park, ultimately protecting and preserving the Southern Appalachians from being completely wiped out by the sawmills. He also helped to route the AT through the Smokies. Kephart is the author of many books, two of the most widely read being *Our Southern Highlanders* and his classic outdoors guide, *Camping and Woodcraft*.

Portrait of Horace Kephart COURTESY OF HUNTER LIBRARY AT WESTERN CAROLINA UNIVERSITY

OUTSIDE THE PARK

5
MAX PATCH

The Appalachian Trail meanders above tree line across Max Patch, a large grassy bald with jaw-dropping views that will have you feeling on top of the world. On clear days you can see Mount Mitchell to the east and the Great Smoky Mountains to the south from the 4,600-foot summit. Max Patch may not be among the tallest of the Southern Appalachians, but if there were awards given for the best Appalachian viewpoint, Max Patch would be in the running. The grassy balds with expansive open sky make for a great spot to catch the sunset or sunrise. This short hike is a direct route to the top of the bald, where you can roam and linger for as long as you like.

DISTANCE: 1.5-mile loop
DIFFICULTY: Easy, but will get you huffing and puffing
TRAILHEAD GPS: 35.7963 / -82.9627
NEARBY TOWN: Hot Springs, North Carolina
HIGHLIGHTS: Incredible 360-degree views, high-elevation grassy bald, history

Max Patch parking lot; 2021

TIPS

- The dirt road to the parking area at the base of Max Patch is rough and difficult for two-wheel-drive vehicles.
- Camping and fires are prohibited at the summit. Roaring Fork Shelter is roughly 2 miles away if you want to camp overnight; stay there.
- This trail is dog-friendly; just keep your furry friends on a leash.
- If you are hiking in the summer, consider sun protection—there is no shade at the summit.
- This special spot is popular for good reason; however, in recent years Max Patch has almost been loved to death. Some people have been disrespecting this Appalachian gem by leaving trash, human waste, and camping equipment scattered about. Restrictions have been put into place to help this beloved mountain begin to heal from overcrowding. Please help Max Patch stay wild and beautiful by walking only on designated trails and adhering to these restrictions, and always practice Leave No Trace principles.

THE HIKE

Take the blue-blazed spur trail that veers left from the parking area and extends roughly 0.3 mile to the Appalachian Trail. Skirting the side of Max Patch, you begin to climb modestly in elevation. During spring and summer, plentiful wildflowers line the path for the entire route. Continue hiking through a shady wooded area until you reach the junction with the AT. Turn right onto the AT and begin walking uphill to the summit. From here, the views are endless. You can see the Great Smoky Mountains to the southwest. Look to the east and you will see Mount Mitchell rising in the distance, with the Craggies standing in front of it. Peaks in the Great Balsam and Unaka Mountains are also visi-

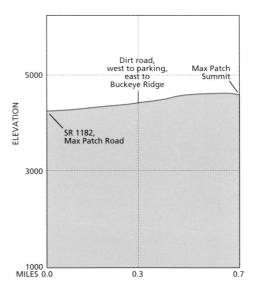

ble. You will most likely encounter others enjoying the far-reaching views, picnicking, tossing a Frisbee, and basking in the serenity.

When you are ready to return, follow the white blazes painted on wooden posts across the bald until you reach another spur trail that leads back down to the parking area.

Blaze on Max Patch, looking toward Bluff Mountain; 2021

Max Patch summit, Mile 255.1 northbound; 2021

Blaze on Max Patch; 2021

TALES FROM THE TRAIL: HIKING IN RECORD SNOWFALL

by Jamie Gault ("Strider," 2014)

Hailing from Australia, my idea of snow was half-frozen slush that comes around two months a year on our tallest mountains. So when I woke up the morning after Halloween in North Carolina, I couldn't wrap my head around the knee-deep snow that had appeared out of nowhere. Chilimac and myself had plans on pushing an easy 20 that day, but boy, did we fall short. Trudging through deep powder, we managed a paltry pace of 1 mile per hour. At first it was fun, part of the adventure, but soon our thoughts turned purely to survival, and we sought the nearest trail hostel and a hot meal. After 6 hours of hiking, we at last made it to the Laurel Trading Post. Wet, cold, and downright miserable, we cranked the heat and slept all afternoon. It was yet another reminder of how little we need out on-trail and how easy it is to satisfy a grumpy hiker. Soon it became a memory we were blessed to have as we hiked through North Carolina's biggest November snowfall on record.

6
BIG FIRESCALD KNOB

This hike will take you along the ridgeline from Jones Meadow parking area to Big Firescald Knob, an exposed ridgeline full of boulders and iconic views in 360 degrees. The out-and-back hike is 4.0 miles long. It is short but sweet and offers a lot. Big Firescald is among our favorite hikes; being so close, we can see this ridgeline from our homestead. With everything you get to see, it's the best bang for your buck timewise.

DISTANCE: 4.0 miles out and back
DIFFICULTY: Moderate due to elevation gain
TRAILHEAD GPS: 36.031330 / -82.705361
NEARBY TOWN: Hot Springs, North Carolina
HIGHLIGHTS: Excellent views, rock outcrops

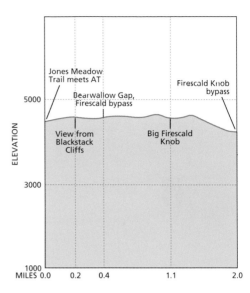

On Big Firescald Knob the morning after a winter storm; 2016

View from Jones Meadow parking lot toward Camp Creek Bald; 2021

MILEAGE MARKERS (NORTH TO SOUTH)

SECTION	MILES FROM SPRINGER MOUNTAIN	LANDMARK	ELEVATION (IN FEET)
0.0	298.1	Jones Meadow Trail meets AT	4,480
0.2	298.3	View from Blackstack Cliffs	4,501
0.4	298.5	Bearwallow Gap; Firescald bypass to the west reconnects with AT 1.5 miles north	4,421
1.1	299.2	Big Firescald Knob, view	4,566
2.0	300.1	Firescald Knob bypass to the west; reconnects with AT 1.5 miles south	4,208

THE HIKE

Starting from the parking lot atop Viking Mountain at Jones Meadow, you are presented with a lovely view of Blackstack Cliffs in front of you looking out over Tennessee and behind you a view of the communication towers on Camp Creek Bald just above the AT.

View from Jones Meadow parking lot toward Blackstack Cliffs; 2021

Bad-weather bypass trail, Mile 298.5 northbound; 2021

Rock outcropping that becomes the trail, en route to Big Firescald; 2021

Rock stair set, en route to Big Firescald; 2021

Mundo on Big Firescald; 2021

Below this area was an old mine that eventually led to the construction of what was hoped to be a ski lodge. That construction was ultimately unsuccessful, and the land was eventually purchased by the USDA Forest Service. It is now a beautiful location to park and link into a variety of hiking trails located on and around this stretch of the AT through Madison County, North Carolina.

The meadow below the parking lot as you walk toward Blackstack Cliffs leads you to a blue-blazed trail that is also a bit of a 4×4 road. Follow this until the road narrows to trail, and turn right when you come to an intersection of trails with a double blue blaze on a tree, indicating to take a right. This will take you about 100 feet to the intersection of this blue-blazed trail and the AT. Take a left (north on the AT) and in a short time arrive at a side trail that heads 0.1 west to Blackstack Cliffs. The cliffs are great if you want to add a stop to this hike. As you continue on, you will come to the intersection of Jerry Miller Trail and the AT at Bearwallow Gap. Just past this location you will see a trail marked as the AT Bypass bad-weather trail, which reroutes you away from the rocky ridgeline during snow or particularly bad weather. This trail reconnects with the AT a bit farther than our out-and-back hike goes; however, you can turn this hike into a semi-loop by continuing across Firescald and taking the bad-weather trail back to this location.

Continuing on, you will be presented with a diverse landscape of laurel and oak trees. The trail hugs beautiful tunnellike outcroppings of rocks, and an endless array of awesome shrubs and flowers will keep the mind wandering all the way down the trail to our destination. Nearing Big Firescald, you will start having to traverse a bit of rock. Some of these areas are a little strenuous and can be a bit dangerous if wet. Take extra care as you reach the exposed ridgeline; there are plenty of drop-offs and tricky footholds, but overall, this is still a casual hike for most hikers. Once along the top, you are presented with views that rival some of

Jarred Douglas, Jared Sims, James Reisen, and Mac Owens at Jerry Cabin Shelter during a snowstorm; 2010

the best on the AT, the sea of western North Carolina mountains to your right and long rolling hills of Tennessee to your left. Anywhere you are able to take a seat is a great place for lunch or a break before heading back. A short way down the ridgeline, you will reach Howard's Rock memorial—a perfect turnaround point—or continue on for more rock scrambles and great views. Make your way to the northern end of the bad-weather trail and loop back to the AT, or turn around and head back to Jones Meadow to conclude your out-and-back hike.

View of the mountains toward Viking Mountain summit the morning after a winter storm; 2016

by Joshua Niven

January 23, 2016. A winter storm is coming and is going to slam into the western North Carolina mountains along the North Carolina–Tennessee border. Having been three years off my thru-hike, I had a serious itch for some adventure at this time in my life and decided to try to figure out the best location on the AT in my region to try to land right in the storm for an overnight in the snow. Remembering back on my hikes over the years through North Carolina, I had a few places come to mind, but one stuck out the most, and that was Big Firescald. Back in 2010 I had taken a winter trip with the guys in this section and happened to get hit by a winter storm in this exact location. I wasn't carrying the best camera gear and was unable to document the occasion as I would have liked, but I remembered how walking this exposed ridgeline in the snow was incredible. I must go today to relive it and try to get some awesome pictures. After some extensive digging on Google Maps around this span of mountains in Madison County, I determined that the Fork Ridge Trail was the closest access by car from the lowest elevation to avoid getting stuck in my vehicle and access Firescald the fastest. I set out with my gear in my Nissan Pathfinder and headed up Highway 26. It was already snowing outside and accumulating in Asheville, North Carolina, as I left. I didn't know if getting to the trail was feasible, but decided that if the highway was still black, I'd commit to making it to the trailhead parking lot. As I got closer and closer, now winding through the back roads in Madison County, it started to become clear that this was a lot of snow. Once I reached the forest service road, I had to cross through a couple of creeks to make it to the trailhead. At this point I figured if I was able to drive in, there would be no reason I couldn't drive right out tomorrow, so I committed and set out on the Fork Ridge Trail to intersect the AT.

Parking lot at the Fork Ridge Trailhead; 2016

Within a few minutes of hiking, I realized the snow was up to just under my knee, and hiking practically straight up this trail was outrageously hard. I had spent time hiking in deep snow before but was not expecting it to be quite this bad. It took me way longer to make it to the top of the ridgeline and link up with the AT than I thought it would. It now being the middle of winter, the second half of the day was setting in, and I knew the sun was going to start dropping soon. Making my way along the ridgeline, I was thankful to not be increasing in elevation anymore, but the snow got deeper and deeper.

At one point I was filming a video in waist-deep snow in a drift around a bend in the trail. It was getting darker, and I wanted to make it to the exposed ridgeline of Big Firescald Knob and try to find a nook to throw my tarp up on. Having not been there in a few years, I wasn't sure if there would even be enough room for me to pitch when I arrived. It was getting dark quickly, so I started to decide that making it all the way wasn't an option. As the elevation started to change and rocks started to seem more abundant through the snow, I started to think that if I went too much farther, finding a viable spot to sleep might not be possible, and I wouldn't have time before dark to turn around and come back to find one. I decided to head off-trail and aim for the flattest spot possible; seemed like an easy task, but now with a foot to 2-plus feet of snow on the ground, it proved to not be. I ended up a good 100 feet off-trail, digging out a hole to pitch in. Not ever owning a tent and always using tarps has served me over the years, but this evening I was wishing I had an enclosed tent. Luckily, the berm of snow I was in did a relatively decent job of cutting the wind. I had a great sleeping bag with a thick wool blanket inside, so I was confident it would still be a comfortable night. I made dinner,

Appalachian Trail approaching Big Firescald Knob; 2016

Frozen hiking boots and candle in tarp tent; 2016

took some pictures, and enjoyed the solitude until morning.

I have realized that most of my stories I tell people about my time on the AT seem to be stories of what not to do. This story is no exception. Waking up, the snow had passed, and my God, the scenery was beautiful. I was jaw-dropped at the views of the frozen trees and the massive amounts of snow I was seeing through the ends of my tarp tent. Then my heart dropped as I realized I had forgotten to completely undo the laces of my hiking shoes and put them under me while I slept. I knew I had screwed up because I had encountered this problem before. I had photographed the condition of my shoes the evening before and had intended on dealing with them before I slept, But I didn't. It is literally impossible to get your feet into shoes this frozen. Luckily—and feeling tickled I had prepared for this—I just happened to have put an extra pair of trail running shoes and waterproof socks in my pack, just in case the worst happened. So I laced up and headed out to make my way to the exposed portion of the ridgeline.

After a bit of a rock scramble, I popped up out of the trees onto the ridgeline and it was incredible; everything was frozen unlike anything I had seen before. The snowstorm from my previous trip was burned in my brain, but this time was even better. Thrilled, I started photographing and doing my thing and then, getting cold, decided to pack up and start making my way back down the mountain to my vehicle. A few minutes in, I started to get annoyed with one of my feet; having waterproof socks on top of wool socks inside my running shoes was a tight fit and was driving me crazy. I finally decided to try to loosen them and adjust, so I stopped and tried to adjust my left shoe because it felt the worst. I wasn't expecting what I saw when I pulled my foot out of the deep snow. The whole sole of my shoe had opened from the front end and was packed solid with snow. At this point I'm starting to realize that the reason I couldn't move my toes on this foot wasn't because the shoe was too tight—they were completely numb. Alarmed, I ripped everything off my foot and assessed; it seemed OK, but, man, I couldn't feel a thing.

Knowing that I was only about 15 minutes from the Fork Ridge Trail to head down, I loosened up the snow and figured that I'd move fast and get the blood flowing and see if my toes got any better as I walked. I dealt with the pain for about 10 minutes and started to panic a bit because I realized that, being distracted by all the picture

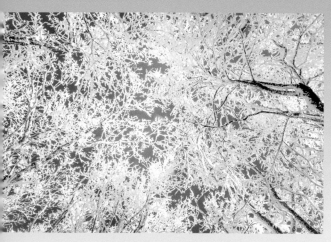

Canopy near Big Firescald Knob; 2016

Trail blaze on the trail approaching Big Firescald Knob; 2016

taking and landscape and having my feet at least a foot under the snow, I had no idea how long my foot had been like that. I decided that maybe it had been numb for a lot longer than I thought and I needed to fully address this now. I threw my pack off, threw my tarp on the ground, pulled out my sleeping bag, took everything off, and got my lower half inside the bag right in the middle of the trail.

Here it gets a little blurry. I couldn't do anything to get feeling back; rubbing, kicking, and trying to move my toes as much as possible wasn't doing much, but I stayed consistent. After what felt like a lifetime, I started to feel sharp pins and needles turning into actual sensation. What relief! I really thought I had screwed up this time in the worst way. Frostbite can happen fast, and I was in the world of great concern for a solid half hour there. Now that I had gotten to the other side of things, I knew the broken trail runner shoe was no longer an option. I pulled my knife out and cut all the frozen laces and tongue out of my hiking shoe, shoved my foot in, tied it with paracord, and made my way down to the comfort of my vehicle at the bottom of the mountain. Having now made the frozen boot mistake twice in my life, I vowed this would be the last.

Trail approaching Big Firescald Knob; 2016

Big Firescald Knob; 2016

The Appalachian Trail passes directly through the middle of Hot Springs, North Carolina. It's a sleepy mountain town that comes alive during hiking season, buzzing with hikers, kayakers, hot tub–soakers, and others seeking a mountain retreat. Nestled in a valley surrounded by Pisgah National Forest, Hot Springs is a haven for those who love the outdoors.

The town of Hot Springs may be small, but don't let the size fool you. Hot Springs has a lot to offer, with access to many popular hiking spots such as Lover's Leap and Max Patch. There are numerous lodging options, including campsites along the river, charming inns, the Hot Springs Resort and Spa, and the historical Iron Horse Station, which has a restaurant and a shop full of local arts and crafts. Blue Ridge Hiking Company's bunkhouse is located right on the AT, a short distance from downtown, and offers gear rentals and shuttle services in addition to overnight accommodations.

There are several local eateries to choose from. You can enjoy a meal at The Iron Horse or by the creek at the Spring Creek Tavern, sprawl out in the open courtyard at Big Pillow Brewing with a cold local beer and tacos, or opt for a scrumptious cheese platter at Vaste Riviere. Located on Bridge Street, the main drag, you will find a welcome center, local hardware shop, library, post office, and Bluff Mountain Outfitters.

Bluff Mountain is a favorite resupply spot for hikers. They have an incredible selection of gear, backpacking food, clothes, gifts, toys, books, and more. Thru-hikers are often seen gathering outside, most likely pondering if they will take a "nero" after resupplying or continue onward.

Big Pillow Brewing; 2021

The famous natural hot water springs have been a big draw to this little town for many years. The mineral water, first discovered and used by Native Americans, is believed to have restorative, healing benefits. Talk about a great way to rest tired legs after hiking! Paint Rock, a Native American pictograph, is nearby and is believed to be related to the hot springs. The French Broad River, the third-oldest river in the world, runs along the edge of downtown. Campers set up along the banks, enjoying the mountain scenery as they watch rafters float by and hikers crossing the bridge above to reenter the woods.

Hot Springs is the nearest town to us. We love it here and owe the Appalachian Trail for leading us to our mountain home. I probably would not be here if it weren't for the Appalachian Trail. I'm writing this book from our cozy log cabin outside of Hot Springs. We bought our home because it reminded us both of being on the Appalachian Trail. It's an old wooden building, reminiscent of an AT shelter, with a view of a small stream and thick woods from the front porch—a short drive to Tanyard Gap. When we first moved in, we didn't have electricity, hot water, plumbing, or cell service. We used an outhouse and took cold baths in the creek for months. We had frequent critters visit inside the house, including wolf spiders, flying squirrels, birds, mice, snakes, frogs, and lots of insects. It was just like living on the AT, except I was pregnant and the closer I got to giving birth, the less I enjoyed "roughing" it. Now we have light switches, hot water, indoor plumbing, and even a washer and dryer, oh, and two kids! Living in the woods is not for everyone, but it sure does feel right for us. I guess sometimes wandering can lead you home.

View of Bluff Mountain Outfitters, which is physically on the AT; blaze on the electricity pole; 2021

In 2005 Jennifer Pharr Davis completed a northbound thru-hike on the Appalachian Trail, but it was just the beginning for her. She hiked the AT again in 2008, setting the record for the fastest thru-hike by a woman—fifty-seven days. In 2011 Jennifer set the overall speed record by completing the trail in forty-six days. Nothing seems to slow down this trailblazer! Since her first thru-hike, she has hiked more than 14, 000 miles in six continents, penned many books, started Blue Ridge Hiking Company, and given birth to two children, both of which she carried and nursed while hiking. She is an inspiration to so many, especially mothers who have big dreams to pursue. Jennifer Pharr Davis will go down in history as an internationally recognized trailblazer, record-setter, mother, business owner, keynote speaker, and, in our opinion, a cool and kind human being.

Jennifer Pharr Davis
COURTESY OF BARBARA PHARR

Big Bald, Mile 326.2 northbound; 2013 thru-hike

Jarred Douglas on Unaka Mountain, Mile 358.1 northbound; 2013 thru-hike

Campsite on Unaka Mountain, Mile 358.1 northbound; 2013 thru-hike

Roan High Knob Shelter, Mile 379.0 northbound; 2013 thru-hike

Roan High Knob Shelter, Mile 379.0 northbound; 2013 thru-hike

Roan High Knob Shelter, Mile 379.0 northbound; 2013 thru-hike

7

ROAN HIGHLANDS

CARVERS GAP TO GRASSY RIDGE BALD

Located at the convergence of the Pisgah and Cherokee National Forests are the famed Roan Highlands. The highlands are a 20-mile massif, rising above 5,000 to 6,000 feet, making them the Appalachian region's longest stretch of grassy balds and one of the highest ranges in the Southern Appalachians. The views are exceptional year-round. Throughout the summer, enjoy walking through a tunnel of rhododendron and mountain laurel blooms. You can also find an abundance of other flowering and fruiting plants, including wild blueberries and bright red-orange flame azalea growing throughout this area. This hike is ideal for wildflower photographers and for those seeking mountaintop views at high elevation.

Bryan Anderson hiking northbound in the Roan Highlands, approaching Grassy Ridge; 2013 thru-hike

DISTANCE: 4.2 miles out and back (option to extend hike)
DIFFICULTY: Moderate due to elevation gain
TRAILHEAD GPS: 36.1068 / -82.1106
NEARBY TOWN: Roan Mountain, Tennessee
HIGHLIGHTS: Incredible 360-degree views, rock outcrops, legendary rhododendron garden, wild berries

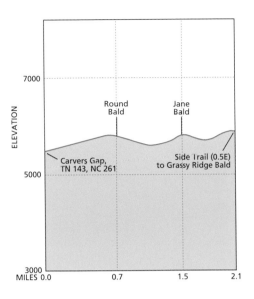

TIPS

- This section stays between 5,500 and 5,900 feet elevation. Be sure to dress in layers and be prepared for all types of weather!
- Asheville, North Carolina, a central creative/business hub of the Appalachian Mountains, is a short drive away.

MILEAGE MARKERS (NORTH TO SOUTH)

SECTION	MILES FROM SPRINGER MOUNTAIN	LANDMARK	ELEVATION (IN FEET)
0.0	380.5	Carvers Gap; TN 143, NC 261	5,512
0.7	381.2	Round Bald; 30 yards east to summit, views	5,827
1.5	382.0	Jane Bald; big rock slab, views	5,808
2.1	382.6	Side trail (0.5 mile east) to Grassy Ridge Bald, views	5,899

THE HIKE

Starting from the parking lot at Carvers Gap, it is apparent that the hike you are about to partake in will be beautiful. The balds you are ascending northbound into are visible from the parking lot; rows of Catawba rhododendron and pine trees welcome you as you enter the trail and start your way up to the ridge. As you climb, views of the bald ridgeline tease you as you go in and out of groves of rhododendron, nearing the top. Next you make your way into a beautiful tunnel of pine trees. During the right time of year, this moist covering provides a haven for myriad species of mushrooms

Jarred Douglas crossing the Roan Highlands northbound; 2013 thru-hike

to thrive, contrasting this small stretch of your hike with the landscape you will soon experience for the rest of the day. Popping out of the back side of the pine tunnel, you climb another couple hundred feet to the apex of the ridgeline. Finally, you have made it to Round Bald; rolling mountains in 360 degrees around you, grassy fields, and rocks provide an endless bounty of things to stare at.

Being upwards of 5,500 feet in elevation, the weather and experience up here can vary tremendously. Arriving on a day when the whole ridge is in a cloud with the wind whipping over the face can offer an exhilarating experience, although coming on a perfectly clear day in early to midsummer when the rhododendrons are in bloom is something hiking enthusiasts in this region show up in droves hoping to see. These peaks provide some of the most dynamic views that Tennessee and North Carolina have to offer. Over the next 1.3 miles, you will cross the ridgeline, seeing a diverse selection of plant

Roan Highlands; 2013 thru-hike

life. A bit of a rocky roller coaster, the elevation changes are still slight and easily traversed by most. Before arriving at the intersection of the AT and the Grassy Ridge Bald Trailhead, you will pass Jane Bald—a perfect spot to perch out and take a break, with an excellent view of Grassy Ridge Bald across the landscape.

When you arrive at the intersection of the two trails, you will see the blue blaze indicating the trail that leads off to the east. The route to Grassy Ridge Bald is about 1 mile, but plenty of destinations along the way can serve as a perfect ending to your hike.

As you approach, you enter a seriously deep rhododendron tunnel that will pop you out right on top of Grassy Ridge. At this point, its name will be an understatement, for this vast paradise in the sky is covered in grass and pines. Eventually you will arrive at the apex of Grassy Ridge Bald, where the Cornelius Rex Peake dedication plaque is positioned on a giant outcropping of rocks. This is where our hike concludes. If you want to explore further, you can make your way along the ridge, exploring side paths and enjoying the plants and views. To return, retrace your steps.

Intersection of Grassy Ridge and the Appalachian Trail, Mile 382.6; 2021

Deer on Grassy Ridge looking at Grandfather Mountain; 2021

Camping on Grassy Ridge; 2021

> **DID YOU KNOW?**
>
> The Roan Highlands are home to 1,200 acres of pink and purple Catawba rhododendron, making the highlands the largest natural rhododendron garden in the world.

Grassy Ridge; 2021

Grassy Ridge; 2021

TALES FROM THE TRAIL: LIGHTNING ON THE RIDGE

By Joshua Niven

It's summer 2010, and I am on a monthlong section with the guys. This was before trail names. This was back when the AT was just the AT for us; the lingo, the traditions, they hadn't been revealed to us yet. It was just friends in the woods following white blazes, bouncing from blue blaze to blue blaze for water, and just living, just being free. Approaching the parking lot at TN 91 and the AT's intersection, Jarred Douglas (Douglas), Jared Sims (Sims), Joel Dallas, Mack Owens, and myself have just landed on the Nelson Chapel/Walnut Baptist Trail Magic box. This famous box is large, made of metal to protect it from bears, cooler inside, and features three cutouts of crosses in the sheet metal on the top of the box. Spray painted with bright orange paint, this box can't be missed, and it is a sad day for anyone who does overlook it, because this box is packed full of trail treats for hikers. Take a drink, take a snack. I scored an orange soda and Swiss Cake Rolls. Taking our snacks to the parking lot, it is misty, dark, and starting to rain, so we huddle under the info map kiosk. Mack decided to continue just at the right time as the rest of us decided to wait for the rain to chill out a bit.

Nelson Chapel Trail Magic box, Mile 449.0 northbound; 2010 section hike

Ahead of us, the trail makes its way up a bald ridge; this beautiful ridge is maintained as a wheelchair-accessible 0.5 mile of trail, with benches along the way for enjoying the views. As we debated making our way, the rain subsided and bits and pieces of sun rays blasted out of holes in the stormy sky above. Thunder started to reveal its presence in the distance. Although the rain had settled, the sky was wild and turned a bit more sinister in appearance. I was stoked—ready to go. It looked to me like it was going to be an exciting hike over the ridge.

Nelson Chapel Trail Angel sign, Mile 449.0 northbound; 2013 thru-hike

Joel started telling us that the storm approaching contained lightning and that going out onto the balds in a lightning storm was not something he wanted to sign up for. This was a wise decision after he explained that his father had informed him today on a call that a couple had been struck the day before on a bald near us. One of them suffered a fatal injury from the strike. We didn't necessarily disagree with him, but we were out there for adventure. Douglas, Sims, and I decided to head up the hill. Walking up this ridge was spectacular. The weather in these moments felt great—breezy, but eerily calm. As we worked our way up in elevation, we could see behind us that the sky was getting darker and darker. Eventually we reached the apex and had a good look at what was going on. It was now clear that a massive storm was rolling in. Lightning danced inside the clouds, making the sky appear as one big strobe light. The parking lot we had ascended from was getting covered by the ominous clouds, and then the thunder started clapping louder. At this point Sims and I had caught up to Douglas, who was ahead of us a bit, and we started talking about whether we thought Joel had stayed under the kiosk or had decided to head up. We grew concerned, because for the last 20 minutes the weather had seemed fine and we knew Joel couldn't see what we were seeing coming over the top of him. The clouds were growing thicker, and the thunder and lightning strikes were gaining in intensity and frequency in the near distance. Ahead of us we could see the trail line; the trail was like a dark tunnel going into the woods, and with the intensity of the light against the trees, it made for quite a cinematic view. Sims decided it would make a great picture if Douglas and I ran to the tree line and stood in the tunnel so that he could take a picture from where he was standing. Douglas and I ran to the tree line, and we got the shot.

Joshua Niven and Jarred Douglas at tree line, just before the sky opened up; 2010 section hike

As we wait for Sims to close the gap between us, things started to progress at an alarming rate. Rain began pouring from the sky, and we heard flash-bangs coming from multiple directions. When Sims reached us we were all becoming concerned with the situation. We had never seen weather change so fast; it felt like something different than anything we had ever experienced. We started talking about Joel and if we should wait for him. After a couple of minutes of contemplation—and progression of the storm—I realized that I had to get out of there immediately. At some point in these moments, one of the guys said, "Three of us don't need to stand here and wait for him." Double Springs Shelter was 2.2 miles north of us, and I decided it was time to get out of there. (When asking Sims years later what happened between the time we were debating on what to do to my deciding it was time to get out of there, he recalled: "You just couldn't take it. It was just getting too real, and you looked terrified. It was as if you were thinking, *I am not gonna just stand here. We've gotta get to the shelter. I'm gone. Peace.*") At that moment I turned around and started hiking fast. Within a minute of turning and heading toward the shelter, *BOOM*, an explosion behind me, followed by *BOOM*, an explosion ahead of me.

This spot in the story is where things get blurry. My recollection in these moments still remains as the scariest moments of my life. I'm speed hiking like I never have, flying through the woods as lightning strikes on my left and on my right. I'm absolutely terrified, literally verbalizing out loud, screaming to the gods to let me get through this. My recollection of the 2.2 miles to the shelter only allows for little glimpses of the trees whipping and screaming above me and the sound of the strikes all around me, some of the loudest noise I have ever heard. At some point the lightning subsides to a gentle rain, I'll never know exactly how fast I hiked to the shelter, but I remember making note of it probably being the fastest 2 miles I ever hiked on-trail with full pack weight.

Sometime toward dusk, or what felt like dusk due to the cloud cover, I rolled into the shelter to find Mack sitting in its dead center. I looked at Mack and was like, "Woah, dude; that was absolutely insane." He told me that he had made it to the shelter with relief and assumed he was safe, and then lighting struck just across from the shelter. Not knowing what else to do, he just got in the middle of the shelter and waited for the storm to pass. Mack and I sat and reminisced about what we had just experienced, wondering how the other guys were. It started concerning us how long it was taking them to get to the shelter; this didn't help our anxiety as we sat and waited. Finally, Sims rolled in, and he didn't look right— pale in the face and looking like he had seen a ghost. He quickly exclaimed to us that he and Douglas had gotten struck. Within a minute of my turning and leaving, the locust-pole fence along the tree line just a couple of feet from them was hit by a strike. Sims explained that the strike went up his hiking poles into his arm, lifted him off the ground, and threw him on his back; Douglas was also thrown to the ground by the strike. Sims said he was fine but definitely felt weird. Shortly after his story, Douglas made it to the shelter with a very similar look on his face, followed by Joel just a couple minutes later. Everyone was OK, Joel in particular; after waiting the whole storm out and making the right decision to hang out in the kiosk, he had no issues whatsoever. The storm was gone and we were all relieved, making our time in the shelter that evening a special one. Shelter chats were reminiscent of the experience, what we could have done differently, and joking about the superpowers the guys probably possessed now after being struck.

Times like these on a trail can be scary, and you're always wondering about the decisions you made and if they were wise. As my father always says, "It's all about the story"—but to what end, I sometimes ask myself. Being a responsible hiker is always priority number one, but sometimes the longing for adventure overshadows these responsibilities. I look back at this experience often on-trail as one where the right decisions were not made and we were seriously lucky to all be OK. It's always a reminder when dealing with Mother Nature on a trail.

The next morning, the guys did not feel well. I captured a portrait of Sims, and you could see in his face that he was off from the lightning strike. He agreed that we needed to document this moment before we headed out to cross into Virginia for the first time.

Jared Sims the morning after being hit by lightning, Double Springs Shelter, Mile: 452.2 northbound; 2010 section hike

CREATURE FEATURE: BLACK BEAR

Black bears live in every state the Appalachian Trail traverses. They can weigh up to 600 pounds, consuming nearly anything they can get their grubby paws on. They eat twigs, leaves, bark, fish, insects such as bees and ants, small animals like mice and chipmunks, and at times hiker food. When camping, always hang your food and garbage or store them in a bear canister to avoid nuisance bears. Once sighted by people, bears typically run off into the woods. Encounters become dangerous when black bears are with their young or when they lose their fear of humans.

Black bear in North Carolina; 2013 thru-hike

FLORA FEATURE: CATAWBA RHODODENDRON

The luscious Catawba rhododendron grows in dense thickets throughout the Southern Appalachians in places such as Stover Creek in Georgia and across the ridges of Mount Rogers in southwest Virginia. Flowers typically bloom in ornate clusters from May to June atop the shiny, leathery leaves. The most impressive display of the pink and purple blooms of the Catawba rhododendron can be witnessed at the natural gardens that sprawl across the top of Roan Mountain at the border of North Carolina and Tennessee. Shenandoah National Park is as far as Catawba rhododendron reaches; however, the great rhododendron, with its white flowers, grows beyond northern Virginia and can be seen all the way to New England.

Catawba rhododendron, Roan Highlands; 2021

FEATURED SHELTERS

Mollies Ridge Shelter

Mollies Ridge Shelter is located in Great Smoky Mountains National Park at 4,570 feet. The stone-shelter sleeps twelve in two-level bunks and has a fireplace and a covered area to eat under. Built in 1961, it is maintained by the Smoky Mountain Hiking Club.

Mollies Ridge Shelter, Mile 177.7 northbound; 2013 thru-hike

Cooking in the fireplace, Mollies Ridge Shelter, Mile 177.7 northbound; 2013 thru-hike

Roan High Knob Shelter

At 6,186 feet, Roan High Knob Shelter is the highest shelter on the entire Appalachian Trail. It was built in 1934 and renovated in 1980. The shelter is maintained by the Tennessee Eastman Hiking and Canoeing Club.

Roan High Knob Shelter, Mile: 379.0 northbound; 2013 thru-hike

Overmountain Shelter

Overmountain Shelter, a large converted barn, was a popular place to camp until deemed unsafe in 2019. You can still camp in the fields around the shelter and enjoy views of the Roaring Creek Valley, as long as you are 40 feet from the barn structure. Water is available on the way to the campsite.

Overmountain Shelter, Mile 1,806 northbound, Tennessee; 2021

Laurel Falls, during 2013 thru-hike, mile 421.3 northbound

Elk River, during 2013 thru-hike

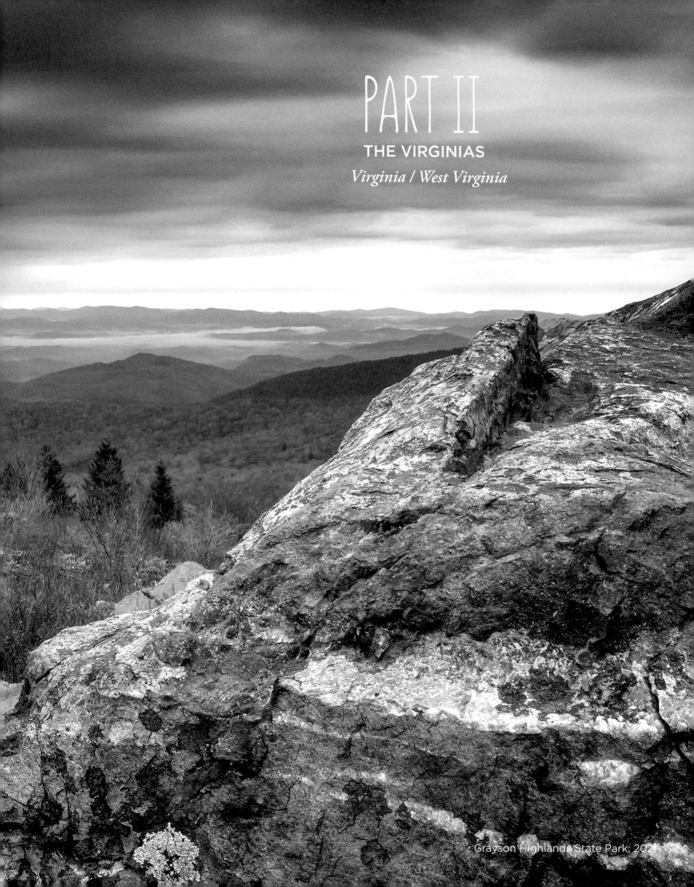

PART II
THE VIRGINIAS
Virginia / West Virginia

Grayson Highlands State Park; 2021

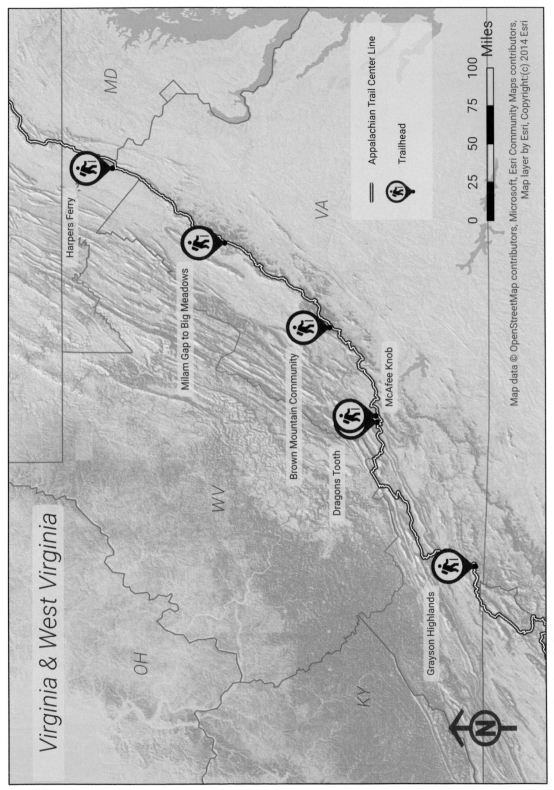

Virginia & West Virginia

MD

VA

WV

OH

KY

Harpers Ferry

Milam Gap to Big Meadows

Brown Mountain Community

Dragons Tooth

McAfee Knob

Grayson Highlands

Appalachian Trail Center Line

Trailhead

Miles

0   25   50   75   100

Map data © OpenStreetMap contributors, Microsoft, Esri Community Maps contributors,
Map layer by Esri, Copyright:(c) 2014 Esri

N

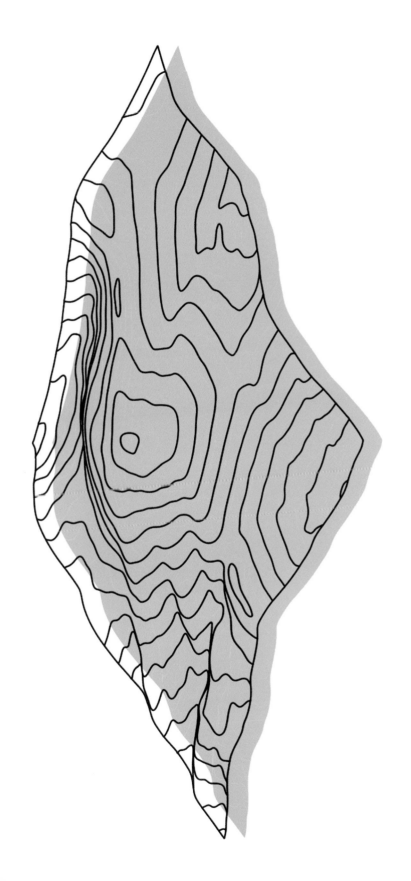

5,729'
MOUNT ROGERS, VA

Blaze at Buzzard Rock, White Top Mountain, Mile 491.6 northbound

Virginia

WELCOME TO VIRGINIA!

The famous state slogan, "Virginia is for Lovers," can be seen on bumper stickers and billboards all around the country. The catchphrase speaks to more than the romantics who travel near and far, seeking a place to plop down with a picnic basket atop the picturesque hills for a lazy lunch together. Virginia seems to have something for everyone. Lovers of mountains, community, wild ponies, history, and hospitality flock to the state each year. The Appalachian Trail travels through Virginia for more than 530 miles. We will explore iconic AT landmarks such as the town of Damascus, wild ponies at Grayson Highlands, McAfee Knob, and more.

Observe as you walk. Be aware that history surrounds you. Keep your eyes and mind open to explore the secrets held by the land.

—Signboard at Brown Mountain Creek, Virginia

DID YOU KNOW?

In addition to northbound and southbound thru-hikers, there is a group of individuals called "flip-floppers." These hikers follow an alternative route by choosing to start on the AT wherever they want. Once they finish the section, they return to where they began and hike in the opposite direction. There are numerous benefits to this approach, such as avoiding large crowds and a longer time frame to complete a thru-hike. Although a flip-flop is a nontraditional thru-hike, that doesn't make it any less of a thru-hike. Check out the ATC's website for sample itinerary options. As always, we encourage you to hike your own hike, whatever that looks like for you.

8

GRAYSON HIGHLANDS

MASSIE GAP TO THOMAS KNOB SHELTER

The hike from Massie Gap to Thomas Knob Shelter is great for hikers of all ages. It's a beautiful hike to take any time of year. During late spring you will find vibrant rhododendron blooms; in summer, blueberries line the path. See the colorful fall foliage and the snowy mountaintops during wintertime. Majestic wild ponies roam the highlands and are often seen grazing alongside the trail. Unique rock outcrops and expansive, sweeping views can be seen from a majority of this trail section.

DISTANCE: 8.4 miles out and back (includes ascent from parking lot)
DIFFICULTY: Moderate
TRAILHEAD GPS: 36.633327 / -81.508759
NEARBY TOWN: Damascus, Virginia
HIGHLIGHTS: Wild ponies, stunning views, rock outcrops

Ponies in Grayson Highlands State Park, 2021

TIPS

- Grayson Highlands State Park is open to day hikers 8 a.m. to 10 p.m.; an entrance fee is required.
- There are several campgrounds located inside the park.
- Be prepared for cool, windy, and potentially inclement weather, as this hike traverses above tree line in lofty lands.

CREATURE FEATURE: WILD PONIES

As you trek along the Grayson Highlands, there is a good chance you will encounter the wild ponies that roam the area. It's recommended that you not feed or get too close to the ponies, but they are sweet and usually have no problem with hikers saying hello. Still, it's always a good idea to stay on guard while enjoying their presence, especially when hiking with a canine.

Pony, Grayson Highlands State Park, Virginia; 2013 thru-hike

MILEAGE MARKERS (NORTH TO SOUTH)

SECTION	MILES FROM SPRINGER MOUNTAIN	LANDMARK	ELEVATION (IN FEET)
0.0	502.8	Massie Gap; 0.2 mile east to parking area	4,910
1.3	501.5	South end of Grayson Highlands State Park; fence, horse trail	5,010
2.0	500.8	Fat Man's Squeeze rock tunnel	5,359
2.3	500.5	Wilburn Ridge Trail (0.1 mile east) to rock outcropping and view	5,449
2.8	500.0	Rhododendron Gap; Pine Mountain Trail to the west	5,396
3.5	499.3	Campsite	5,390
3.8	499.0	Thomas Knob Shelter	5,422

THE HIKE

Begin at the Massie Gap parking lot and hike up the Rhododendron Trail for 0.5 mile. The ridgeline snakes its way through trees and brush, revealing the mountain ranges behind you while building anticipation and teasing you with quick views of the open balds ahead. As you reach the end of the Rhododendron Trail, you are spit out into the most incredible gap between two great ridges. Fields of sporadic rock, pine trees, and berry bushes give you the feeling of truly being in the highlands. This epic landscape only exists in a handful of places in the southern mountains. As you intersect the AT, it becomes apparent that you are in an extraordinary place. Here, at the intersection of the Rhododendron Trail and the AT, you will be taking a left and heading south.

From this point on, there is a high potential of seeing wild ponies. As you make your way south, the landscape continues to blow your mind with views of rock outcroppings framed by pine trees. In about 1 mile you will navigate through the horse gate at the intersection of the AT and a horse trail. From

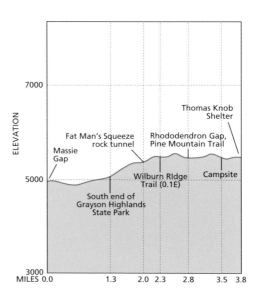

Grayson Highlands State Park; 2021

here, you will ascend a majestic mountainside as the landscape becomes more and more diverse and rocky.

At the peak of the incline, you find yourself in a place of majesty. The rock stacks and outcroppings are a visual joy and could provide a lifetime of gazing and pondering all the unique features. You will eventually run into Fat Man's Squeeze, a tight tunnellike gap in the rocks you will need to navigate through. At this point, you are 1.8 miles from Thomas Knob Shelter and the end of the hike. The landscape continues to provide incredible views as you pass through Rhododendron Gap. Thomas Knob Shelter is a wonderful place to stop and have lunch, get water, and enjoy the beauty of this unique part of the Southern Appalachians. The ponies are often nearby, looking for the occasional overlooked scrap of food. Making your way back to Massie Gap is a pleasant downhill hike. Concluding this hike, you can be confident that you have experienced some of the best of what the Grayson Highlands have to offer.

Jarred Douglas and Jared Sims at Fat Man's Squeeze, Mile 500.8 northbound; 2010 section hike

Grayson Highlands State Park; 2013 thru-hike

Rhododendron Gap; 2013 thru-hike

Steer at Rhododendron Gap; 2013 thru-hike

Bryan Anderson and pregnant pony at Thomas Knob Shelter, Mile 499.0 northbound; 2013 thru-hike

Jared Sims in Grayson Highlands State Park; 2010 section hike

Blaze on the AT in a rainstorm; 2013 thru-hike

Bryan Anderson and Joel Dallas crossing bridge on the AT in a rainstorm; 2013 thru-hike

Dismal Falls after a rainstorm, Bland County, Virginia, Mile 612.0 northbound; 2013 thru-hike

Mack Owens at Dismal Falls; 2010 section hike

9
DRAGONS TOOTH

Geologically-minded hikers will love this short climb to a stone monolith resembling the tooth of a dragon, hence its name. This short but sweet hike is all uphill and provides a great opportunity for some strenuous exercise with a major payoff at the end—one of the best views and most picturesque locations on the AT. Arriving here gives you the feeling you were plucked out of modern times and dropped into a breathtaking prehistoric landscape.

DISTANCE: 5.0 miles out and back
DIFFICULTY: Difficult due to technical terrain
TRAILHEAD GPS: 37.371613 / -80.149864
NEARBY TOWN: Catawba, Virginia
HIGHLIGHTS: Fascinating rock formations, incredible views

TIPS

• Parking at Newport Road is limited. There is an option to start at the Dragons Tooth parking lot and trailhead, which will link up with the AT on the way up the mountain, but parking at Newport Road is ideal for the purposes of this guidebook and avoiding crowds.

Dragons Tooth, Mile 702.1 northbound; 2014

MILEAGE MARKERS (NORTH TO SOUTH)

SECTION	MILES FROM SPRINGER MOUNTAIN	LANDMARK	ELEVATION (IN FEET)
0.0	704.6	VA 624, Newport Road	2,039
0.4	704.2	Scout Trail to the west to Dragons Tooth parking	2,039
1.3	703.3	Rawies Rest Overlook; view	2,482
1.7	702.9	Lost Spectacles Gap	2,520
2.5	702.1	Cove Mountain; Dragons Tooth Trail (0.1 mile east) to stone monolith and views	3,020

THE HIKE

Begin by hiking southbound on the AT, located on the opposite side of the road from the parking area. Hitting the woods, you will immediately begin ascending Cove Mountain. Although short, this hike is straight up the majority of the way, and you will gain 1,210 feet over the 2.5-mile trek. A pretty traditional, slightly rocky terrain will keep you ascending until you pass the Scout Trail, which leads to the Dragons Tooth parking area. Continue another 0.9 mile to Rawies Rest; this is the perfect

Dragons Tooth, Mile 702.1 northbound; 2014

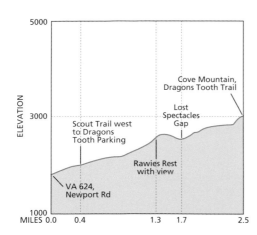

Dragons Tooth, Mile 702.1 northbound; 2014

Dragons Tooth, Mile 702.1 northbound; 2014

Dragons Tooth, Mile 702.1 northbound; 2014

semi-midway point to relax and take a breather before continuing upward. You will have a little reprieve from the uphill as you cruise into Lost Spectacles Gap and then finish your ascent about 0.8 mile straight up. At this point, the trail becomes increasingly difficult, traversing rocks jutting off the path; some iron handholds assist you on the way up.

As you reach the top, you will find the side trail sign for Dragons Tooth; this will take you 0.1 mile to the rock cove, where you will be presented with the massive Dragons Tooth rocks. You have arrived in one of my favorite, if not *the* favorite, locations of the entire Appalachian Trail; these massive rocks provide you with awesome things to view and explore in every direction. Looking at the pictures I have provided, you will see the passion I have for this location. Everything is surreal here and makes you feel like you are in a prehistoric landscape. The "teeth" of Dragons Tooth are Tuscarora quartzite spires shooting roughly 35 feet into the air. This unique geological feature makes this one of the most popular hiking

Four Pines Hostel, Catawba, Virginia; 2013 thru-hike

destinations in Virginia. It can get a little crowded, so visiting in the middle of the week could be beneficial. I have personally never visited on the weekend, and I have never experienced any significant crowds. This location will provide plenty to do and view before making your way back down the mountain to your car. Be careful while exploring the rocks—the drop-offs are sheer, and the potential for injury very real.

Yard art at Four Pines Hostel, Catawba, Virginia; 2013 thru-hike

10
MCAFEE KNOB

VA 311 TO MACAFEE KNOB

Conjure up an image of the Appalachian Trail in Virginia, and you will likely come up with a pair of legs dangling from MacAfee Knob. The iconic overhang is one of the most cherished and photographed spots on the entire AT. This moderate hike begins at VA 311 and traces the AT northbound along Catawba Mountain for 3.7 miles.

DISTANCE: 7.4 miles out and back
DIFFICULTY: Moderate
TRAILHEAD GPS: 37.3801 / -80.0894
NEARBY TOWN: Catawba, Virginia
HIGHLIGHTS: Popular photo spot with amazing views and rock outcrops

Nighttime at McAfee Knob viewing Tinker Cliffs, Mile 714.2 northbound; 2013 thru-hike

TIPS

- This popular hike attracts a lot of people. Consider hiking during the week and early in the morning to avoid crowds.
- Camping or fires are not permitted except at shelters and designated campsites.

MILEAGE MARKERS (NORTH TO SOUTH)

SECTION	MILES FROM SPRINGER MOUNTAIN	LANDMARK	ELEVATION (IN FEET)
0.0	710.5	VA 311 parking area	1,990
0.6	711.1	Footbridge	2,030
1.0	711.5	Johns Spring Shelter	1,957
1.4	711.9	Footbridge	2,110
2.0	712.5	Catawba Mountain Shelter	2,203
2.4	712.9	Trail crosses fire road	2,378
2.8	713.3	Power line	2,617
3.7	714.2	McAfee Knob	3,197

THE HIKE

From the parking area, cross VA 311 to where the Appalachian Trail reenters the woods, and begin hiking north. You will cross a wooden footbridge before passing Johns Spring Shelter and another footbridge before the trail passes Catawba Mountain Shelter. Both of these shelters have unreliable springs, so be sure to carry ample water. From the second shelter, you've hiked 2 miles and have gained slightly in elevation. The trail starts to climb steadily for the next 1.7 miles all the way to McAfee Knob, where amazing views of the Shenandoah Valley await you. Before reaching your destination you will cross a fire road that intersects the AT and hike through a power line clearing. The top of McAfee Knob is a short distance from here. For your return trip, simply retrace your steps southbound to the parking lot.

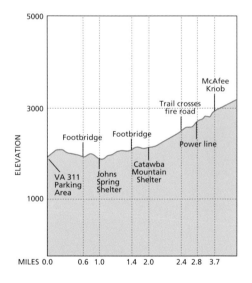

If you have extra time, continue northbound to Campbell Shelter and stay the night. The shelter is less than 1 mile from McAfee Knob. Rise early the next morning and hike to Tinker Cliffs to enjoy the sunrise.

Mark "Twigs" Grubbs at McAfee Knob, Mile 714.2 northbound; 2013 thru-hike

View from McAfee Knob to Tinker Cliffs, Mile 714.2 northbound; 2013 thru-hike

Cinnamon at the James River, Mile 787.1 northbound; 2013 thru-hike

Trail town Glasgow, Virginia, Mile 787.3 northbound; 2013 thru-hike

Bryan Anderson, Virginia, 2013 thru-hike

TRAILBLAZER SPOTLIGHT: BILL IRWIN

Hiking the trail was also a way of understanding the burden of possessing too much, both materially and emotionally. Each day and night, I had a clear mind and time to examine who I was, and long-forgotten memories rose to the surface. For instance, I discovered that I'd never really come to terms with the deaths of my parents. I hadn't started out to do the trail as some sort of quest for healing, but that healing happened.
—Bill Irwin, "Led by Faith to Conquer the Appalachian Trail," *Guideposts*, 2010 (guideposts.org)

On November 21, 1990, a hiker dropped to his knees atop Mount Katahdin to pray and sing "Amazing Grace." There were 150 of his friends and family members to share in his joy and accomplishment. This hiker's name was Bill Irwin, the first person to thru-hike the AT entirely blind. Irwin was inspired to hike after a conversation he had with God. In his book *Blind Courage*, Irwin writes about how he was "led by faith" along with his German Shepherd, Orient. The two became known as "the Orient Express." Irwin shares his newfound spirituality and how the AT helped him recover from the deaths of his parents. Although he lost his battle with cancer in 2014, Irwin continues to be a guiding light for others with blindness to believe they, too, could walk the entire Appalachian Trail.

Bill Irwin on his thru-hike COURTESY OF DEBRA IRWIN

11
BROWN MOUNTAIN COMMUNITY

The Brown Mountain Community hike is a historical stroll through an amazing part of the Virginia backcountry that has a great deal to offer for a simple day hike. An easy to moderate hike brings you to Brown Mountain Creek, the location of the community that used to inhabit this area. Stroll through time and take a dip in Brown Mountain Creek on this awesome hike.

DISTANCE: 3.6 miles out and back
DIFFICULTY: Easy to moderate
TRAILHEAD GPS: 37.7234 / -79.2506
NEARBY TOWN: Buena Vista, Virginia
HIGHLIGHTS: History, scenic creek

MILEAGE MARKERS (NORTH TO SOUTH)

SECTION	MILES FROM SPRINGER MOUNTAIN	LANDMARK	ELEVATION (IN FEET)
0.0	809.1	US 60 Long Mountain Wayside	2,065
1.8	807.3	Brown Mountain Creek Shelter	1,358

Brown Mountain Creek Community history sign; 2021

THE HIKE

Our hike starts at the Long Mountain Wayside on US 60 outside of Buena Vista, Virginia. Leaving the parking area, you will cross the street and hit the trailhead going southbound, downhill. For the next mile you will gently descend through several switchbacks into the valley. As the trail starts to flatten, you will start seeing views of Brown Mountain Creek. Note the banks stacked with rock and a feeling of the presence of humans from a different time all around you. Shortly after the trail flattens out, you will come to the "Living Along Brown Mountain Creek" historical sign (pictured) and a bench, where you can sit and read a bit about the community that used to inhabit these lands. A quote from Taft Hughes, who lived in this community, explains how they made a living in this valley. The sign also informs that the next 1.4 miles of trail has evidence of the old community; with a little imagination, you can have a great time picturing what life here was once like. You will see remnants of old chimneys and rock-stacked fences throughout the landscape as you hike along the creek.

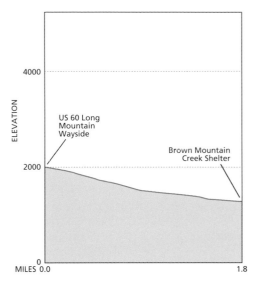

Brown Mountain Community hike trailhead at Long Mountain Wayside, US 60, Mile 809.1 northbound

There is plenty to explore and enjoy as you continue the hike. You eventually come to Brown Mountain Creek Shelter, where you can get springwater. The shelter is a great spot to stay overnight if you are seeking a night in the woods. If you continue on the AT, you will reach a wooden footbridge that crosses the creek, leading to some great spots to get in the water, cool off, and enjoy some creekside fun or have lunch.

This location is where our guided hike ends; you have the option to continue south-bound and explore the area or conclude your hike by making your way back to Long Mountain Wayside. Although this hike is short, once you arrive in this spectacular landscape, you can easily make a day of exploring the area and the creek without the stress of having to get somewhere. This hike is among our favorites for its casual approach and amount of things to explore.

Brown Mountain Creek Community history sign; 2021

Brown Mountain Creek Community ruins; 2021

Mundo at Brown Mountain Creek Shelter, Mile 807.3 northbound; 2021

Amber Niven, River Niven, Indie Niven, and Mundo at the Brown Mountain Creek bridge; 2021

Trail town Buena Vista, Virginia, Mile 809.1 northbound; 2013 thru-hike

The Cathedral, North Fork Piney River, Mile 821.2 northbound; 2013 thru-hike

Jarred Douglas and Herb "Two-Sticks" Manila at Maupin Field Shelter, Mile 843.5 northbound; 2013 thru-hike

SHENANDOAH NATIONAL PARK

The Appalachian Trail roams through Shenandoah National Park, tracing the ridge of the beautiful Blue Ridge Mountains. Much of the trail runs parallel to the renowned Skyline Drive and crosses it numerous times. The park contains nearly 200,000 acres, with trails that lead to incredible vistas, open meadows, and tumbling waters. You may encounter wildlife including deer, back bears, squirrels, and songbirds, which are all abundant in the park.

Over a million annual visitors come to enjoy this park, which has two visitor centers, lodges, campgrounds, gift shops, eateries, and more than 500 miles of trails to explore. As with Great Smoky Mountains National Park, Shenandoah can be

Shenandoah National Park; 2021

All across the nation people are starting out on vacations to be spent in . . . parks. [In] their tents under the stars, with an open fire to cook by, with the smell of the woods, and the winds in the trees, they will not forget the rush and strain of all the other long weeks by the year, and for a short time at least, the days will be good for their hearts and for their souls.

—President Franklin D Roosevelt, park dedication at Big Meadows, 1936

overwhelming when choosing what to do or see. The good thing is that this section has something for everyone! Stargazers, rock scramblers, birders, and hikers alike will all enjoy this highly adored park. You can reach the Appalachian Trail by several side trails or stay on the Skyline Drive to enjoy the views from its many overlooks.

Best time to visit: Summer is a great time to enjoy ripened blackberries, and fall is best for the leaf-peepers. However, if you want to avoid the crowds, consider visiting during the spring, when myriad wildflowers adorn the trails.

TIPS

- There is a $30 fee (per vehicle, as of this writing) to enter the park. Passes are good for seven consecutive days.
- The shelters along the AT are referred to as "huts" in Shenandoah National Park. Overnight permits are required and can be obtained from self-registration sites at the north and south entrance stations and visitor centers. In addition, there are less-primitive accommodations such as cabins and lodges with dining halls.
- Leashed pets are allowed on some trails. Check before you go.

12
MILAM GAP TO BIG MEADOWS

This hike is short and sweet. Elevation changes are minimal, and relaxation spots are ample. It's perfect for those who want to take a midmorning stroll, have a picnic, and walk off lunch while admiring nature's beauty.

DISTANCE: 3.4 miles out and back or 1.7-mile shuttle
DIFFICULTY: Easy
TRAILHEAD GPS: 38.5003 / -78.4457
NEARBY TOWN: Luray, Virginia
HIGHLIGHTS: Grassy meadows, stargazing opportunities

TIPS

- If this hike doesn't suit your needs or desires, you can visit nps.gov to pursue the vast collection of recommended hikes or stop by one of the park's visitor centers to chat with a friendly park ranger.

Milkweed in Big Meadows; 2021

THE HIKE

Park at the Milam Gap parking area, located at mile 52.8 on the west side of Skyline Drive. Locate the AT and turn right to begin hiking north. You will walk through a grove of apple trees and pass many maple, oak, locust, and hickory trees as you make your way to the meadows. Cross Tanners Ridge Road and hike a bit farther to a gravel road that leads 0.2 mile east to Skyline Drive. From here, turn left onto Skyline and walk another 0.2 mile on the road to reach Big Meadows Wayside, where you can grab lunch and enjoy a picnic with views of Big Meadows.

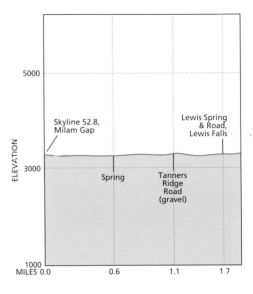

During the spring and summer months, this meadow is a sea of blooms. At different seasons you will find goldenrod, Queen Anne's lace, milkweed, thistle, yarrow, wineberry, and pokeweed. And where there are flowers, there are butterflies and bees!

Amber, Indie, and River Niven at Big Meadows, with Big Meadows Wayside in the background; 2021

If you don't have a car waiting at the wayside, simply retrace your steps to return. Before you leave, check out the visitor center, located adjacent to the wayside. It has a great exhibit about the park and a small gift shop to pick up souvenirs.

This area is great for stargazing! Consider staying the night if you enjoy observing the evening sky. Camping is not permitted in Big Meadows; however, there is a campground (fee) nearby. This is a popular spot, so be prepared for crowds of other people enjoying the beauty of this special spot. Don't worry; there is plenty of room to spread out.

DID YOU KNOW?

Monarchs cannot survive without milkweed. Female monarch butterflies only lay their eggs on milkweed, and monarch caterpillars feed exclusively on the leaves of milkweed, making it the only host plant for this iconic butterfly species. Without milkweed, monarchs cannot complete their life cycle. Without milkweed, there would be no monarchs. Planting milkweed is a great way to help ensure this special species' survival; it also helps other pollinators too, as milkweed provides nectar to a diverse suite of bees and butterflies.

Milkweed close-up, Big Meadows; 2021

Fawn, Byrds Nest #3 Hut,
Mile 941.1 northbound; 2013
thru-hike

Skyline Drive traversing
Shenandoah National Park, 2021

Skyline Drive traversing
Shenandoah National Park;
2021

SHENANDOAH RIVER: DAUGHTER OF THE STARS

The Shenandoah River is 300 miles long, flowing from Front Royal, Virginia, until it meets the Potomac at Harpers Ferry, West Virginia. Thousands of years ago, long before the Appalachian Trail, railroads, or Skyline Drive, Native Americans set up homes and began farming along the banks of the Shenandoah River. According to oral tradition, the name "Shenandoah" comes from "Skenandoah," a great chief of the Oneida Indians.

Another story, although unlikely true, is that Natives Americans named the river Shenandoah, meaning "daughter of the stars," for it was where "the morning stars placed the brightest jewels from their crowns in the river." Imagine what it was like back when the water was so clear and pristine, free of pollution, that when you looked at it, you could see the reflection of the Milky Way.

Some thru-hikers choose to flow with the Shenandoah River as it travels north, bypassing a section of the AT. This is called aqua-blazing. Hikers can enjoy a multiday float on the river via canoe or kayak, giving their legs a rest and their arms a workout. Shenandoah River Adventures services AT aqua-blazing. You can learn more on their website: shenandoahriveradventures.com/a-t-aquablaze.

Aqua-blazing in the Shenandoah River; 2013 thru-hike

Cow aqua-blazing in the Shenandoah River; 2013 thru-hike

Canoe aqua-blazing in the Shenandoah River; 2013 thru-hike

Fording a dam while aqua-blazing the Shenandoah River; 2013 thru-hike

FLORA FEATURE: BLACKBERRY

During the summer, the Appalachian Trail explodes with thickets of deep indigo, ripened blackberries. You can find the thorny bushes growing on hillsides, near road crossings, and many other places throughout the AT. Shenandoah National Park celebrates the arrival of the tasty fruit by hosting Blackberry Delight, an annual celebration with music, festivities, and lots and lots of blackberries.

Wild blackberry bush in bloom; 2021

Wild blackberries on a fruiting bush; 2021

Trail Days and the Friendliest Town on the Appalachian Trail

Downtown Damascus looking toward Mt. Rogers Outfitter, Mile 470.9 northbound; 2010 section hike

Joshua Niven, Amber Niven, River Niven, Indie Niven, and Mundo under the wooden archway leading into Damascus's town park during Trail Days, Mile 470.4 northbound; 2021

Soon after crossing the Tennessee-Virginia border, the AT meanders into the town of Damascus. The trail exits the woods and roams past the visitor center and library then travels under a wooden archway that leads into the town park. The white blazes continue through the center of downtown, where hikers can easily grab a bite to eat, recharge cell phones, and restock provisions at Mt. Rogers Outfitters.

The Appalachian Trail and Damascus have been inseparable since the AT was completed in 1934. It was one of the first designated Trail Communities along the AT. Damascus has been dubbed "the friendliest trail town" on the Appalachian Trail, as well as "Trail Town U.S.A." This hospitable mountain town may be small, with a population of around 1,000 permanent residents and not a single streetlight, but it serves thousands of visitors each year. It has all the necessities and creature comforts for any hiker, plus numerous lodging options, shuttle services, and the newly opened Appalachian Trail Center. Damascus is known for catering to AT hikers, but it is also a hub for six other nationally known trails, including the famed Virginia Creeper and Iron Mountain Trails.

The town has been hosting an annual festival called Appalachian Trail Days for more than thirty years, and it has become the largest festival along the AT. This year (2021) was my eleventh in attendance and Josh's ninth. It has become a tradition we look forward to every May. The festival was canceled last year due to the global pandemic. This year we are bringing our 4-month-old daughter, Indie, for her first time and our son, River. It's his second Trail Days. As soon as we pull into town, we are greeted with smiling faces and warm welcomes. "Welcome home," we hear people cheering over and over again during the three-day weekend. We see these people once a year, but it feels like a family homecoming, and I know others feel the same as we do. We kindred spirits share a bond. It's a simple one, but strong—we all love the AT.

We were told by longtime local, Bill Thomas, about how the festival has grown and evolved over the years. An avid hiker and AT enthusiast, Bill lives a few blocks away from downtown and has worked at *The Tomahawk*, a local newspaper, for sixteen years. Bill and his wife, Bobbie Jean, have been providing us with Trail Magic for almost a decade by feeding us delicious meals and offering up their home as a place to stay, shower, and play. Their house sits in between the Virginia Creeper Trail and the Laurel River, with clear views of Mock's Mill's Falls. It's an eclectic building decorated with all sorts of original AT art, potted plants, and knickknacks Bill has collected. They have hosted many hikers throughout their years of living in Damascus and are two of the most giving people I have ever encountered. Although it comes as no surprise, because that's how most of the folk along the AT corridors are—big-hearted people. The kind of people who will drop everything just to give you a ride to the nearest grocery store if you need it. Bobbie Jean disappears only to come back with one of her jackets to give me. "Here . . . it's chilly. You can have this," she says as she hands me the black zip-up hoodie that appears brand-new. I bundle up myself and the kids as we all get ready to walk to the park together.

Appalachian Trail Days hiker parade, Mile 470.0 northbound

As we stroll around town, zigzagging through laidback hikers and stopping to chat with vendors who make a living by selling crafts inspired by the AT, I'm hit with a wave of nostalgia and sense of belonging. I feel my everyday worries start to fade away the way they do while relaxing on a beach. Being at Trail Days is like a spiritual revival for us hikers. It's

Bill Thomas at his home

Bill Harris, Virginia Creeper Trail Angel and legend, in his happy place on Laurel Creek in Damascus, Mile 471.8 northbound; 2013

one giant pick-me-up that seems to cure a sort of homesickness for the trail.

I'm carrying Indie in one of those front baby carriers. Josh is pushing River in the double stroller that is packed to the brim with baby supplies while also walking our dog, Mundo. "You've got your hands full," people keep repeating as they pass by, giving our pup a pat. We hear it so many times that I have to hold back a laugh, thinking that the universe is playing a cruel trick on us. I silently yet grudgingly reply to the invisible forces that be: *Yes, I get it . . . a thru-hike is not in the cards for us right now.*

It's nice remembering how light our load was a few years back when we would carry everything we needed on our back, providing us with two free hands! I see families with kids a little older than ours and am filled with hope. *OK, soon we won't need so much stuff! We can ditch the diaper bag and emergency blankets and toys and snacks.*

I look past the playground and onward to the stage, where a small band is playing some folk sounds. I see people dancing, eating ice cream, resting their tired hiker legs.

The sense of community buzzes throughout Damascus during the weekend festivities of Trail Days. It electrifies the whole town. AT alums bestow wisdom on the current hikers on the trail. Trail enthusiasts gain even more of a hunger for hiking as they watch thru-hikers parading around drenched in sweat and dirt, seemingly without a care in the world. Many are hobbling around with sore ankles and blistered feet, their eyes wide with stories to tell—proof they have been living life to the edge of their limits. One can't help being drawn to them as if under a spell. Curiosity is another thing that bonds us hikers. We just can't help ourselves; we want to know: *How's your hike? What have you experienced? Seen? Learned? What's next?*

Inner flames are stoked. Like dying embers reignited by a slight breeze, sleepy, worn-out hikers become recharged with inspiration and motivation. The thing is, we all know that to completely quench our thirst for being on the AT, there is only one thing to do: Get out there! Our own two feet hitting the dirt is the one thing that will cure hiking fever. But Trail Days will do for now. As we make the trip home to North Carolina, toddler and newborn in tow, we feel our inner fire glowing anew, lighting the way back to the Appalachian Trail. Once we return, we order a second kid carrier so we can hit the trail as a family.

FEATURED SHELTER: PUNCHBOWL SHELTER

Punchbowl Shelter is located at 2,500 feet in the George Washington National Forest. Built in 1961, it is maintained by the Natural Bridge Appalachian Trail Club.

Bryan Anderson and Many Waters at Punchbowl Shelter, Mile 797.8 northbound; 2011 section hike

Pond at Punchbowl Shelter, Mile 797.8 northbound; 2013 thru-hike

By Sarah Jones Decker ("Harvest," Georgia–Maine, 2008, 2018–19)

There are many labels for how people enjoy the AT: day hiker, flip-flopper, Northbounder, section hiker, Southbounder, thru-hiker, weekend warrior, etc. I like to think of myself as a lifer. The trail has influenced my creative work for over twenty years, starting back in high school, when I would hike up to Bears Den in Virginia to watch the sunset and practice photography after class. At the time, I could never have guessed that narrow, white-blazed trail would become such a big part of my life.

When I was 16, my 71-year-old grandpa invited me to hike the Presidential Range section of the AT in the White Mountains of New Hampshire. A B-26 navigator in Korea and an adventurer at heart, he had taken all of his children, my young father included, and some of his grandchildren up and over those rocky peaks for decades.

Sarah Jones Decker with her daughter, Josephine COURTESY OF SARAH JONES DECKER

My grandpa and I arrived at the hut on a sunny August afternoon, with snow starting to fall that night. Far from a simple lean-to, I stayed at the famous Lakes of the Clouds Hut with travelers from around the world. I was in awe of the whole experience. That evening, we met a towering hiker named "Lorax," a gentle bearded traveler who was on his way to finishing the whole trail from Georgia to Maine; he was the first thru-hiker I had ever met. Months later he sent me his summit photo of Katahdin when he finished. And just like that—I was hooked.

I thru-hiked from Georgia to Maine myself eleven years later, in 2008, with my friend Kris "Scout" Powers after we both finished graduate school. When I passed Lakes of the Clouds the next time, as a "late in the season" hiker, the hut was silent and shuttered for the season. We had the mountain to ourselves and stayed in the dank "Dungeon" while we listened to the wind howl outside. That night, we were able to get a call out from a small flip phone to my grandpa, now in his 80s. I described to him the sun that was slowly setting in front of us, warming the hut and the surrounding lakes with deep yellows and oranges in the cold mountain silence. It was like he was there again on top of the world with us, sharing two totally different experiences together in the same special place.

I now live near the AT outside of the beloved trail town of Hot Springs, North Carolina. The trail runs the northern border of my county from two iconic trail locations—Max Patch to Big Bald. After I had my daughter in 2017, I started hiking the trail again locally as a way to reconnect with my postpartum body. I set out with the goal of hiking the trail once a month. This eventually led to my section hiking in all fourteen states again in 2018–19 for my book *The Appalachian Trail: Backcountry Shelters, Lean-tos, and Huts*, documenting every shelter on the trail.

Back on the trail for my ten-year "trailsversary," I felt like I was experiencing the trail for the first time all over again. As a day hiker, section hiker, and thru-hiker, the trail is always a new experience. I always come back to a quote I love by Greek philosopher Heraclitus: "No man ever steps in the same river twice, for it's not the same river and he's not the same man." This could be said for the AT. The trail is always changing, and we are changed because of it.

TRAILBLAZER SPOTLIGHT: SARAH JONES DECKER ("HARVEST")

Sarah Jones Decker is a farmer, photographer, and writer based in Madison County, North Carolina. She thru-hiked the Appalachian Trail in 2008 and again in sections in 2018–19 for her book *The Appalachian Trail: Backcountry Shelters, Lean-tos, and Huts,* which documents all the shelters on the trail. Sarah has her MFA in Photography from Savannah College of Art & Design and a BA in Journalism and Creative Writing from Virginia Tech. Sarah and her husband, Morgan, own Root Bottom Farm in Marshall, North Carolina. She is a trail maintainer with the Carolina Mountain Club. If she isn't hiking, you can probably find her on the river. Her work can be found at sarahjonesdecker.com.

Self-portrait of Sarah Jones Decker

DID YOU KNOW?

Northbound thru-hikers trek 33 miles from Vandeventer Shelter (Mile 437.7 northbound) into Damascus, Virginia, in a single day and call it the "Damascus Dash."

Bears Den, a beautiful and accommodating hostel in Bluemont, Virginia, Mile 1005.5 northbound; 2013 thru-hike

Lael "Manywaters" House, Trail Angel and legend on the AT in Virginia; 2013

View from the north end of the Shenandoah River
Bridge, Mile 1025.1 northbound; 2013 thru-hike

West Virginia

WELCOME TO WILD AND WONDERFUL WEST VIRGINIA!

The Appalachian Trail travels through the state of West Virginia for less than 4 miles. It's a short section, but it does not lack in sites to see. The trail goes right through the heart of Harpers Ferry, a small town with a lot to offer. The Appalachian Trail Conservancy headquarters is located a short walk off-trail (0.25 mile) and is a popular place to visit. Thru-hikers and trail lovers are often seen posing for a picture with the sign outside the ATC visitor center. At the confluence of the beautiful Shenandoah River and the mighty Potomac is a place called "The Point," where you can look upon the joining of these two major rivers as well as the convergence of three states: West Virginia, Maryland, and Virginia. Even though it's not technically the midpoint for the AT, thru-hikers know Harpers Ferry to be the "psychological halfway point" and look forward to reaching this milestone for many miles.

Harpers Ferry may be quiet and quaint, but this mountain town is not-so-sleepy. It's not only alive with a charming downtown and vibrant natural setting but also has a dramatic, harrowing history that will forever live on as part of its story.

The entire town is part of Harpers Ferry National Historical Park. Full of historical buildings, landmarks, and notable battlefields, it's a popular destination for history buffs. It's most famously known as the place of John Brown's raid, when the American abolitionist led a small group of men in an attempt to seize all weapons from the federal armory in October 1859. Although the raid failed, and Brown was captured and tried for treason, his revolt was one of many acts of conflict that triggered the Civil War. Many historians believe the raid was ultimately the catalyst for ending the institution of slavery. Aha, so it seems John Brown did succeed after all!

Woods are not like other spaces. To begin with, they are cubic. Their trees surround you, loom over you, press in from all sides. Woods choke off views & leave you muddled & without bearings. They make you feel small & confused & vulnerable, like a small child lost in a crowd of strange legs. Stand in a desert or prairie & you know you are in a big space. Stand in the woods and you only sense it. They are vast, featureless nowhere. And they are alive.

—Bill Bryson, *A Walk in the Woods: Rediscovering America on the Appalachian Trail*

13

HARPERS FERRY HISTORICAL HIKE

This hike is a walk to remember. It passes historical landmarks and buildings that stand to tell stories of African-American history and the Civil War as it winds through hallowed ground. Much of this hike takes place on paved roads. However, there are some steep stone stairs and a small section of relatively narrow trail. Otherwise, it's a lovely walk. You don't have to take this route to explore Harpers Ferry. The town has a lot to offer and plenty of sites that are wheelchair accessible and stroller friendly. We recommend hitting the Appalachian Trail Conservancy headquarters and then visiting "The Point," located at the confluence of the Potomac and Shenandoah Rivers—both are exciting stops and offer great photo ops! This area is swarming with historical exhibits, beauty, and access to the footbridge that leads into Maryland! Keep your eyes peeled for peregrine falcons, ospreys, and bald eagles that may be soaring above the river or perched overhead. Great blue herons can be seen along this stretch as well.

> **DID YOU KNOW?**
>
> A third of the nation lives a half day's drive from some part of the Appalachian Trail.

Remains of St. John's Episcopal church on the Hike through History; 2021

DISTANCE: 2.8-mile loop
DIFFICULTY: Easy to moderate due to some steep steps and uphill walking
TRAILHEAD LOCATION: 799 Washington St., Harpers Ferry (ATC headquarters)
HIGHLIGHTS: History, views, photo ops

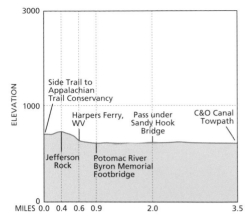

TIPS

- Parking is available along Washington Street.
- This hike is dog friendly. It gets hot in the summer; be sure to bring water for yourself and your pet.
- Climbing on Jefferson Rock is prohibited.

THE HIKE

This hike begins at the Appalachian Trail Conservancy headquarters and visitor center, located on Washington Street. Take a left out the front door of the ATC and follow the blue blazes along the road before reaching a redbrick path that passes Storer College, the first school of higher learning that allowed all races and genders. It originated after the Civil War left nearly 30,000 former enslaved without an education. What started as a small, one-room school building expanded into a campus with multiple buildings that enriched the lives of thousands of students. Storer College was open from 1857 to 1955.

Before you reach the Appalachian Trail, you will pass more historical buildings such as the Odd Fellows Lodge, so named because it was odd to do kind things for the less fortunate at the time, as well as the Brackett House and the Lockwood House. You can read more about these sites and others at the interpretive waysides and exhibits scattered throughout the town.

Entrance to the Appalachian Trail Conservancy headquarters, Mile 1025.4 northbound; 2013 thru-hike

Jefferson Rock history plaque; 2021

Jefferson Rock, with Harpers Ferry and converging rivers in the background, Mile 1025.8 northbound; 2021

View from The Point, where the Shenandoah and Potomac Rivers converge, Mile 1026.3 northbound; 2013 thru-hike

Continue following the blue blazes down the steep stone steps until you officially reach the Appalachian Trail. Take a left to begin hiking north on the AT. Soon you will come to Jefferson Rock, where Thomas Jefferson once sat and admired the view of the Potomac and Shenandoah Rivers. He is famously quoted as saying this view was "worth a voyage across the Atlantic" to see.

Follow the white blazes as they lead into "Lower Town." You will pass the crumbling remains of St. John's Episcopal church, which served as a hospital during the Civil War, on your left and the ornate St. Peter's Catholic church on your right. Be extra careful as you descend very steep steps that were carved into the stone in the 1800s. Cross the lower end of Washington Street (where the hike started) and follow the blazes painted on old-fashioned lampposts. This area of Harpers Ferry is bursting with exhibits and museums where you can learn more about the town's dramatic history. Be sure to check out John Brown's Fort and read about how this building served as his refuge during his 1859 raid.

Once you reach the end of Potomac Street, turn right and make your way to The Point. This is where the Potomac and Shenandoah Rivers converge. Enjoy the view before continuing across the footbridge that rises above the Potomac. Once you get to the end of the bridge, follow the spiral staircase down to the river and turn left onto the Chesapeake & Ohio Canal National Historical

Park towpath for roughly 0.5 mile before reaching the sign pointing to Maryland Heights. This is your turnaround point.

Option: If you have extra time and energy, you can extend this hike by turning right at the bottom of the staircase instead of left. By turning right, you will continue on the AT, following the white blazes, and enjoy more hiking along the Potomac River and the historic Chesapeake & Ohio Canal Towpath, which shares this trail with the AT. If you hike until you reach railroad tracks, congratulations! You just hiked the flattest 3 miles of the entire AT.

To return, retrace your steps over the bridge back to John Brown's Fort, continue up to Potomac Street, then upward to High Street (which will eventually turn into Washington Street), and back to the ATC headquarters, where you started. Don't forget to snap a photo at the famous wooden sign outside the ATC headquarters building.

CREATURE FEATURE: EASTERN BOX TURTLE

Box turtles are a common sight along the Appalachian Trail. You may see them near the edges of ponds and streams or hanging around other wet areas. However, you could walk past one without even noticing—the coloring and pattern on their shells help them camouflage brilliantly with the earth, especially when they are among damp fallen leaves. Box turtles live long lives, typically 25–30 years, although some live much longer.

Eastern box turtle

Time, distance, terrain, weather, and the Trail itself cannot be changed. You have to change. Don't waste any of your energy complaining over things you have no control over. Instead, look to yourself and adapt your mind, heart, body, and soul to the Trail. Remember, you will be a guest in someone else's house the entire journey.
—Warren Doyle

Trail legend, endurance hiking mentor, and Appalachian Trail educator, Warren Doyle has hiked the entire Appalachian Trail a record of eighteen times. That's more than any other person has ever roamed the AT. He has walked more than 38,000 miles since his first hike in 1972.

Doyle is the founder of the Appalachian Long Distance Hikers Association and creator of the Appalachian Trail Institute and SmartHikes (warrendoyle.com), where he has helped well over a thousand hikers prepare for thru-hiking. Many have called him the Yoda of the AT for his boundless wisdom and his photographic memory of the entire trail. In 2020 he was inducted into the Appalachian Trail Hall of Fame.

Warren Doyle

FUNGI FEATURE: NORTH AMERICAN REISHI

Reishi is a fungus that can be found growing on old trees and stumps along the Appalachian Trail. It is a large mushroom with a dark red, glossy exterior that grows in a semicircular shape. Reishi is loved by many throughout the Appalachian region for its purported medicinal properties. Another related species, found in Asia, is highly regarded as the "herb of spiritual potency."

North American reishi; 2013 thru-hike

PART III

MID-ATLANTIC

Maryland | Pennsylvania | New Jersey | New York

AT blaze in New York,
northbound; 2013 thru-hike

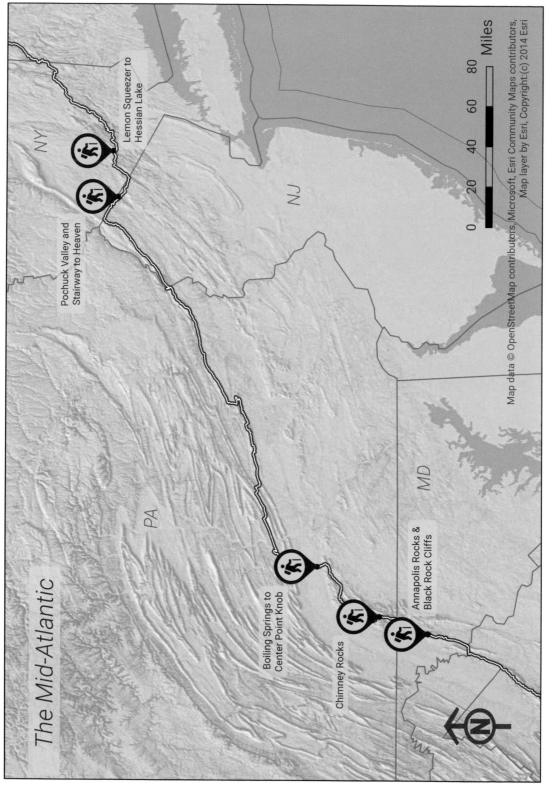

The Mid-Atlantic

Lemon Squeezer to Hessian Lake

Pochuck Valley and Stairway to Heaven

NY

NJ

Boiling Springs to Center Point Knob

Chimney Rocks

PA

Annapolis Rocks & Black Rock Cliffs

MD

Miles

0   20   40   60   80

Map data © OpenStreetMap contributors, Microsoft, Esri Community Maps contributors,
Map layer by Esri, Copyright:(c) 2014 Esri

Created by Mark Hylass, hylasmaps.com

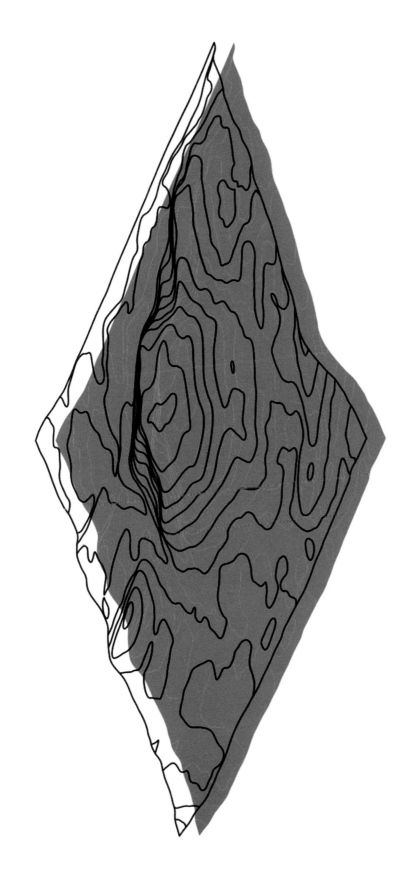

1,283'

BEAR MOUNTAIN, NY

View from Black Rock Cliffs, Mile 1051.5 northbound; 2013 thru-hike

Maryland

WELCOME TO MARYLAND!

You can hike through Maryland in three to five days, since the Appalachian Trail travels through it for approximately 41 miles. The southernmost end of the state contains the flattest section on the entire AT. The whole route is on gentle terrain and makes for great terrain for beginners to test out backpacking. Highlights include hiking along the Potomac River and unobstructed views from Annapolis Rocks and Black Rock Cliffs. Thru-hikers celebrate crossing the Mason-Dixon Line at the Pennsylvania border.

Remote for detachment, narrow for chosen company, winding for leisure, lonely for contemplation, [the Appalachian Trail] beckons not merely north and south, but upward to the body, mind, and soul of man.

—Harold Allen, early AT volunteer

14

ANNAPOLIS ROCKS AND BLACK ROCK CLIFFS

A relatively easy day hike with two amazing views, this route is a great option for trail running or for a peaceful sunrise hike. A shelter is close by if you want to turn this trip into an overnighter.

DISTANCE: 6.6 miles out and back
DIFFICULTY: Easy due to mostly flat trail and little elevation change
TRAILHEAD GPS: 39.5353 / -77.6035
NEARBY TOWNS: Boonsboro, Maryland; Smithsburg, Maryland
HIGHLIGHTS: Scenic views, rock outcrops

Annapolis Rocks, Mile 1050.5 northbound; 2014 Photo by Rick Adams

TIPS

- No-parking zones are strictly enforced by the trailhead.
- This trail is only an hour away from Washington, DC, and is heavily trafficked. Consider visiting during the weekday or early morning if you want to avoid crowds.

MILEAGE MARKERS (SOUTH TO NORTH)

SECTION	MILES FROM SPRINGER MOUNTAIN	LANDMARK	ELEVATION (IN FEET)
0.0	1048.2	US 40 parking	1,239
0.7	1048.9	Pine Knob Shelter	1,378
2.3	1050.5	Annapolis Rocks	1,756
3.3	1051.5	Black Rock Cliffs	1,779

View from Black Rock Cliffs, Mile 1051.5 northbound; 2013 thru-hike

THE HIKE

From the parking area at US 40, make your way north on the AT as you leave the noisy roadway and enter the woods. In less than 1 mile you will reach a short side trail that leads to Pine Knob Shelter. The path becomes significantly steeper for the next 0.5 mile past the spur trail but then levels out all the way to Annapolis Rocks, located just over 2 miles from the trailhead. Annapolis Rocks is a popular hike in Maryland, with beautiful views of the surrounding mountains and Greenbrier Lake. If you are seeking solitude, consider coming in the early morning. The vista sits at roughly 1,750 feet and has a campsite nearby that's used by many thru-hikers.

Hike 1 mile farther north to reach a second view at Black Rock Cliffs for an extra treat. This overlook also has expansive views of the valley below. Enjoy open skies and the green and brown mosaic patchwork of farms and forests. When you are ready to return, retrace your steps by following the white blazes back to the parking area.

Gathland State Park War Correspondents Monument, Mile 1036.0 northbound; 2013 thru-hike

Washington Monument plaque, Mile 1045.4 northbound; 2013 thru-hike

Washington Monument, Mile 1045.4 northbound; 2013 thru-hike

by Evans "Jukebox" Prater, owner of Mount Inspiration and AT thru-hiker

I first heard about the Appalachian Trail as I was flipping through channels on a hungover Sunday during my first summer in college at FSU. I remember being equal parts fascinated and enthralled by the thought of walking 2,000-something miles.

Who the hell would ever do that? What kind of insanity is in these people's minds? Ticks . . . Rattlesnakes . . . Bears . . . No thank you. But still, I kept watching. I mean, damn, what a feat. What an accomplishment. What. A. Crazy. Thing. To. Do.

Fast-forward—dropping out of college six months later, making a bed in the back of my Ford Explorer, loading up my worldly possessions, and hitting the road westward with just $1,000 in my bank account . . . I was doing a crazy thing by conventional societal standards, at least. But after three months bumming around the Southwest, from Phoenix to Flagstaff to the Grand Canyon to Vegas to L.A. to Yosemite to San Francisco, polishing it off with a week on US 101 down to San Diego, a tide was changing deep inside. I was learning that the world was much bigger than Tallahassee, Florida. I became more self-sufficient and OK with being alone for long periods and learning how to live on beans, rice, and whiskey. I was growing up.

I got a job at YMCA Camp Surf as a camp counselor and ocean lifeguard. I met people from all over the world. People who were a lot more like me than the people I had left behind in Tallahassee. World travelers. Eccentrics. Surfers, rock climbers, mountain bikers. And all—every single one of them—kinder than anyone I had ever met. The leadership at Camp Surf was there to help the staff grow and learn as much as it was for the campers. I learned so much about life and communication and being nice to people through that experience, which I genuinely feel was the most formative time of my life. I also learned that it's OK, in fact, it's natural, to want to travel, to move, to see the world. You're not a weirdo or a crazy person for wanting to get out of the

The trail taught me that I can do anything as long as I want it bad enough. That, yes, anything worth pursuing will include (quite a few) shitty days, quite a few happy days, quite a few boring days, and quite a few regular-ass-days. It taught me that even with average athletic ability, there is no match for determination. Motivation. Passion. Desire—to do something great, be great, to have epic stories and live an epic story. You just can't do something like hike the Appalachian Trail without those things.
—Evans Prater ("Jukebox," Georgia–Maine, 2014

town you grew up and went to college in. You're lucky—because most people go to school, graduate, get jobs, get married, have kids, keep working, go on two weeks' vacation, keep working, have more kids, buy houses, keep working, go on two weeks' more vacation, retire. Play spades. Die. Yeah, if you wanna get out, you're lucky.

From there I spent a semester at the University of Hawaii, lived in a cave, and wrote about it for the school paper. It was fun. I kept growing. I went back to school and finished without a plan. I had half-assedly pursued a comedy magazine internship my last two semesters in college, which didn't translate to a "real" job, so I putzed around my parents' house, lifeguarded for some cash, and thought about my next move. Then, a buddy of mine, an entrepreneur, invited me on a camping trip to Cloudland Canyon, Tennessee, in late September. I had nothing better to do and hadn't been to North Georgia/Tennessee in many years, so I obliged.

During a 7-mile hike on that trip, he told me about how he had completed the Georgia section of the Appalachian Trail that previous spring. I didn't know he had done that until he started talking about it. After all my experiences traveling around the United States and meeting so many great people—so many wild, fun, kind people (as Gary Sizer says: "eccentric go-getters")—the AT sounded less foreign to me, more like a place I'd like to be. His stories of Trail Magic, a concept unbeknownst to me at the time, and all the crazy characters he met . . . the pure pleasure of being alone on a rock face in the sun, staring out at a vast expanse of trees and mountains, eating whatever you want whenever you want. I was, once again, equally fascinated and enthralled. This time, however, I knew I needed to get on that damn trail.

On the way home, I bought every piece of gear he suggested and stopped in REI for some boots. I was on a Greyhound to Atlanta seven days later; eight days later, I was at Springer Mountain.

That first section hike led me to Mile 309, where, after the trials and tribulations of sleeping outside alone for the first time—postholing through Hurricane Sandy snow in the Smokies, meeting Southbounders who were finishing their thru-hikes, carrying a 60-pound pack—I was spent. I remember legitimately thinking, *How the hell do people do this all the way to Maine.*

I ended up spending a year and a half in Asheville, North Carolina, bartending and waiting tables, saving up money to attempt my thru-hike. I didn't do much of anything but work, exercise, and work some more. It was hell, which is excellent preparation for a thru-hike.

April 1, 2014, I was back at Springer with a real backpack and real gear, totaling about 30 pounds with food. I didn't know if I'd make it to Katahdin; I didn't know what would happen over the next 2,185.3 miles. But I knew that if I just kept walking, I'd get there eventually. So I started walking.

CREATURE FEATURE: CICADA

Periodical cicadas emerge and begin singing their song after living underground as nymphs for thirteen or seventeen years, depending on their cycle. Since the periodicals surface en masse, their chorus can be deafening. They are primarily black with bulging red eyes and orange-hued, veined wings. Annual cicadas tend to be larger than periodical cicadas and are mainly black, brown, and green, with green coloring on their wings.

Cicada exoskeleton; 2013 thru hike

Cicada on AT blaze; 2013 thru-hike

TRAILBLAZER SPOTLIGHT: WALKIN' JIM STOLTZ

The crystal morning's broken with the cooing of a dove, and you head up on the trail to the highlands up above, where the colors of the rainbow are the flowers at your feet, and your heart sings a song with every beat.

—Walkin' Jim Stoltz

In 1974, Jim Stolz hiked the entire Appalachian Trail from Georgia to Maine. Inspired by his journey, he kept walking once he reached Katahdin. The *Wall Street Journal* called him the "Music Man of the Wilderness," but most people know him as Walkin' Jim.

During his long-distance hikes, Walkin' Jim produced and performed shows with original songs, music, and photos of his travels to advocate for the environment. The heart of his work was sharing the beauty he found through the wilderness. He walked a total of 29,000 miles and peacefully advocated for the justice of all wild things as a trailblazer, musician, and artist for forty-five years before he passed away in 2010. In 2020, Walkin' Jim was inducted into the Appalachian Trail Hall of Fame. His music, poetry, and photography are still loved and enjoyed today. Learn more about his life and work at walkinjim.com.

Walkin' Jim Stoltz COURTESY OF LESLIE STOLTZ

FLORA FEATURE: BLACK-EYED SUSAN

Black-eyed Susan has been Maryland's state flower since 1918. A member of the Sunflower family, these golden yellow wild-flowers with a dark center are common throughout Maryland. Black-eyed Susan grows all along the AT and can be found blooming in meadows between May and August.

Black-eyed Susan; 2021

FEATURED SHELTER: PINE KNOB SHELTER

Pine Knob Shelter is less than 1 mile north of the footbridge over I-70 in Maryland. It's a popular spot for those hiking to Annapolis Rocks, which sits roughly 1.5 miles south of the shelter. If you are seeking solitude, try visiting during the week. The shelter was built in 1939 by the Civilian Conservation Corps (CCC) and is currently maintained by the Potomac Appalachian Trail Club.

Pine Knob Shelter Photo by Sarah Jones Decker

The infamously rock-laden AT in Pennsylvania; 2013 thru-hike

Pennsylvania

WELCOME TO PENNSYLVANIA!

Follow the ridges east of the Allegheny Mountains as the Appalachian Trail winds through the state of Pennsylvania for more than 200 miles. The northern part of this state is known to test weary thru-hikers—the rugged terrain is rough on weak ankles, and at times the sea of stones seems endless. It's so notorious for boulder fields and rocky terrain that it gained a nickname: "Rocksylvania." However, you will soon discover that this state is more than just a jumble of stones. Some of the smoothest parts of the entire AT lie within Pennsylvania. The southern part courses through scenic farmlands, state parks, and recreation areas. Highlights of this section include the AT Museum in Pine Grove Furnace State Park (also home of the "ice cream challenge"), the AT midway point, and the picturesque town of Boiling Springs.

> Jumping from boulder to boulder and never falling, with a heavy pack, is easier than it sounds; you just can't fall when you get into the rhythm of the dance.
>
> —Jack Kerouac, *The Dharma Bums*

TIPS

- Avoid visiting in the fall, as the AT passes through game lands managed for hunting. You are required to wear fluorescent-orange material from November 15 to December 15 while on state game lands in Pennsylvania. For more information about hunting safety along the AT, visit appalachiantrail.org/hunting.

> **DID YOU KNOW?**
>
> The total elevation gain of hiking the entire Appalachian Trail is equivalent to climbing Mount Everest sixteen times.

- Camping regulations vary considerably throughout the state, so be sure to plan ahead for your hike. Only AT thru-hikers may camp on Pennsylvania Game Commission lands.

15

CHIMNEY ROCKS

Chimney Rocks is located in central Pennsylvania, roughly 10 miles north of the Mason-Dixon Line. It's an excellent out-and-back day hike to a beautiful vista overlooking the park and town below. The name comes from the limestone towers on top of the mountain that resemble chimneys. According to local lore, there is a "chief seat" created by flat stones on top of one of the limestone "chimneys" that was used by the local Native American chiefs as a lookout spot.

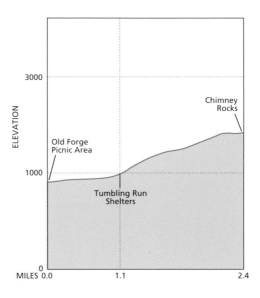

View from Chimney Rocks, Mile 1076.5 northbound; 2013 thru-hike

DISTANCE: 4.8 miles out and back
DIFFICULTY: Moderate due to rocky incline
TRAILHEAD GPS: 40.1478 / -77.1241
NEARBY TOWNS: South Mountain, Pennsylvania, and Waynesboro, Pennsylvania
HIGHLIGHTS: Scenic views, rock outcrops

TIPS

- Parking is available at the picnic area.
- Avoid the crowds and enjoy a peaceful sunrise or sunset hike. Bring your headlamp!

MILEAGE MARKERS (SOUTH TO NORTH)

SECTION	MILES FROM SPRINGER MOUNTAIN	LANDMARK	ELEVATION (IN FEET)
0.0	1074.1	Old Forge Picnic Area	899
1.1	1075.2	Tumbling Run Shelters	1,081
2.4	1076.5	Chimney Rocks; view to the east	1,900

View approaching Chimney Rocks, Mile 1076.5 northbound; 2013 thru-hike

THE HIKE

From the Old Forge Picnic Area, locate the AT and begin hiking north. In roughly 1 mile you will pass Tumbling Run Shelters; one shelter is designated for snoring hikers and the other is for non-snorers. A spring is west of the shelters if you need water. Continue following the white blazes as the trail ascends another mile to Chimney Rocks, where amazing panoramic views await. Enjoy the views. When you are ready to return, retrace your steps on the AT back to the picnic area.

Bryan Anderson in a sea of ferns on the AT in Pennsylvania; 2013 thru-hike

Bryan Anderson checking out the trail log at the AT midpoint sign, Mile 1096.5 northbound; 2013 thru-hike.

AT Museum "Signs of the Times" exhibit at Pine Grove Furnace State Park, Mile 1104.6 northbound; 2013 thru-hike

16
BOILING SPRINGS TO CENTER POINT KNOB

This wonderful hike in southern Pennsylvania is an easy-paced hike with lots to do. Experiencing the spring-fed lake in the heart of town and being able to end your hike with a dip in the cool water from "The Bubble"—a constantly flowing 52°F artesian spring in the heart of town—makes this one a must-see. An out-and-back hike up to the original midway point of the Appalachian Trail brings you to creek crossings, through corn fields, and a pleasant jaunt through the woods to the summit of Center Point Knob.

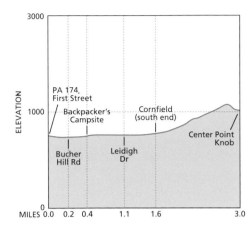

DISTANCE: 6.0 miles out and back
DIFFICULTY: Moderate
TRAILHEAD GPS: 40.1478 / -77.1241
NEARBY TOWN: Boiling Springs, Pennsylvania
HIGHLIGHTS: Friendly trail town, picturesque lake, iconic Midway Rock (original AT midpoint)

Appalachian National Scenic Trail information sign at former ATC mid-Atlantic regional office, Mile 1123.9; 2021

TIPS

- Parking is available in town alongside the main road.
- Carlisle, Pennsylvania, is a short drive away with access to more restaurants and shops as well as art galleries, museums, and more.

MILEAGE MARKERS (NORTH TO SOUTH)

SECTION	MILES FROM SPRINGER MOUNTAIN	LANDMARK	ELEVATION (IN FEET)
0.0	1123.9	PA 174, First Street	500
0.2	1123.7	Bucher Hill Road	501
0.4	1123.5	Backpacker's campsite	515
1.1	1122.8	Leidigh Drive	553
1.6	1122.3	Cornfield (south end)	562
3.0	1120.9	Center Point Knob	1,060

THE HIKE

Our hike begins in the parking lot of the ATC visitor center on First Street. The ATC visitor center provides information about the AT through information plaques and functions as a meeting location for thru-hikers. Hike south on the AT, passing the "Appalachian National Scenic Trail" information sign on your right as you

Entering a cornfield outside of Boiling Springs, southbound; 2021

follow the white blazes through the park. Enjoy the ducks and geese hanging out in Children's Lake, a spring-fed man-made lake with cool, crystal-clear water year-round. The lake is fed by "The Bubble," a constantly flowing artesian spring that gave this town its name.

Once you reach tree line, you will make your way across a well-flowing creek and then across Mountain Road. Be sure to pay attention when crossing the road—the AT is not well marked in this location; look for the double blazes indicating which direction the trail leads across the bridge. From here, you will make your way out of the trees to your first view of the cornfields. What time of year you arrive will determine how majestic this view will be. In my experience of being here in midsummer, the corn is tall and beautiful, making for a truly unique experience not often seen on the AT. The patterns across the landscape of repeating rows of tall corn stalks make for quite a cinematic experience. Make your way through the fields for about 0.75 mile and cross Leidigh Drive. As you head left up the road, you will see the blazes at the edge of the field on your right. Continue hiking toward the trees and ridgeline of mountains in front of you. From here, you are about 0.5 mile from where the cornfields end and will soon enter the woods.

From the tree line you start to climb and tackle the only real incline in this hike, 1.4 miles to the summit of Center Point Knob, gaining roughly 500 feet in elevation. Once at the summit, you will arrive at the Center Point Knob dedication plaque, stating the history of this location. A side trail to the east will take you 0.4 mile to a view at White Rock Cliffs, a great place to enjoy a view and rest before heading back to town.

"Epic" relaxing in a hammock at the Center Point Knob plaque, the original midpoint of the AT, Mile 1120.9 northbound; 2013 thru-hike

Once you make your way back down the mountain and through the cornfields, you can take a break and cool off in one of the creeks. Or visit The Bubble, located across First Street from the ATC, by following the concrete strolling path. This hike is unique for its access to all the town offers, such as excellent fly fishing and unique geographic features right on the trail. This one is a must-see. Be sure to visit TCO Fly Shop across from the ATC for gear and information on fly fishing in the area.

The Historic Doyle Hotel, Duncannon, Pennsylvania; 2013 thru-hike

AT blaze on rock climb approaching Superfund site, Palmerton, Pennsylvania; 2013 thru-hike

Jarred Douglas, Nick Browne, and Joel Dallas on top of Superfund site, Palmerton, Pennsylvania; 2013 thru-hike

Trail blaze on the AT in Pennsylvania; 2013 thru-hike

By Amber Adams Niven ("Dandelion")

It's the end of August. I've been on the Appalachian Trail for nearly three months, and my spirit is tired. I just encountered the most giant black bear I've ever seen while camping at a church in New Jersey. His huffing and gruffing are still echoing in my head. Now I am stuck looking at my feet so that I don't fall while scrambling through Pennsylvania's boulder fields. Stories of hikers returning home are surfacing more and more. The pain, fatigue, monotony, mosquitoes, body odor, and lack of water have got the best of me. Who knew that thru-hiking would be weeks of misery? Not me. I knew there would be bad days, but I was unprepared for these relentless mental challenges.

Trail life had grown wearisome. The adventure had become lackluster, and I had lost my purpose for why I was out in the woods. The reality that Springer was still hundreds of miles away was hitting me hard. It was challenging to keep my mind off home. I needed something to break this spell, and I needed it fast, because the thoughts of catching a ride home were tempting. A cozy bed, a home-cooked meal, warm showers, light switches, and Wi-Fi at my command; all the creature comforts were calling my name!

I had the midway blues.

We hunkered down in Hamburg, Pennsylvania, until I recovered from my lack of enthusiasm about hiking.

Don't be fooled—the physical demands of long-distance hiking are rigid. Still, the mental aspect of hiking is far more challenging. Sure, physical pains play a part, but the combination of the rain, the cold, the monotonous routine of camp chores, and counting miles is hard on the hiker spirit. It takes a lot of energy to stay positive on the trail.

While writing this book and reminiscing about the hard days, the ones that seem to outnumber the easy times, I can't help but laugh a little at my past self. Much like anything in life, going through some challenging experience forces us to become stronger, braver, and more rooted in ourselves. What's that phrase Dolly Parton always says? You know, something about storms making trees grow deeper roots. She also says that "if you want the rainbow, you gotta put up with the rain." Amen, Ms. Parton.

We didn't hike through much rain while in Pennsylvania, but we did wander through a sea of rocks. Reading the trail registers made me feel better, because it seemed that everyone was feeling the same. We all cursed the rocks, which I'm sure Mother Nature didn't appreciate. (Sorry about that, Mama E). One hiker hated Pennsylvania so much that she decided to do a flip-flop, meaning she skipped to Georgia and is hiking back to Pennsylvania, leaving it for last. The general consensus of Southbounders is that Pennsylvania is one of the least-favorite sections. However (according to my Northbounder husband), there are actually hikers who enjoy it! He claims it to be "entertaining and fun." Naturally, this sparks a friendly debate. He argues that Pennsylvania was like a playground for him after coming from the flat terrain of northern Virginia. He liked being all Jack-be-nimble. Of course all I could think about was how the rocks were beating up my already weak ankles. I imagine him and the other jolly NOBOs playing a version of "the floor is lava." I can see the scene playing out in my head: a bunch of charismatic hikers getting in touch with their inner kid, hopping, skipping, and jumping from rock to rock, imagining being surrounded by oozing, molten rock.

It only took a few days for me to completely loathe Rocksylvania; *ahem*, excuse me, Pennsylvania. I blamed the rocky terrain for my thru-hiking downfall because, unfortunately, I never bounced back from the midway blues. I continued hiking, but my spirit was crushed by the boulders. If I could do it again, I would definitely join in on the lava game. Sore ankles or not . . . might as well have some fun! And as some wise hikers who came before me once said as they were giving me thru-hiking advice: "EMBRACE THE SUCK." And that's my story about discovering perspective on the AT. Thanks, Pennsylvania.

CREATURE FEATURE: TIMBER RATTLESNAKE

Timber rattlesnakes are most commonly sighted in Virginia and Pennsylvania, but can be found anywhere on the AT from southern New Hampshire to Georgia. They love basking in the sun in dry, rocky areas. They feed on mice and hunt mainly during the night. If you see or hear a rattler, keep your distance—these snakes are venomous.

Timber rattlesnake, Pennsylvania; 2013 thru-hike

TRAILBLAZER SPOTLIGHT: DAVID MILLER ("AWOL")

In 2003 David Miller left everything behind to hike the entire length of the Appalachian Trail. He became known as "AWOL" and later penned a hiking memoir, *AWOL on the Appalachian Trail*. As a former software engineer, Miller noticed an opportunity to create a guidebook for the AT unlike others that were out on the market—one that was both functional and aesthetically pleasing. So he created *The A.T. Guide*, which became the most popular guidebook for AT thru-hikers. You can get the latest version, as well as a copy of his hiking memoir, at theatguide.com.

David "AWOL" Miller

FLORA FEATURE: SCARLET BEE-BALM

You are likely to come across a colony of bee-balm if you are hiking through the mid-Atlantic region in the summertime. The brilliant red flowers grow on four-sided stems that tower to 3 to 4 feet tall. Bee-balm is an aromatic herb that is part of the Mint family. Hummingbirds are attracted to their blossoms, as well as insects that can reach the nectar. You can find bee-balm putting on a spectacular show along the AT from Georgia to New York.

Bee-balm patch; 2021

FEATURED SHELTER: QUARRY GAP SHELTERS

The Quarry Gap Shelters are located in Caledonia State Park, near the AT midway point. They are connected by one long roof, with a common area in the middle. Built in 1934 by the CCC as two separate shelters, they are now maintained by the Potomac Appalachian Trail Club.

Robin "Violet B" Harlow filtering water at the Quarry Gap Shelters, Mile 1087.4; 2013 thru-hike

Sunset at backpacker's campsite, Mile 1301.4 northbound; 2013 thru-hike

New Jersey

WELCOME TO NEW JERSEY!

Nearly 72 miles of the Appalachian Trail lie within the state of New Jersey. The AT travels through Delaware Water Gap National Recreation Area, Wallkill Nature Preserve, and across the largest wetlands the AT traverses, the Pochuck Valley boardwalk. You can hike to Sunrise Mountain, one of New Jersey's highest peaks, or take a short side trail to explore the Appalachian Mountain Club's Mohican Outdoor Center. No matter where you choose to adventure throughout this section, you will surely find beautiful scenery and maybe a large black bear.

If you are free, I recommend a hiking trip on a wilderness footpath. How inspiring it is to walk all day in the sunshine and sleep all night under the stars. What a wonderful experience in simple, natural living. Since you carry your food, sleeping equipment, etc., on your back, you learn quickly that unnecessary possessions are unnecessary burdens. You soon realize what the essentials of life are—such as warmth when you are cold, a dry spot on a rainy day, the simplest food when you are hungry, pure cool water when you are thirsty. You soon put material things in their proper place, realizing that they are there for use, but relinquishing them when they are not useful. You soon experience and learn to appreciate the great freedom of simplicity.

—Mildred Norman ("Peace Pilgrim"), *Peace Pilgrim, Her Life and Works in Her Own Words*

Swamp pond in New Jersey; 2013 thru-hike

Jarred Douglas on the wooden tower facing High Point Monument, atop the highest point in New Jersey, Mile 1340.0 northbound; 2013 thru-hike

View from the wooden tower toward High Point Monument, Mile 1340.0 northbound; 2013 thru-hike

17

POCHUCK VALLEY BOARDWALK AND STAIRWAY TO HEAVEN

Hike across an elevated boardwalk that extends over the largest wetland area on the Appalachian Trail before climbing the "stairway to heaven," a series of rock slabs that switch back and forth, leading to a vista from Wawayanda Mountain.

DISTANCE: 7.4 miles out and back
DIFFICULTY: Moderate due to boulder terrain at end
TRAILHEAD GPS: 41.2357 / -74.4805
NEARBY TOWNS: Vernon Township, New Jersey; Glenwood, New Jersey
HIGHLIGHTS: Wetlands beneath a boardwalk and a rock staircase leading to a mountain view

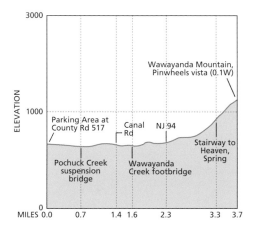

View of the Pochuck Boardwalk; 2013 thru-hike

TIPS

- We rated this hike as moderate for the boulder terrain near the end. However, the beginning section is easy; it is on level wooden boards, making it wheelchair friendly, stroller friendly, and a great walk for little tots.
- Parking is limited. Respect the "No Parking" signs to avoid tickets.

MILEAGE MARKERS (SOUTH TO NORTH)

SECTION	MILES FROM SPRINGER MOUNTAIN	LANDMARK	ELEVATION (IN FEET)
0.0	1,357.3	Parking area at CR 517	428
0.7	1,358.0	Pochuck Creek suspension bridge	394
1.4	1,358.7	Canal Road	410
1.6	1,358.9	Wawayanda Creek footbridge	401
2.3	1,359.6	NJ 94	450
3.3	1,360.6	Stairway to Heaven, spring	973
3.7	1,361.0	Wawayanda Mountain; Pinwheels vista (0.1 mile west)	1,340

Pochuck Boardwalk; 2013 thru-hike

THE HIKE

Begin at the parking area and enjoy a scenic walk across the 6,000-foot raised board-walk. The Appalachian Trail crosses a 144-foot suspension bridge over Pochuck Creek and through the swampy wetlands for roughly 1 mile. Look for turtles and other wildlife that seek refuge here. The boardwalks help protect this sensitive ecosystem. The trail is lined with tall grasses and wildflowers, making it a picturesque walk, and the terrain stays flat and relatively easy for the first 2 miles of the hike.

You start to gain elevation once you reach the first step of the "Stairway to Heaven," a series of rock slabs that ascends to the top of Wawayanda Mountain. After the steep switchback staircase, you will reach the peak of the 1,340-foot mountain. From the top, you can hike 0.1 mile west to reach Pinwheels vista, a great place to rest your legs and enjoy some lunch.

To return, retrace your steps by hiking southbound on the AT back to the parking area.

Option: You can continue to walk north for 1.7 miles, down the mountain and onward to Barrett Road, which leads west to New Milford, New York. Just be sure you have transportation figured out beforehand.

Pochuck Creek Suspension Footbridge, Mile 1358.0 northbound; 2013 thru-hike

TALES FROM THE TRAIL: THE BREAKFAST CAKE

By Amber Adams Niven ("Dandelion")

The sun wakes me up as it brightens the inside of our tent. We are somewhere in the mid-Atlantic region at low elevation. It's hot and humid. I look up and see the raindrops from last night's storm and the mosquitoes buzzing between the rain fly and the tent's mesh. I don't want to get up. I don't want to pack up a soaking wet tent and lug the extra water weight with me. I don't want to hike today. I'm sweaty and sore. I want a shower and clean clothes. I want to rest my painful ankle and tend to my blistered feet.

Getting out of the tent and packing up was the most challenging part of the day. But once I got moving, I remembered why I was out there. My morning Pop-Tart became a ritual I looked forward to every morning—a little sweet treat to get the dopamine flowing. Yet for some reason, this morning, the Pop-Tart wasn't doing the trick.

My mind starts to wonder: *Why am I doing this? Why am I putting myself through all of this? What is the purpose?* All the views had begun to look the same, and the conversations around the campfire were the same. Life on the trail had started to feel like life in the real world—monotonous, lots of work, and little play. In an attempt to muster up some sort of motivation, I roll over on my stomach and reach for our *AWOL* guide. I'm hoping there is a cool view or river crossing to look forward to. But nope; it's just going to be a long day of hiking in the understory to the next campsite. Darn. Oh, well, guess it's time to cash in on the breakfast cake that Mom sent in the last mail drop. I had been saving it for a rainy day.

I shimmy out of my sleeping bag and start deflating my air mattress. Then I throw my gear out of the tent so I can pack it up. Finally, I carefully place my breakfast cake on a rock to enjoy after packing up the tent and filtering water for the day. My little individually-wrapped reward was going to send me into endorphin euphoria and help me cope with the onset of hiker blues.

After the tent is put away and the pack is repacked, I sling it over my shoulder, grab my trekking poles, and reach for my treat. . . . Wait, where is it!? My little silver lining is nowhere to be found. I cry out to my group, "Has anyone seen a little breakfast cake? I laid it right here on this rock. It looks like something you get at a gas station in the doughnut section. Please! Anyone?"

FireSquirrel pops his head up as he's buckling the last clip on his pack and calls out, "Oh, I ate that."

"You what?" I reply in disbelief.

"I thought you laid that out for me," he says confidently.

This was heartbreaking; I would have to soldier on sugar-free. Lesson learned: Keep your sweets close and your ambitions closer. I wasn't out here to consume sugar; I was out here to commune with nature. So, with the help of songbirds, I walked off my frustration and remembered nothing is sweeter than a walk in the Appalachian Mountains.

CREATURE FEATURE: EASTERN COTTONTAIL

If you see a rabbit while hiking the AT, chances are high it's an eastern cottontail, the most common rabbit species in the United States. A pair of cottontails can produce 350,000 rabbits in just five years. However, since they rank low on the food chain, most do not live past one year. Cottontails are named from their distinctive white fluffy tail. You can spot them in meadows, near marshes, and around farmlands.

ARTWORK BY JEN TOLEDO

FLORA FEATURE: TALL GOLDENROD

Tall goldenrod is commonly seen from Georgia to New York along the Appalachian Trail; however, it can also be spotted in some places throughout New England. The towering 6- to 7-foot stem bears tiny yellow flowers that begin appearing in August and stay until November. You are likely to encounter goldenrod in open areas such as meadows, grasslands, and along roadsides.

Goldenrod; 2021

TRAILBLAZER SPOTLIGHT: MILDRED NORMAN ("PEACE PILGRIM")

The inspiration for the pilgrimage came at this time. I sat high upon a hill overlooking rural New England. . . . I saw, in my mind's eye, myself walking along and wearing the garb of my mission. . . . I saw a map of the United States with the large cities marked—and it was as though someone had taken a colored crayon and marked a zigzag line across, coast to coast and border to border, from Los Angeles to New York City. I knew what I was to do. And that was a vision of my first year's pilgrimage route in 1953!

—Mildred Norman, later known as "Peace Pilgrim"

In 1952 Mildred Norman packed up and embarked on a long journey that resulted in a name change and a lifetime of walking for peace. After walking the entire length of the Appalachian Trail in less than five months and becoming the first woman to hike the whole trail in one season, Mildred changed her name to Peace Pilgrim and kept walking. Her famous pilgrimage began on January 1, 1953, in Los Angeles and extended well over 25,000 miles from 1952 to 1981. (She stopped counting miles in 1964, having completed 25,000 miles that year. Her total mileage was probably double that or more.) She journeyed without food, money, or clothes except for what she was wearing, keeping faith that her needs would be met (they always were). Her pilgrimages may have seemed strange to some, but Peace Pilgrim knew she was a pioneer of sorts and didn't mind if others thought her mission odd. In her last interview, the day before she "passed into a freer life," Peace Pilgrim talked about how much she loves people despite what they think. She said, "I see the good in [people], and you're apt to reach what you see. The world is like a mirror. If you smile at it, it will smile at you." She believed there is goodness in everyone—and that taking a step toward peace within ourselves is a step toward collective peace.

Peace Pilgrim was not only the first woman to complete the entire AT but also the first one to complete a flip-flop hike. Dick Lamb accompanied her during her AT hike, and together they finished the first flip-flop hike by walking from Mount Oglethorpe to Harrisburg, Pennsylvania, then going to Katahdin and walking back to Harrisburg. Peace Pilgrim was inducted into the Appalachian Trail Hall of Fame and the New Jersey Hall of Fame in 2017. Her legacy lives on through countless lecture videos, books, art, and more through the nonprofit Friends of Peace Pilgrim, an organization dedicated to sharing her message of world peace.

Peace Pilgrim
PHOTO BY JIM BURTON, COURTESY FRIENDS OF PEACE PILGRIM

FEATURED SHELTER: HIGH POINT SHELTER

High Point Shelter, built by the CCC, is located north of High Point State Park and a short distance from the highest point in New Jersey (1,803 feet). High Point Monument tower, a memorial to New Jersey veterans, is located at the top and offers views of the Pocono Mountains, Catskill Mountains, and the Wallkill River Valley.

High Point Shelter PHOTO BY SARAH JONES DECKER

The Appalachian Trail in New Jersey; 2013 thru-hike

View from the AT somewhere in New York; 2013 thru-hike

New York

WELCOME TO NEW YORK!

The Appalachian Trail meanders through the state of New York for more than 90 miles. This section stretches across enchanting woodland areas, swimming lakes, and past interesting rock formations. The trail goes through Harriman State Park, New York's second-largest state park, where you can see distant views of the New York City skyline, and travels through Bear Mountain State Park, where there is a trailside museum and zoo. There are numerous road crossings for a chance to catch a ride into town to resupply, take a shower, and enjoy some grub. You can even catch a train into the Big Apple!

Now I see the secret of making the best person; it is to grow in the open air and to eat and sleep with the earth.

—Walt Whitman

18
LEMON SQUEEZER TO HESSIAN LAKE

This overnight hike has fun written all over it. It travels through two state parks, passes a trailside zoo, and ends with an epic granite staircase. The walk is on nice dirt paths lined with ferns and peppered with flowers. It crosses over boulders flush with the earth and over flat pavement in some places. You will have to navigate through some tight boulders during the famous "Lemon Squeezer" as well as climb the beautiful, yet grueling stairs up to Bear Mountain. This hike concludes at the Trailside Museums and Zoo.

Entering forest at Elk Pen Trailhead parking lot, Mile 1387.1 northbound; 2021

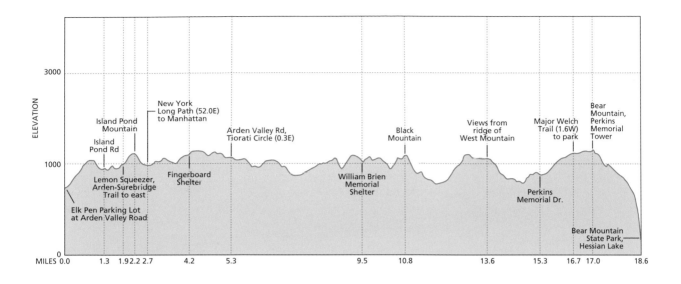

DISTANCE: 18.6 miles one-way
DIFFICULTY: Moderate for avid hikers; beginners may find this strenuous.
TRAILHEAD GPS: 41.2649 / -74.1544
NEARBY TOWNS: Southfields, Harriman, and Fort Montgomery, New York
HIGHLIGHTS: Unique rock formations, AT history, swimming lake

TIPS

- There are plenty of access points if you want to do any of this stretch as a day hike; some parts are wheelchair accessible.
- A trail on the summit of Bear Mountain includes a 0.4-mile section of wheelchair-accessible trail that leads to a vista overlooking the Hudson Valley, where you can see views of the Catskill Mountains on a clear day. Begin at the parking area near the Perkins Memorial Tower.
- Be careful while hiking rocky areas on wet days. They can be slippery and hazardous.
- This stretch of the AT is heavily trafficked, as it goes through two popular parks—Harriman State Park and Bear Mountain State Park. Consider hiking during the week for fewer crowds.
- For shuttle services in this area visit myharriman.com/harriman-shuttle-bus.
- There is no fee to walk through the Trailside Museums and Zoo. Bring some cash to drop in the donation box.

MILEAGE MARKERS (SOUTH TO NORTH)

SECTION	MILES FROM SPRINGER MOUNTAIN	LANDMARK	ELEVATION (IN FEET)
0.0	1387.1	Elk Pen parking lot at Arden Valley Road	594
1.3	1388.4	Island Pond Road	1,008
1.9	1389.0	Lemon Squeezer; Arden-Surebridge Trail to the east	1,088
2.2	1389.3	Island Pond Mountain; view	1,298
2.7	1389.8	New York Long Path (52.0 miles east) to Manhattan	1,055
4.2	1391.3	Fingerboard Shelter; unreliable spring	1,348
5.3	1392.4	Arden Valley Road; Tiorati Circle (0.3 mile east)	1,196
7.4	1394.5	Footbridge, spring	836
7.5	1394.6	Seven Lakes Drive	850
9.5	1396.6	William Brien Memorial Shelter; unreliable spring	1,075
10.8	1397.9	Black Mountain; views of New York City skyline	1,192
11.6	1398.7	Palisades Parkway, busy four-lane divided highway	680
13.6	1400.7	Views from ridge of West Mountain	1,137
15.3	1402.4	Perkins Memorial Drive	794
16.7	1403.8	Major Welch Trail (1.6 miles west) to park	1,289
17.0	1404.1	Bear Mountain, Perkins Memorial Tower	1,305
18.6	1405.7	Bear Mountain State Park, Hessian Lake	189

THE HIKE

Begin at the trailhead located at the Elk Pen parking lot off Arden Valley Road and follow the white blazes as you travel northbound on the AT, climbing steadily. In the spring and summer, the trail is lined with a variety of flowering plants, including steeplebush and butter-and-eggs. Cross Island Pond Road and shimmy your way through the Lemon Squeezer, a narrow corridor created by two massive boulders. You may have to take your pack off and hold it over your head to get through, and don't be surprised if there are people waiting in line to enter! This section has gained in popularity over the years.

Ascend to the top of Island Pond Mountain to catch some views before you go back down and pass the intersection for the New York Long Path, a trail that leads 52 miles east to Manhattan. Journey over giant boulders that lie flush with the ground, making for a smooth walking path as you make your way to Fingerboard Shelter, a wide stone lean-to with two fireplaces. If you decide to camp here, be sure to use the bear cables—this shelter has a history of frequent bear activity from hikers' improper food storage.

The hike continues to offer up beautiful scenery as it travels through lush meadows and woodland areas with tall grasses. The trail descends down to Arden Valley

The Lemon Squeezer Photo by Rebecca Harnish

Island Pond, Mile 1388.4 northbound; 2013 thru-hike

Trail intersection sign on the way to Lemon Squeezer; 2013 thru-hike

Road and then to Seven Lakes Drive before passing William Brien Memorial Shelter and heading back up to Black Mountain. This is a great stop for lunch with a view. On clear days, you can see the New York City skyline in the distance. Descend the mountain and use extreme caution while crossing the Palisades Parkway, a busy four-lane divided highway that leads into New York City.

> **DID YOU KNOW?**
>
> The first section of the Appalachian Trail was blazed in New York at Bear Mountain State Park back in 1923. This section of the trail became so popular that hundreds of volunteers rallied together in 2004 to help create a more sustainable footpath and save the mountain from being "loved to death."

If you are jonesing for a sweet treat, there is a visitor center with snack machines located in the median, a short distance off-trail.

Keep following the blazes north, crossing Beechy Bottom Brook and then climbing steeply up to West Mountain. The shelter at the top is a fantastic place to camp; it sits on a giant stone slab and offers amazing views of the Hudson River. See the twinkling lights of New York City on the horizon at night. As you descend the ridge of West Mountain, drink in more amazing views before the trail drops to 610 feet elevation as it crosses Seven Lakes Drive and Perkins Memorial Drive. Yep, this road travels to the summit of Bear Mountain. There will be cars and people in flip-flops at the top, so just prepare yourself for that as you begin your heart-pumping ascent to the Perkins Memorial Tower, which sits at more than 1,300 feet elevation on top of Bear Mountain. The steep descent to the base of the mountain is made easier by the stone staircase, a project that took many years and volunteers to complete. This hike ends at the base of the mountain, where you will find crowds of people enjoying Hessian Lake and picnics by the water. Bear Mountain Inn is a short walk away, as are parking areas for Bear Mountain State Park. Those who want to stay at the famous Bear Mountain Inn should consider visiting during the week; prepare to book far in advance for weekends.

If you have the extra time and energy, you can keep following the AT as it winds through the Trailside Museums and Zoo. It's a lovely walk on a paved path that leads by many exhibits with animals and plants native to New York. The lowest elevation point on the entire AT (124 feet) is near the bear cage. In addition to the animals and gardens, several stone buildings house small museums. We highly recommend the Nature Study Museum and stopping by the Geology Museum to learn more about the boulders found throughout this stretch of the AT.

Soon after the zoo, the trail leads over Bear Mountain Bridge, with stunning views of the Hudson River and then back into the woods, where more adventure awaits you!

Trail Side Museums and Zoo Entrance, Mile 1406 northbound; 2021

Bear cage—at 124 feet, the lowest point on the entire AT; 2021

Nature Study Museum; 2021

Interior, Nature Study Museum; 2021

Bald eagle; 2021

View of the Hudson River from Bear Mountain Bridge; 2021

Remains at Dennytown Road, Mile: 1421.2 northbound; 2013 thru-hike

Nick Browne at the AT railroad station that will take you to New York City, Mile 1451.8 northbound; 2013 thru-hike

By Amber Adams Niven ("Dandelion")

It's early morning on August 15, 2014. I'm eager to get packed up and moving because today is the day we take a train into the big city. My best friend, Lillie, and her boyfriend, Dan, will be hosting us at their apartment in Brooklyn.

I've never been to New York City. It never made it on my bucket list, but I can't pass up an opportunity to visit Lillie. We've been best friends since kindergarten and have been through everything together. Plus, I could use some female companionship after hiking for a month with four men.

We trek 15.3 miles to the train station in Pawling, New York, and then enjoy a long ride into the city. It's strange coming from the woods and into so much hustle and bustle. However, I don't feel out of place as I stand in busy Grand Central Station. I'm just another fish in the sea of people. I make eyes with Lillie, who guides us to the subway and back to her apartment. I notice that no one seems to care that we have large packs on, look disheveled, and stink to high heaven. No one is gawking at us as they sometimes do in the small mountain towns where we resupply.

Finally, we arrive at her apartment, where we swap stories and later explore her neighborhood. As a small country girl from east Tennessee, I'm fascinated by her lifestyle. It's minimal living, kind of like the trail, but posh. She keeps limited groceries on hand—due to limited storage, I suppose—but the market is only a few blocks away. Her clothes are washed at a laundromat across the street. *Hey, urban life is proving to have some interesting parallels to thru-hiking.* Their pad is so small it might as well be a two-person tent. My brother, Fire-squirrel, and I sleep shoulder to shoulder on the floor outside her bedroom.

It was a great break from the hike—full of joy, unexpected kindness, culture, and options. OK, maybe not the options part.

After we do the touristy things like visiting Times Square, walking across the Brooklyn Bridge, and paying for overpriced cookies, we make our way to Whole Foods to grab stuff for a picnic in Central Park. It's been well over two months of eating the same thing every day—Clif Bars, Pasta Sides, and rice and beans. And when we go into small trail towns, there are usually two vegetarian options for me—a veggie burger or pizza; occasionally a place will have nachos. So here I am, in food heaven—the mecca of organic, fresh, vegetarian food options. I feel my stomach doing cartwheels in excitement. My taste buds cry out in exuberant glee, *Yes! Yes! We finally get to taste new flavors and feel new textures!*

I beeline to the hot bar and then visit the fresh fruit. I check out the salads and the house-made salsas. I spend way too much time perusing the vast collection of cheeses and take a gander at the pre-made sandwiches before making my way back to the hot bar. I don't know how long this route took, but I completed it more than once.

Seeing my crew leave, I panicked. I was in option-overload-land (not a great place to be if you are an indecisive person). I gave myself a pep talk: *OK, Amber, you don't have to consider the shelf life or how heavy items are or if they are calorie-dense. Shoot, you can finally enjoy a fresh salad or pop a can of peaches or chow down on a plate of spaghetti. Pick something—something good!* I was limitless for the first time in months. It was overwhelming, so I went with the usual and walked out with one slice of cheese pizza. *Sorry, taste buds.*

I make my way to the park. It's just like in the movies. Huddles of people in their own little world enjoying the green patch that serves as a haven for city dwellers. It's crowded but still enjoyable. We watch people fly kites, toss Frisbees, and sunbathe. It's peaceful. I'm glad New Yorkers have a place to retreat from the stress of city life. It's hard to imagine living someplace with so few natural areas. *I wonder how many of these parkgoers have been on the AT.*

Feeling both energized and drained from our "Big Apple" excursion, it was time to get back on the AT. New York was neat, but we were ready to be in the woods where we belonged. So we said goodbye to Lillie and Dan (who have since moved back to the mountains) and caught a train back to Pawling.

FLORA FEATURE: ECHINACEA (CONEFLOWER)

From early summer to late fall, bright blooms of Echinacea appear along the Appalachian Trail. These perennial flowers grow in open wooded areas, pasturelands, and at road crossings. Their common name is coneflower, but many people know them by their botanical name. Echinacea is most commonly seen in the mid-Atlantic and southern regions, often accompanied by pollinators such as bees and butterflies. Mountain folk value this plant for its immune-boosting properties and use it as an herbal remedy during cold and flu season.

Echinacea; 2021

Founder of the Appalachian Trail, Benton MacKaye, published an article in 1921 presenting his ambitious idea of creating a footpath through the Appalachian Mountains. One hundred years ago, the Appalachian Trail was merely a dream, and although MacKaye's full vision hasn't come to completion, much of it has. Like a true trailblazer, MacKaye set out to create a new way of living, and we are so grateful he did. He pioneered the idea of land preservation for recreation and conservation purposes and was a strong advocate of balancing human needs with those of nature. His influence still lives on as we find ourselves continuously on the Appalachian Trail.

Benton MacKaye FROM THE ATC ARCHIVES

CREATURE FEATURE: LUNA MOTH

The range of the eye-catching Luna moth includes every state on the Appalachian Trail. The moths live in rich, deciduous forests. You may see one flying around or perched on a leaf anywhere from Maine to Georgia. They are exquisitely beautiful, with light to lime-green wings that taper into long tails. Their wings' bright pink borders, four eyespots, and furry antennae make them hard to miss.

Luna moth PHOTO BY JEN TOLEDO

FEATURED SHELTER: WILLIAM BRIEN MEMORIAL SHELTER

The William Brien Memorial shelter was built in 1933 by the Civilian Conservation Corps. It's one of the oldest shelters on the Appalachian Trail, with double bunks and a fireplace.

William Brien Memorial Shelter PHOTO BY SARAH JONES DECKER

View from Glastenbury Mountain Lookout Tower in Vermont, Mile 1624.3 northbound; 2013 thru-hike

PART IV

NEW ENGLAND

Connecticut | Massachusetts | Vermont

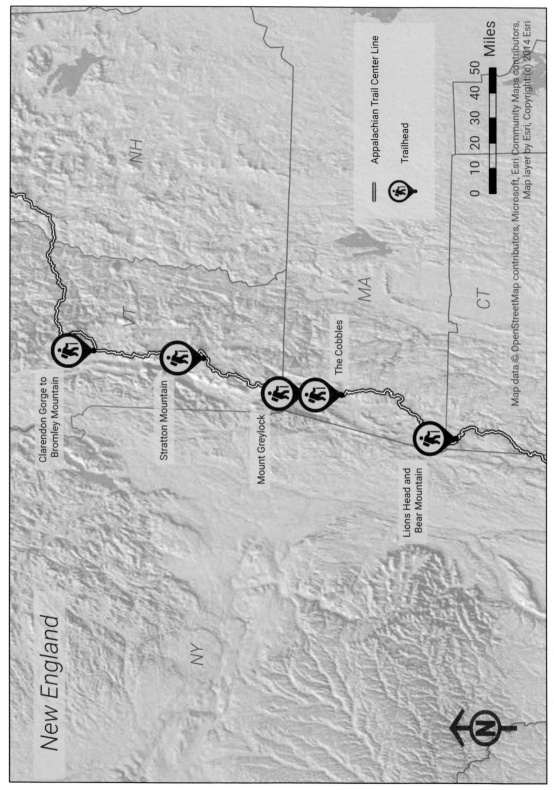

New England

NH

VT

NY

MA

CT

Clarendon Gorge to
Bromley Mountain

Stratton Mountain

Mount Greylock

The Cobbles

Lions Head and
Bear Mountain

Appalachian Trail Center Line

Trailhead

Miles

0   10   20   30   40   50

Map data © OpenStreetMap contributors, Microsoft, Esri Community Maps contributors,
Map layer by Esri, Copyright (c) 2014 Esri

N

Created by Mark Hylass, hylasmaps.com

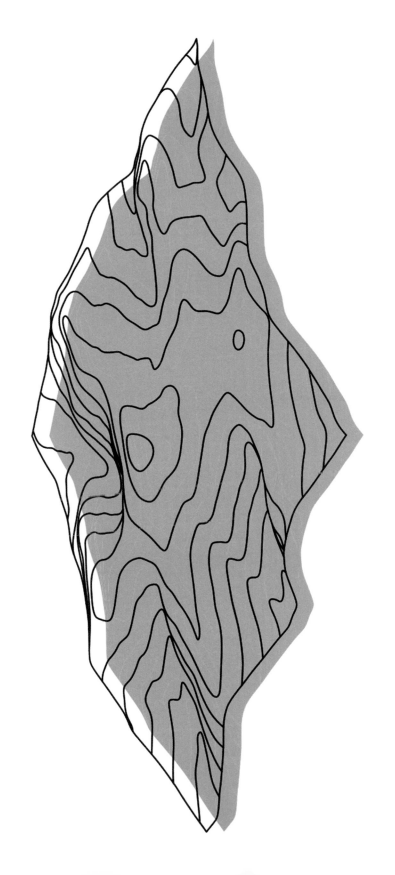

4,236'
KILLINGTON PEAK, VT

On the AT in Connecticut; 2013 thru-hike

Connecticut

WELCOME TO CONNECTICUT!

The Appalachian Trail travels 48 miles through the state of Connecticut. Enjoy sights of wonderment with moderate elevation changes as the trail roams along the Housatonic River and through the Taconic Range. Highpoints include St. Johns Ledges, Hang Glider View, Rand's View, Lions Head, and Bear Mountain. Fall is a beautiful time to experience this section of the AT as the hardwood forests explode with vibrancy.

> ### DID YOU KNOW?
> A flat section of the AT along the Housatonic River in Falls Village, Connecticut, was the first part of the trail to be universally accessible.

America needs her forests and her wild spaces quite as much as her cities and her settled places.

—Benton MacKaye

19
LIONS HEAD AND BEAR MOUNTAIN

This hike makes for a great, long day hike or a comfortable overnight trip. Enjoy two outstanding mountain views from the top of Lions Head and the highest peak in Connecticut, Bear Mountain. Fall is the best time to go, as the hardwoods in the valley below put on a heck of a show. If you are short on time, you can simply hike the 2.3 miles to Lions Head and still have a great time!

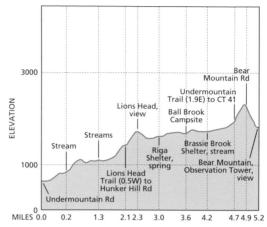

DISTANCE: 10.4 miles out and back or overnight (your choice!)
DIFFICULTY: Moderate due to slight elevation gain
TRAILHEAD GPS: 41.9941 / -73.42685
NEAREST TOWN: Salisbury, Connecticut
HIGHLIGHTS: Incredible scenery from multiple vistas

View from Riga Shelter, Mile 1505.9 northbound; 2013 thru-hike

TIPS

- Parking is available at Undermountain Road.
- Campfires are prohibited.
- Camping is permitted only at designated sites.

MILEAGE MARKERS (SOUTH TO NORTH)

SECTION	MILES FROM SPRINGER MOUNTAIN	LANDMARK	ELEVATION (IN FEET)
0.0	1502.9	Undermountain Road	720
0.2	1503.1	Stream	828
1.3	1504.2	Stream (multiple)	1,110
2.1	1505.0	Lions Head Trail (0.5 mile west) to Hunker Hill Road	1,496
2.3	1505.2	Lions Head; view	1,729
3.0	1505.9	Riga Shelter; spring	1,646
3.6	1506.5	Ball Brook Campsite	1,720
4.2	1507.1	Brassie Brook Shelter; stream	1,733
4.7	1507.6	Undermountain Trail (1.9 east) to CT 41	1,834
4.9	1507.8	Bear Mountain Road	1,920
5.2	1508.1	Bear Mountain; observation tower, view	2,316

THE HIKE

Begin at the trailhead on Undermountain Road and start hiking northbound on the AT. You will reach Lions Head in less than 3 miles after a short climb that will get your heart racing. Take in the views and rest a while before carrying onward to Bear Mountain for more views.

From Lion's Head, hike down to Riga Shelter, an eastward-facing shelter with a nice view. This would be a great spot to camp out and catch a sunrise. If you don't plan on staying the night, you can hike the additional 2 miles to reach Bear Mountain. The last 0.25 mile is fairly steep. At the top you'll find a stone "tower" that looks more like a large cairn, which you can stand on top of for far-sweeping views of the valley below. To return, backtrack the 5.2 miles on the AT to Undermountain Road.

TALES FROM THE TRAIL: FOREST SOUNDS

by Amber Adams Niven ("Dandelion")

Babbling brooks and chirping crickets are two of my favorite sounds to enjoy in the forest. Unlike the noises of civilization, the low hum of nature soothes and relaxes. Being enveloped in soft ambient sounds of flowing water and the wind blowing through the trees is like getting a sound bath from nature. No bathtub required. It is such a nice break from listening to modern sounds like zooming cars, chatter in crowded grocery stores, and clicking keyboards. The crackling of the campfire, the pitter-patter of raindrops hitting the tent, joyful noises of the songbirds, even the unzipping of sleeping bags all work together to create a sort of symphony that softly plays throughout the background.

Walking in the forest gives you an immersive experience as you soak in the sounds and vibrations of nature. Everyone knows how peaceful the sounds of the forest can be. It's why almost every sound machine on the market today has a setting with crashing waves or chirping birds. Yet, let's talk about the uneasy forest sounds for a moment. Leave the enchanted forest behind and enter the dark woods—the place where mysterious thumps and crinkles in the leaves stir your slumber.

Here's the cool thing about a long-distance hike: Typically, you get to experience myriad forest sounds—the enchanting calls of distant whip-poor-wills and peaceful lake loons as well as the mysterious thumps and crinkles in the leaves of the dark forest. I've certainly heard my fair share of spooky, unknown noises.

There was a night that I woke up to the sound of my brother, Tucker, frantically fighting off a ravenously hungry mouse. Unfortunately, he had left a Snickers bar in the mesh pocket of his tent, and the mouse had eaten straight through to get to the coveted gas station treat! Although it spooked and frustrated Tucker, it was entertaining to watch as he tried to chase the determined mouse away.

The most nerve-rattling night was the evening we camped by an old logging road in Maine. In the middle of the night, I was awakened by my dad, asking us if we heard "that."

"Heard what, Dad? We were sound asleep and didn't hear anything," I quickly replied, feeling a little uneasy.

"I thought I heard footsteps around my tent . . . might have been a moose, but I think we should pack up and move on. I'm not getting a good feeling."

My dad was in law enforcement for thirty-two years, so when he gets spooked, I trust his gut. We packed up everything and headed south for a more peaceful spot to rest. We didn't even consider looking at the terrain ahead during the commotion. So to our unfortunate surprise, we had to ford a raging

MOUSE PHOTO BY JEN TOLEDO

river and then climb steeply up the side of the mountain. To make matters even more, hmm, shall I say, adventurous, the batteries in my headlamp went dead while I was crossing the river. I'm not sure how long we hiked, but it was long enough for us to settle on pitching our tents on the side of the mountain. We fell asleep to rabbits thumping in the leaves, but at least it wasn't the sound of ominous footsteps. A few days later we found out that our friends Bug Out and Clam had been attacked in the middle of the night by a deer, or maybe even a moose, in the same spot. They weren't sure what it was, but the animal made a large hole in their tent that they had to repair in Hanover.

During an evening in New Jersey, we had our first bear encounter. We weren't actually in the forest. Yep, we were in town. FireSquirrel and I were camping on the lawn of a church hostel with Opi and the Slug Squad, our SOBO thru-hiker friends, when a 600-pound "townie bear" visited us. FireSquirrel woke me up to the sound of the bear grunting and snorting. After the beast grazed the side of our tent, FireSquirrel looked out the door just in time to make eye contact with him. Waking me up, he screamed, "THERE'S A BIG A** BEAR BY OUR TENT!" FireSquirrel yelled to alert the other hikers and, in doing so, scared the bear away. We all got out of our tent to watch him cross into a nearby parking lot, and we spent the next hour packing up our stuff to sleep in the church basement.

One of the most memorable nights of forest sounds was in Massachusetts, when porcupines invaded our camp. Dad, Tuck, and I set up our tents in a semicircle with a tree in the middle. Around two o'clock in the morning, I heard something crawling around our tent. I was already on high alert, since we had just spent the evening talking to our friends about the night something attacked their tent— something big. I woke up FireSquirrel, and we carefully reached for our headlamps to investigate what was making all the noise. Paralyzed with fear, we yelled out to Badweather and TallMilk, "Y'all hear that?!" Our screams made one of the critters run for safety up the tree. The four of us shined our headlamps at the tree from inside our tents. We could hardly see anything but the silhouette of its body.

"Oh, gosh; it's a baby bear," I yelled. My heart started racing with fear that the momma bear may be nearby. "No . . . I think it's a porcupine," said Badweather. I didn't know porcupines could climb trees, but I was relieved to find out they could. I would much rather deal with a porcupine than a baby bear. We waited for him to climb down so we could sleep soundly without the fear of being quilled, but he kept teasing us by climbing down and then back up again. Eventually, we all fell back to sleep. The porcupines were gone in the morning. We later googled to learn that porcupines cannot throw their quills. Phew!

Don't let the inevitable scare you too much, in any case. The dark forest is part of the journey. It can be spooky, but it's mostly harmless and a great chance to discover a sense of courage as you face your fears of the unknown. Unless, of course, you come across one of our Appalachian Mountain creatures like Bigfoot or the Bell Witch—well, then you'd better run.

CREATURE FEATURE: BROOK TROUT

Take a dip in the cool, clear waters of any mountain stream and you are likely to encounter a brook trout. These freshwater fish have beautiful bright colors and a marbled pattern, giving them a distinctive appearance. Brook trout are one of the most popular fish to catch while fly fishing. You can fish along the Appalachian Trail with the appropriate state fishing license.

Brook trout ILLUSTRATION BY DANNY REED

FLORA FEATURE: BLOODROOT

Bloodroot can be spotted in early spring in forested areas from Georgia to Maine. It grows close to the forest floor, with white petals and leaves furled around its stem to keep warm. Bloodroot gets its name from the toxic red sap found within its roots and stem. Native Americans used bloodroot as a natural dye, face paint, and insect repellent.

Bloodroot; 2013 thru-hike

TRAILBLAZER SPOTLIGHT: EMMA GATEWOOD ("GRANDMA GATEWOOD")

By Ricky J. Adams ("Chief Badweather")

I get faster as I get older.
—Emma Gatewood

In 1955 Emma Gatewood, known as Grandma Gatewood, became famous as the first solo female thru-hiker. ("Solo" being the keyword, as a woman named Peace Pilgrim had thru-hiked it three years prior with a comrade.) At the ripe age of 67, Grandma Gatewood hiked the entire rugged 2,100-mile length of the Appalachian Trail. She walked for 146 days through 14 states, lost 30 pounds, and went through 7 pairs of shoes.

Emma Gatewood FROM THE ATC ARCHIVES

You may be thinking, *If she can do it, I can do it.* But before you buy a bus ticket for Springer Mountain, know that Grandma Gatewood was not your typical rocking-chair granny. She was raised on a farm and worked on it tirelessly while raising eleven children and surviving a life of harsh domestic abuse. Her story has inspired countless hikers. After hiking the trail in 1955, she thru-hiked it again two years later and then section-hiked it in 1964, making her the first person to complete the trail three times.

FEATURED SHELTER: RIGA SHELTER

The Riga Shelter has an amazing east-facing view, which makes it a perfect spot to catch a sunrise. Built in 1990, the shelter is maintained by the Appalachian Mountain Club—Connecticut Chapter.

Riga Shelter PHOTO BY SARAH JONES DECKER

AT view in Massachusetts; 2013 thru-hike

Massachusetts

WELCOME TO MASSACHUSETTS!

The Appalachian Trail runs through Massachusetts for approximately 90 miles. As the trail winds across the Berkshire region of western Massachusetts, it passes through shaded woodlands, along ponds and streams with intricate beaver dams, over hills with scenic views overlooking the Housatonic River valley, and through several charming mountain towns. The highest peak, Mount Greylock, sits at nearly 3,500 feet.

We do not go to the green woods and crystal clear waters to rough it, we go to smooth it. We get enough rough at home, in towns and cities.

—G. W. Sears

Beaver dam on the AT in Massachusetts; 2013 thru-hike

Gore Brook / Gore Pond, Mile 1577.1 northbound; 2013 thru-hike

Gore Brook / Gore Pond, Mile 1577.1 northbound; 2013 thru-hike

20

THE COBBLES

The Cobbles is a short hike to a vista with wide, sweeping views and stone outcroppings composed of white Cheshire quartzite. From the top of The Cobbles you can see views of Mount Greylock, the Hoosic River valley, and the town of Cheshire. This moderately trafficked trail is a great day hike from the friendly trail town of Cheshire.

DISTANCE: 7.2 miles one way
DIFFICULTY: Moderate due to slight elevation gain
TRAILHEAD GPS: 42.48207 / -73.17859
NEARBY TOWNS: Dalton, Massachusetts; Cheshire, Massachusetts
HIGHLIGHTS: Scenic views, rock outcrops

TIPS

- For a shorter hike to The Cobbles, you can hike southbound on the AT. Park at the Ashuwillticook Rail Trail parking area in Cheshire and follow the AT southbound (east) on Church and East Main Streets to Furnace Hill Road. It's roughly 1 mile, all uphill, from there.

Rick Adams at The Cobbles, Massachusetts, Mile 1579.3 northbound; 2014 thru-hike PHOTO BY AMBER ADAMS NIVEN

MILEAGE MARKERS (SOUTH TO NORTH)

SECTION	MILES FROM SPRINGER MOUNTAIN	LANDMARK	ELEVATION (IN FEET)
0.0	1573.2	Gulf Road parking area	1,180
2.2	1575.4	Spring	1,920
3.1	1576.3	Power lines	1,906
3.2	1576.4	Crystal Mountain Campsite (0.2 mile east)	1,951
3.9	1577.1	Gore Brook, outlet of Gore Pond	2,032
5.0	1578.2	Stream	1,986
5.4	1578.6	Stream	1,816
6.1	1579.3	The Cobbles	1,846
7.2	1580.4	Furnace Hill Road	1,046

THE HIKE

From the trailhead, follow the white blazes as you travel north on the AT. In roughly 2 miles you will pass a spring and then power lines 1 mile later. A short distance from the power lines, you will reach a side trail to the Crystal Mountain Campsite. If you camp here, be sure to bring water in the summer—the spring tends to run dry. Continue following the white blazes as the trail passes Gore Brook and gains elevation. Finally it dips down, passing four more streams before reaching The Cobbles.

Enjoy the view of the countryside while standing on top of the famed Cheshire quartzite. From the outcropping, the AT dives down to Furnace Hill Road and follows the road. Continue on AT to the Ashuwillticook Rail Trail where this hike concludes.

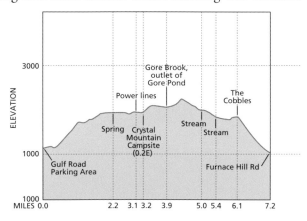

21
MOUNT GREYLOCK

With an elevation of nearly 3,500 feet, Mount Greylock is the highest peak in Massachusetts. It's situated in the state's only boreal forest and nestled within Mount Greylock State Reservation, a 12,500-acre state forest reserve that contains 70 miles of trails for hiking, mountain biking, backcountry skiing, snowshoeing, and snowmobiling.

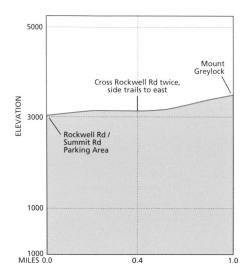

DISTANCE: 2.0 miles out and back
DIFFICULTY: Moderate due to elevation gain, although avid hikers may find this relatively easy.
TRAILHEAD GPS: 42.63770 / -73,17076
NEARBY TOWN: Adams, Massachusetts
HIGHLIGHTS: Incredible 360-degree views, history, stone monument

Topographic sculpture at the summit of Mount Greylock, Massachusetts; 2013 thru-hike

TIPS

- Mount Greylock is only 3 hours away from Boston, and many people use this place as a base camp while exploring the Berkshires.
- An auto road leads to the summit, where there is water, food, and restrooms.

MILEAGE MARKERS (SOUTH TO NORTH)

SECTION	MILES FROM SPRINGER MOUNTAIN	LANDMARK	ELEVATION (IN FEET)
0.0	1588.2	Rockwell Road / Summit Road parking area	3,025
0.4	1588.6	Cross Rockwell Road twice; side trails to the east	3,144
1.0	1589.2	Mount Greylock summit	3,491

THE HIKE

From the trailhead, hike northbound on the AT, following the white blazes. In less than 0.5 mile you will cross Rockwell Road twice, noticing side trails leading to the east. From the road crossings, you will begin the short climb to Mount Greylock. In slightly over 0.5 mile you will reach the summit.

Perched atop Greylock is a 90-foot lighthouse-like memorial tower honoring World War I veterans. The tower may be closed due to recent restrictions. However, you don't have to get any higher to see incredible views of the neighboring mountain ranges. Also located at the summit is the artfully crafted Bascom Lodge.

Trail maintenance crew with generator pack on the trail approaching Mount Greylock; 2013 thru-hike

The rustic stone lodge was built in the 1930s by the Civilian Conservation Corps during the height of the Depression. It's simple yet elegant, and offers hikers a wonderful place to retreat while adventuring in the surrounding area. When you are ready to leave, simply backtrack on the AT, following the white blazes.

View from summit of Mount Greylock, Mile 1589.2 northbound; 2013 thru-hike

View from summit of Mount Greylock, Mile 1589.2 northbound; 2013 thru-hike

By Rebecca Harnish ("V-Dub"), artist and AT thru-hiker, 2018

Torrential rain surrounded us, but we were dry and (relatively) warm huddled on the porch of the homey shelter by Upper Goose Pond in Massachusetts. Cigarette smoke hung in the air amid the hum of conversation just audible over the rain, punctuated by the occasional crack of a beer being opened. It was easy to be right there in the moment; there was nowhere else to go, yet it felt liberating. We found a chessboard and cards, we laughed at the dumbest jokes, and when the rain let up, we raced to the water to swim and canoe to the island in the middle. We stacked rocks in the shallows and sunbathed on warm rocks. We played like the kids we once were—and healed from wounds old and recent.

We often forget how to play as adults; the thought of wasting our time doing silly things can be painful in our productivity-driven society. But taking a break from our carefully built egos and external expectations is so crucial for our well-being. This is the

Rebecca Harnish on the AT

most valuable thing I've taken away from the Appalachian Trail, and as I learned to prioritize play above fear, I was oriented toward pursuing what I love: painting. It was always my intention to paint along the trail with a tiny watercolor kit, but the culture is what was motivating and inspiring. As someone who has trouble not being very critical of my own art, the atmosphere of play made it easier to embrace a more loose and expressive style. Thru-hiking and trail culture will always be one of my main inspirations as an artist, as well as staying connected to my creative and playful side.

Artwork by Rebecca Harnish

CREATURE FEATURE: OPOSSUM

Opossums are strange-looking creatures, primarily gray with a long pointy head and black, hairless ears. Their prehensile tail, also naked, is long and thin. They are scavengers who eat anything they can get their paws on—insects, frogs, mice, nuts, berries, food scraps, and more. They have the most teeth of any North American mammal and are also North America's only marsupial (an animal that carries its young in a pouch). Opossums live in every state the AT travels through; however, you will most likely only encounter them on a night hike, as these creatures are primarily nocturnal.

Joey Opossum PHOTO BY JEN TOLEDO

FEATURED SHELTER: UPPER GOOSE POND CABIN

Upper Goose Pond Cabin is located in the northern end of the AT in Massachusetts, approximately 1,550 miles from Springer Mountain. The lowest-elevation shelter in the state, the cabin sits next to a pristine, undeveloped pond that is perfect for swimming. This multilevel shelter can sleep up to sixteen people in bunks and also has tent platforms. The cabin has a fireplace, a covered porch, and an outdoor food-prep area. There is a caretaker on-site from mid-May to mid-October. There's no charge to stay at Upper Goose, although donations are accepted. The cabin is maintained by the Appalachian Mountain Club—Berkshire Chapter.

Upper Goose Pond Cabin, Mile 1551.6 northbound
Photo by Amelia Cary

FLORA FEATURE: AMERICAN POKEWEED

Pokeweed is a tall, bushy plant with vibrant color that can be found along the Appalachian Trail at the edge of forests, fields, and fences. Pokeweed has bright green leaves that shoot out from a magenta stem and long clusters of grapelike berries that turn from green to indigo during summer. Birds love them, but they are toxic to humans.

Pokeweed

FEATURED SHELTER: TOM LEONARD SHELTER

The Tom Leonard Shelter was constructed in 1988 by a group of volunteers. It has bunks, a loft, skylights, and a bear box. A nice view near the tent platform overlooks the ravine. The shelter is maintained by the Appalachian Mountain Club—Berkshire Chapter.

Tom Leonard Shelter, Mile 1530.3 northbound Photo by Sarah Jones Decker

Glastenbury Mountain lookout tower, Mile 1624.3 northbound; 2013 thru-hike

Vermont

WELCOME TO VERMONT!

Vermont, also known as the Green Mountain State, is revered for its dense forest, where the unbroken canopy shades most of the trail and ferns are as high as your waistline. Vermont is enchanting with its lush, green forest paths, but may test your patience as you trek through muddy sections during the wet season. The Appalachian Trail travels through this state for roughly 150 miles, with elevations diving as

Every Vermonter is a mountaineer . . .
—James P. Taylor

low as 400 feet and climbing more than 4,000 feet. Vermont is also well loved for its maple syrup, cheddar cheese, and Ben and Jerry's ice cream! So be sure to hit up a roadside farm stand before or after you hit the trail.

At 3,748 feet elevation, Glastenbury Mountain is one of Vermont's tallest peaks. Atop the mountain is a lookout tower reaching far above the tree line and providing jaw-dropping views. The tower was initially constructed in 1927 and renovated in 2005. In the 1800s, a thriving community once inhabited this allegedly haunted piece of wilderness. Now it's a ghost town, with abandoned buildings the earth is reclaiming. According to local lore, the area of Glastenbury is home to paranormal activity, Bigfoot sightings, a disappearing community, and other mysterious happenings.

DID YOU KNOW?

Once you cross the Massachusetts-Vermont border, you are hiking not only one long-distance trail but two! The Appalachian Trail and the Long Trail run concurrently for roughly 100 miles northbound.

Glastenbury Mountain lookout tower,
Mile 1624.3 northbound; 2013 thru-hike

Jarred Douglas atop Glastenbury
Mountain lookout tower, Mile
1624.3 northbound; 2013 thru-hike

Hiking the Appalachian Trail was the first time I've separated myself from the secular world extensively, even though I was mingling with one of the most interesting "societies" out there. Being on the Trail allowed me to be present and see more of everything rather than going through the motions of life. Understanding the environment, resourcefulness, accepting my flaws, and embracing others is the template behind the deeper meaning of my six-and-a-half-month trek. It was the greatest experience, in every sense of the word, of my 35 years of existence.

—Jarred Douglas

22
STRATTON MOUNTAIN

KELLY STAND ROAD TO STRATTON MOUNTAIN

This hike will take you to the top of Stratton Mountain, southern Vermont's highest peak. From the 3,936-foot summit, you can enjoy outstanding, far-reaching views of the White Mountains, the Adirondacks, the Berkshires, and the Green Mountain Range. Stratton is also known as the cradle of the Appalachian and Long Trails. History buffs will love experiencing the mountain that inspired James P. Taylor, founder of the Long Trail, and Benton MacKaye, founder of the AT, to create long-distance trails so many people enjoy every day.

DISTANCE: 7.6 miles out and back
DIFFICULTY: Moderate due to elevation gain
TRAILHEAD GPS: 43.0611 / -72.9678
NEARBY TOWN: Stratton, Vermont
HIGHLIGHTS: Incredible 360-degree views, fire tower, AT history

Stratton Mountain lookout tower, Mile 1640.3 northbound; 2021

TIPS

- Camping at the summit is not permitted.
- The Appalachian Trail shares this section with the Long Trail.

MILEAGE MARKERS (SOUTH TO NORTH)

SECTION	MILES FROM SPRINGER MOUNTAIN	LANDMARK	ELEVATION (IN FEET)
0.0	1636.5	Parking area at Kelly Stand Road; campsite (100 yards north), Daniel Webster Monument (0.3 mile east)	2,230
1.5	1638.0	Logging road	2,584
3.8	1640.3	Stratton Mountain; lookout tower, caretaker cabin, side trail (0.8 mile east) to Stratton Mountain Resort gondola	3,936

THE HIKE

Begin hiking northbound from the parking area at Kelly Stand Road. The trail gently ascends as you trek through the mixed hardwood and softwood forest. After crossing an old logging road, begin a steeper climb up the mountain. The AT follows the ridgeline and levels out for a bit before the last final push. Finally, the white blazes lead through a series of switchbacks before reaching the top of Stratton Mountain. Climb the fire tower for breathtaking views of the majestic Green Mountain Range, and say hello to the caretaker if you are there in summer or fall. A side trail about 1 mile long leads to a gondola that

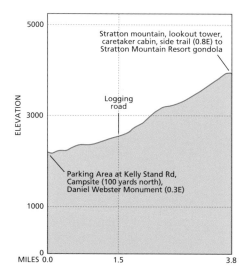

carries people up and down to Stratton Mountain Resort, a popular skiing destination.

Once you finish exploring, retrace your steps on the AT to return to the parking area.

Stratton Mountain lookout tower,
Mile 1640.3 northbound; 2021

Stratton Mountain lookout tower,
Mile 1640.3 northbound; 2021

Stratton Pond, Mile 1643.5
northbound; 2013 thru-hike

23

CLARENDON GORGE TO BROMLEY MOUNTAIN

VT 103 TO VT 11 & 30 NEAR MANCHESTER CENTER

This backpacking trip traverses the majestic Green Mountains for nearly 33 miles. Starting with a suspension bridge that towers above beautiful swimming holes, this hike then crosses several streams and rustic wooden footbridges to an interesting display of stone cairns before finishing off with spectacular views atop Bromley Mountain.

DISTANCE: 32.4 miles one way
DIFFICULTY: Moderate due to elevation gain
TRAILHEAD GPS: 43.5214 / -72.9258
NEAREST TOWN: North Clarendon, Vermont; Manchester Center, Vermont
HIGHLIGHTS: Swimming holes, suspension bridge, lake, incredible views

TIPS

- This section of the AT is shared by the Long Trail.
- Camping at the summit of Bromley Mountain is not permitted.
- If you're hiking here in the summer, you can stop by the Manchester Farmers Market, held every Thursday in Adams Park, downtown Manchester.

Clarendon Gorge suspension bridge, Mile 1686.3 northbound; 2021

MILEAGE MARKERS (NORTH TO SOUTH)

SECTION	MILES FROM SPRINGER MOUNTAIN	LANDMARK	ELEVATION (IN FEET)
0.0	1686.4	VT 103 parking area	860
0.1	1686.3	Clarendon Gorge; suspension bridge	808
2.7	1683.7	Minerva Hinchey Shelter; spring	1,611
3.3	1683.1	Footbridge, stream	1,648
4.6	1681.8	Bear Mountain	2,228
6.3	1680.1	VT 140; footbridge, stream	1,105
7.1	1679.3	Bully Brook, Keewaydin Trail to the west	1,424
7.8	1678.6	Greenwall Shelter (0.2 mile east); spring	2,095
8.4	1678.0	Stone cairns; trail (0.2 mile west) to White Rocks Cliff	2,276
11.6	1674.8	Footbridge, stream	1,938
12.6	1673.8	Little Rock Pond Shelter; water at caretaker platform	1,835
12.7	1673.7	Homer Stone Brook Trail to the west	1,854
14.8	1671.6	Danby-Landgrove Road; parking	1,517
17.1	1669.3	Spring	1,956
17.6	1668.8	Lost Pond Shelter; water	2,192
19.7	1666.7	Baker Peak Trail to the west	2,642
21.8	1664.6	Griffith Lake tenting area	2,600
22.3	1664.1	Peru Peak Shelter; water	2,597
23.6	1662.8	Peru Peak	3,429
25.3	1661.1	Styles Peak	3,394
26.9	1659.5	Mad Tom Notch	2,446
29.4	1657.0	Bromley Mountain; skier warming hut	3,260
30.4	1656.0	Bromley Shelter	2,535
32.4	1654.0	VT 11 & 30	1,840

THE HIKE

From the parking area on VT 103, find the trailhead and make your way south. Soon you will cross the 30-foot suspension bridge that hangs directly above Clarendon Gorge. This area is a popular swimming hole and may be crowded during warmer months. After the bridge, the trail climbs steadily, crossing several streams and passing beautiful cascades. As you hike past Minerva Hinchey Shelter, the course begins to

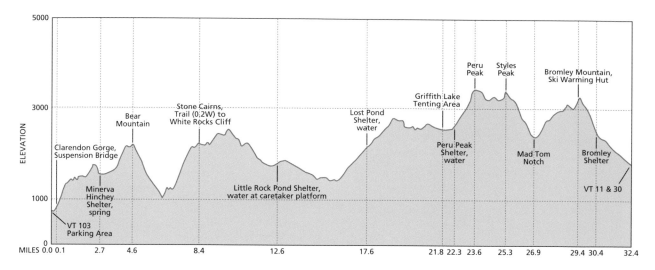

climb Bear Mountain. Once you descend from the 2,228-foot peak, you will cross Sugar Hill Road just pass VT 140. From this point, Greenwall Shelter is about 1.5 miles away—an excellent spot to camp for the night. Get water at Bully Brook before the shelter, as the spring at Greenwall tends to run dry. Next, hike roughly 0.5 mile to enjoy a creative display of stone cairns surrounding the trail sign for White Rocks Cliff; a 0.2-mile blue-blazed spur trail leads to a view.

From the cairns, continue trekking south toward Bromley Mountain. You will pass four shelters within the next 10 miles as the trail gently dips and then climbs again through the forest. On the way up to Peru Peak is a peaceful area to camp next to Griffith Lake, roughly 7.5 miles from Bromley Mountain. From Griffith Lake, traverse over Peru Peak and Styles Peak, and then descends to Mad Tom Notch at 2,446-feet. From the notch, climb 2.5 miles up to Bromley.

Once you reach the 3,260-foot peak, savor the views and enjoy some food. Take refuge in the skier warming hut if it's cool and windy. You can camp here for the night and enjoy watching the sunset from the summit. Or continue onward to Bromley Shelter, about 0.5 mile farther. Once you reach the shelter, the trail begins to descend gradually. After you cross a footbridge, the parking area is less than 1 mile away and where you will end this hike.

Take a ride into downtown Manchester Center for a delicious post-hike meal. This town is bursting with local eateries and shops, including a well-stocked outfitters. Book-lovers, don't miss the family-owned Northshire Bookstore, housed in a multilevel building that might as well be literature heaven.

DID YOU KNOW?

Killington Mountain, located in central Vermont, is the first time the AT reaches above 4,000 feet in elevation since Tennessee.

View from Clarendon Gorge suspension bridge, Mile 1686.3 northbound; 2021

View from Clarendon Gorge suspension bridge, Mile 1686.3 northbound; 2021

Cairn garden at White Rock Cliff Trail, Mile 1678.0 northbound; 2013 thru-hike

Peru Peak Shelter, Mile 1664.1 northbound; 2013 thru-hike

Northbound directional sign at Peru Peak Shelter, Mile 1664.1 northbound; 2013 thru-hike

Bromley Mountain summit, Mile 1664.1 northbound; 2013 thru-hike

Poem on Maine Junction Sign, Northern intersection, Mile 1664.1 northbound; 2013 thru-hike

Waterfall in Vermont; 2013 thru-hike

By Nick Browne ("Brownie," Georgia-Maine, 2013)

My trip on the Trail taught me this—just go for it.

I didn't grow up dreaming of hiking the AT. Nor did I plan for years before leaving. I didn't discover it until Bari, a battle buddy of mine, casually brought it up one night. He said, "Dude, I just watched a documentary on this backpacking trip in the United States called the Appalachian Trail; it's 2,000 miles, and people do the whole thing. We should do it!"

I replied, "No way. That's impossible, right . . . ? Maybe pro athletes or something, but no normal person is hiking 2,000 miles. That's insanity."

He turned the documentary on, and we decided right then we'd do it when we got out of the military. I'm not sure if he ever did any more research. But I did. It took about 3 hours for me to figure out that we should leave in late March.

Day 0 went like this: We showed up at what we thought was the Springer Mountain trailhead. Unfortunately, it's snowing, and I'm wearing shorts and a T-shirt. Note to self: *It snows in Georgia.*

We start arguing once we hit the waterfall . . . there is NOT a waterfall in the guide I'm using. It should only be a few miles to the summit of Springer. I think they dropped us off at the wrong trailhead. It turns out there are several trails to Springer. We added 13 miles to keep up with our original planned campsite.

It's almost dark when we finally arrive. There's no room to pitch our tents. There must be forty people camping here.

Bari packed the cutting board and kitchen knife; I had the potatoes and canned chili—neither of us brought a camp stove. "We'll just cook on an open fire, right?" Unfortunately, the snow made it difficult to start a fire. So we ate cold chili in silence—suffocated by doubt.

I summited Katahdin on September 19 with a stove and a lesson that informs my life to this day. Just go for it. Dive in. You don't need permission. You don't need to read another book or buy better gear. Preparation is overrated. And the answers are always in the process. All you have to do is go.

CREATURE FEATURE: GREAT BLUE HERON

The great blue heron can be seen hanging out in calm, slow-moving rivers and near the shores of lakes along the Appalachian Trail. They are easy to spot, towering out of the water, often motionless, as they wait for dinner to get within reach. These spectacular birds make their home as far north as Canada and return south during the winter. With a wingspan of 70 inches, the great blue heron appears majestic in flight.

Great blue heron PHOTO BY JEN TOLEDO

FEATURED SHELTER: STRATTON POND SHELTER

Stratton Pond Shelter is located at the base of Stratton Mountain and a short walk from beautiful Stratton Pond. Built in 1999, it has a sleeping capacity of twenty people. There is an overnight fee to stay here.

Stratton Pond Shelter PHOTO BY SARAH JONES DECKER

James P. Taylor is the founder of the Green Mountain Club and father of the Long Trail. An avid hiker, Taylor became frustrated with the lack of trails in Vermont's Green Mountains and was inspired to create a "long trail." Interestingly enough, he conceived his idea at Stratton Mountain—the same place Benton MacKaye envisioned the AT in 1900.

The Long Trail extends 272 miles along the spine of the Green Mountains and shares roughly 100 miles with the AT. Built between 1910 and 1930, it was America's first long-distance trail and the first linear trail, predating the Appalachian Trail. The builders of the AT adopted techniques from Taylor, such as using paint to mark the trails. There is no doubt that Taylor's vision was part of the inspiration behind the AT, as well as other trails that followed.

James P. Taylor

FUNGI FEATURE: OYSTER MUSHROOM

Oyster mushrooms are commonly seen growing in hardwood forests on trees and stumps along the Appalachian Trail. They have a light brown to white cap with whitish-yellow gills and arise from a stub-like stalk. Their illustrious oyster-like shape gives them their name.

Oyster mushroom

Mount Monroe; 2013 thru-hike

PART V

THE WILD NORTH

New Hampshire / Maine

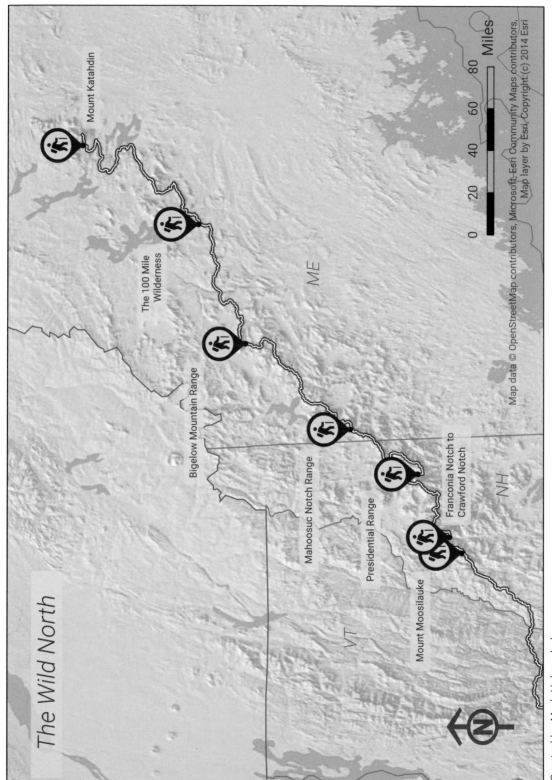

The Wild North

Mount Katahdin

The 100 Mile Wilderness

Bigelow Mountain Range

ME

Mahoosuc Notch Range

Presidential Range

Franconia Notch to
Crawford Notch

Mount Moosilauke

VT

NH

Miles

0   20   40   60   80

Map data © OpenStreetMap contributors, Microsoft, Esri Community Maps contributors,
Map layer by Esri, Copyright:(c) 2014 Esri

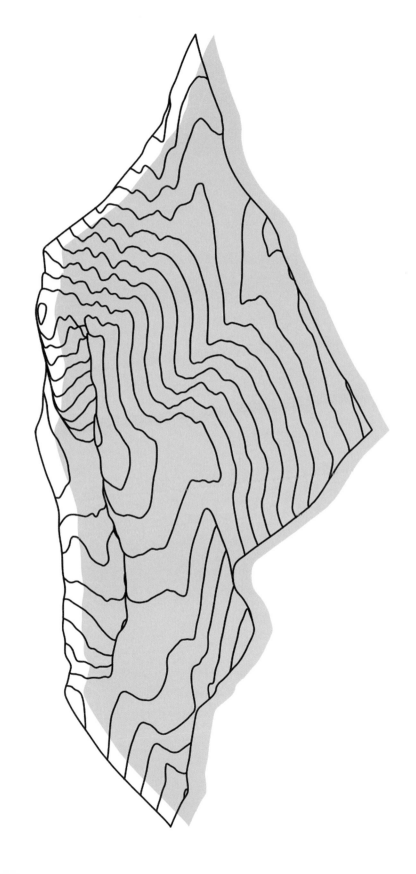

5,267'

MOUNT KATAHDIN, ME

The AT in New Hampshire; 2013 thru-hike

New Hampshire

WELCOME TO NEW HAMPSHIRE!

The Appalachian Trail traverses New Hampshire for approximately 160 miles. This state holds the most mileage above tree line than any other state on the AT. New Hampshire is commonly referred to as the Granite State and the White Mountain State. Their mountains are as dramatic as their state motto, "Live free or die," which is inscribed on every license plate. Locals here are self-reliant outdoor adventurers, and hiking is just one of the many ways they play outside. The Granite State is famed for skiing, snowboarding, snowmobiling, rock climbing, horseback riding, zip-lining, kayaking, and more. Many people travel to New Hampshire to visit the White Mountain National Forest ("the Whites"), prized for its many peaks above 4,000 feet, technical topography, and friendly huts.

> It is the love of country, the love of primal nature and of human nature, the lure of crestline and comradeship, which we like to think of as being indigenous to our own homeland. In short, the object of the Appalachian Trail is to develop the Indigenous America.
>
> —Benton MacKaye

This section of the Appalachian Trail has so much to offer. The mountains are steep, rugged, and rocky—challenging at times. However, there is still a plethora of comfortable ridge-walking to offset the sharp, vertical climbs and descents. Whether you choose to trek the ridgeline of the Presidential Range, which includes Mount Washington, the highest peak in the northeastern United States, or climb up Mount Moosilauke, you will need strong legs to get up and down New Hampshire's steep mountains.

EXTREME WEATHER

Hikers should carefully plan passage through New Hampshire, since the weather often changes on a whim and much of this section is on exposed ridges. It's best to trek these rugged mountains when you are in good condition and well equipped.

Ball field near trailhead in Hanover, New Hampshire, Mile 1751.7 northbound; 2013 thru-hike

Ball field near trailhead in Hanover, New Hampshire, Mile 1751.7 northbound; 2013 thru-hike

Hikers Welcome Hostel, Glencliff New Hampshire; 2013 thru-hike

Smarts Mountain fire tower, Mile 1774.2 northbound; 2013 thru-hike

24
MOUNT MOOSILAUKE

KINSMAN NOTCH TO NH 25

This is a very challenging hike, and although there are alternate routes up Mount Moosilauke, none are as rewarding as this one. It's perfect for avid hikers looking for a challenge and wanting to see a great high-elevation view.

DISTANCE: 9.3 miles one way
LEVEL OF DIFFICULTY: Strenuous due to steep, technical terrain and alpine conditions
TRAILHEAD GPS: 44.0398 / -71.7921
NEARBY TOWN: North Woodstock, New Hampshire
HIGHLIGHTS: Shelter with a view, beautiful cascades, panoramic views from the mountaintop

Looking back at Mount Moosilauke during descent; 2013 thru-hike

TIPS

- Contact the Appalachian Mountain Club if you are interested in staying in a hut. The AMC also has a hiker shuttle that you can schedule by calling (603) 466-2727. If you are thru-hiking, ask about the AMC Thru-hiker Pass program for discounts on campsites and other perks.
- Camp in designated sites or at least 200 feet from water, trails, and facilities.
- Do not camp above tree line (where trees are 8 feet tall or less) or within a Forest Protection Area (FPA).
- Fires are not permitted above tree line.

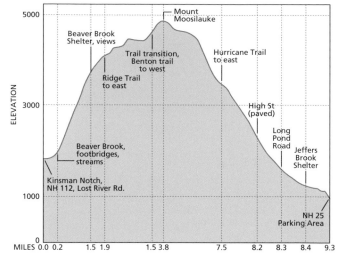

MILEAGE MARKERS (SOUTH TO NORTH)

SECTION	MILES FROM SPRINGER MOUNTAIN	LANDMARK	ELEVATION (IN FEET)
0.0	1803.7	Kinsman Notch; NH 112, Lost River Road	1,870
0.2	1803.5	Beaver Brook; footbridges, streams	1,877
1.5	1802.2	Beaver Brook Shelter; views	3,728
1.9	1801.8	Ridge Trail to the east	4,042
3.5	1800.2	Trail transition; Benton Trail to the west	4,581
3.8	1799.9	Mount Moosilauke	4,802
7.5	1796.2	Hurricane Trail to the east	1,665
8.2	1795.5	High Street (paved)	1,345
8.3	1795.4	Long Pond Road	1,329
8.4	1795.3	Jeffers Brook Shelter	1,308
9.3	1794.4	NH 25 parking area	1,043

Joel Dallas, Nick Browne, and Jarred Douglas ascending Moosilauke; 2013 thru-hike

THE HIKE

Begin this hike at the Beaver Brook Trailhead at Kinsman Notch. We recommend using trekking poles or a walking stick, as the terrain is very steep. Shortly after you set out, you will pass a sign warning of the difficulty of the terrain. The trail crosses a footbridge over Beaver Brook and ascends rapidly past a series of beautiful cascades. You won't find switchbacks here, but there are hand rungs and stairs bolted into the rock face to assist you in your climb. After a grueling 1.5 miles from the trailhead, you will encounter Beaver Brook Shelter, built by the Dartmouth Outing Club. This shelter is an excellent spot to rest while enjoying stunning views of the Franconia Ridge. The trail continues to climb, but it is less steep than the first portion of the hike. From here, Mount Moosilauke is roughly 2 miles away, where great 360-degree views and a meadow of alpine grass await you. It's often windy at the summit, so come prepared.

Once you are ready to leave Moosilauke, descend the mountain and hike 5.5 miles to the parking area at NH 25.

Ascending Mount Moosilauke; 2013 thru-hike

Approaching summit of Mount Moosilauke; 2013 thru-hike

Sign at summit of Mount Moosilauke, Mile 1799.9 northbound; 2013 thru-hike

Nick Browne at summit of Mount Moosilauke, Mile 1799.9 northbound; 2013 thru-hike

Descending Mount Moosilauke; 2013 thru-hike

Descending Mount Moosilauke; 2013 thru-hike

TALES FROM THE TRAIL: BILL ACKERLY, THE ICE CREAM MAN

by Sean Kamp ("P-Diddy," Georgia–Maine, 2015)

My favorite day on the Appalachian Trail occurred in Lyme, New Hampshire, in late June 2015. It was a wet and rainy day, and I felt like I was walking through a car wash as the waist-high, lush, and overgrown foliage lining the trail brushed against me with every step. Soon my hiking partners and I saw a sign indicating free ice cream just down a side path that led to a house not far off the trail. We stood on the back porch for a second, not sure if we should knock. Before we could knock, however, we saw movement from inside a sliding glass door, and soon an elderly man in glasses cheerfully greeted us. With a slow but excited wave, and an incredibly big smile, we were ushered inside.

His name was Bill Ackerly. For fifteen years he had been providing a quick reprieve from the trail and loved to share frozen treats. Still standing up, and soaking wet from the rain, we devoured our ice cream and thanked Bill for his kindness. We didn't want to linger too long, but he assured us it was fine to seek refuge from the storm outside. He beckoned us to sit at his dining room table. Bill guided our conversation through myriad topics spanning classical music, food, travel, Eastern philosophy, and, of course, the Appalachian Trail. Occasionally I glanced around, noticing books and records and all kinds of cool items around his house. I could tell Bill had lived an interesting life, and I could tell he was highly educated yet very down to earth. Later, I found out he had been a dedicated and respected psychiatrist. I loved every minute of our conversation. Bill was in his late 80s, and while he moved slowly, his words and thoughts raced about and our conversation never missed a beat. Time flew by; we had been there 4 hours. Bill had a way of seamlessly connecting his life to everything and finding common ground with us all. My hiking partner, Mozart, was from Germany. Bill told us about his father, who had been captured by German soldiers during WWI. They showed him kindness and compassion, and for that reason he considered every German his friend. Bill saw the beauty and love in everything.

Sean Kamp

The rain began to let up, and although I didn't want to leave such wonderful company, it was time to go. As I left, Bill turned to me and said, "Come back and see me in ten years; I'd love to see where life has taken you." I quickly replied, "I will." A wide smile slowly crept across Bill's face and he said with a laugh, "I'll be dead, silly."

Bill was the most interesting person I met on the Appalachian Trail, and I often think of his kindness and how he made our rainy day much brighter. A year after meeting Bill, I came across an article online celebrating his life. Bill had died recently at the age of 87. His words as he joked about meeting again to catch up had sunk deep. I hope we do meet again.

By Amber Adams Niven ("Dandelion")

After Mount Moosilauke, the terrain levels out for Southbounders and changes from fewer boulder fields to more grassy areas. Checking for ticks became a daily ritual for me and my hiking family, or should I say my "tramily." The last week in New Hampshire was bittersweet—no, really. It was full of sugar! I felt like I was floating on a big, fluffy cloud, high on sweetness and scenes of beauty. I didn't want to leave, ever, but I knew the crash was coming. We stayed at Mount Cube Farm, where Maple Jimmy and owner, Pete, gave us a tour of their facility. They've been tapping trees to make maple syrup and sugar since the 1950s. They had an outdoor shower rigged up outside. It wasn't exactly private, but my skin, layered with dirt and grime, was itching to wash the trail off. Now was not the time for modesty. Now was the time to take full advantage of a Maple Jimmy's backwoods shower.

We enjoyed camping on their lawn and waking up to pancakes, which were accompanied with a generous amount of maple syrup. An army of slugs had found their way into the crevices of Dad's egg-crate sleeping pad. After fighting them off, we made our way to trail legend Bill Ackerly's house. He is famous for

Mount Cube Farm; 2014 thru-hike PHOTO BY STACEY MCDERMID

giving hikers free ice cream in exchange for a game of croquet. After I introduced myself as Dandelion, he lit up with excitement. His delighted face made it clear he wanted to tell me something: "Have you ever tasted dandelion wine? I made some. Would you like a taste?" I said "sure," and he hurried off, but he never returned with his homemade wine. I assumed he got distracted with other hikers, who seemed to trickle in until sundown.

We spent the evening eating ice cream, meeting new friends, laughing with old ones, and watching hikers play croquet from a picnic table that sat under a string of prayer flags. A pink sunset colored the sky. It was a night I will remember forever. The next day we planned to hike into Hanover, New Hampshire, for a celebratory zero day before crossing the border into Vermont.

We arrived in Hanover late at night, minutes before a thunderstorm. The town has an excellent reputation on the trail. Every Northbounder we passed raved about all the free stuff hikers get. We had all been looking forward to experiencing the "big trail town" since leaving Gorham. Aside from doing laundry and resting, my favorite thing about Hanover was discovering carrot cake pancakes at Lou's. I loved them so much, I ordered them twice. After filling our bellies with pancakes, we toured the "big trail town." We explored the Hood Art Museum and the rest of the Dartmouth campus, spent hours in a bookstore, and took advantage of the free slice of pizza and doughnuts for thru-hikers. I also found a funky clothing boutique and bought a new, clean outfit that I planned on wearing for the remainder of the trip.

The many people, cars, urban noises, and busy pace of the city had us in a bit of a shock. Coming from the mellow woods, everyone in town seemed to be in a rush. We saw other hikers just staring in the distance and realized we were not alone; we were all in sensory overload.

We returned to the trail with our freshly restocked (very heavy) packs and our senses processing everything we had just experienced. As we crossed the border into Vermont, we snapped a quick photo, and I heard my younger brother, Tucker, say, "You don't know it, but you've changed." He was speaking for all of us, and I couldn't agree more. Tucker is the type that always thinks before he speaks, careful not to waste anyone's time with nonsense small-talk. So when he drops a truth bomb, everyone is all ears. This one reverberated in my mind all day. Nature was indeed changing me.

As fellow AT hiker Peace Pilgrim said in her book, "You soon put material things in their proper place, realizing that they are there for use, but relinquishing them when they are not useful. You soon experience and learn to appreciate the great freedom of simplicity." Visiting trail towns along our journey was a way to see how life in the woods was such a counterbalance to modern living. Both special, with much to give.

South Kinsman Mountain; 2013 thru-hike

Lonesome Lake; 2013 thru-hike

25
FRANCONIA NOTCH TO CRAWFORD NOTCH

Located in the White Mountains National Forest, Franconia Ridge is one of the most popular hikes in New Hampshire. This strenuous traverse takes you over three of the state's 4,000 footers, offering endless views.

LENGTH OF HIKE: 27.4 miles one way
DIFFICULTY: Strenuous due to steep, technical terrain and alpine conditions
TRAILHEAD GPS: 44.1002 / -71.6825
NEARBY TOWN: Lincoln, New Hampshire
HIGHLIGHTS: Alpine hiking with breathtaking views, beautiful waterfall, Zealand Falls Hut

TIPS

- Contact the Appalachian Mountain Club if you are interested in staying in a hut. The AMC also has a hiker shuttle that you can schedule by calling (603) 466-2727. If you are thru-hiking check-in about the AMC Thru-hiker Pass program for discounts on campsites and other perks.
- Camp in designated sites or at least 200 feet from water, trails, and facilities.
- Do not camp above tree line (where trees are 8 feet tall or less) or within a Forest Protection Area (FPA).
- Fires are not permitted above tree line.
- You can easily extend this hike to traverse the Presidential Range.

View from Haystack Mountain toward Mount Lincoln, Mile 1824.7 northbound; 2013 thru-hike

MILEAGE MARKERS (SOUTH TO NORTH)

SECTION	MILES FROM SPRINGER MOUNTAIN	LANDMARK	ELEVATION (IN FEET)
0.0	1820.0	Franconia Notch	1,421
0.7	1820.7	Flume Side Trail to the east	1,834
1.2	1821.2	Streams	2,033
2.6	1822.6	Liberty Spring Campsite (overnight fee), reliable water	3,856
4.7	1824.7	Little Haystack Mountain; Falling Waters trail to the west (AT is above tree line for the next 2 miles.)	4,729
5.4	1825.4	Mount Lincoln, Franconia Ridge	5,089
6.4	1826.4	Mount Lafayette; Greenleaf Hut (1.1 miles west)	5,246
9.5	1829.5	Garfield Pond	3,857
10.3	1830.3	Garfield Ridge Shelter and Campsite (0.2 mile west); reliable water	3,923
10.8	1830.8	Franconia Brook Trail (2.2 miles east) to Thirteen Falls Campsite, reliable water	3,428
13	1833.0	Frost Trail to Galehead Hut	3,800
13.8	1833.8	South Twin Mountain; North Twin Spur Trail to the west	4,902
15.8	1835.8	Guyot Shelter (0.7 mile east) on Bondcliff Trail (overnight fee)	4,517
15.9	1835.9	Mount Guyot; view to the east	4,578
18.3	1838.3	Zeacliff Pond to the east	3,786
19.3	1839.3	Whitewall Brook; many streams leading to falls	3,155
19.9	1839.9	Zealand Falls Hut	2,624
22.3	1842.3	Stream; Thoreau Falls to the east	2,478
23.5	1843.5	Footbridge; stream	2,632
24.8	1844.8	Ethan Pond Campsite, water source is in the inlet to the pond and is reliable	2,861
27.2	1847.2	Ripley Falls (0.5 mile east)	1,578
27.4	1847.4	Railroad tracks, parking	1,428

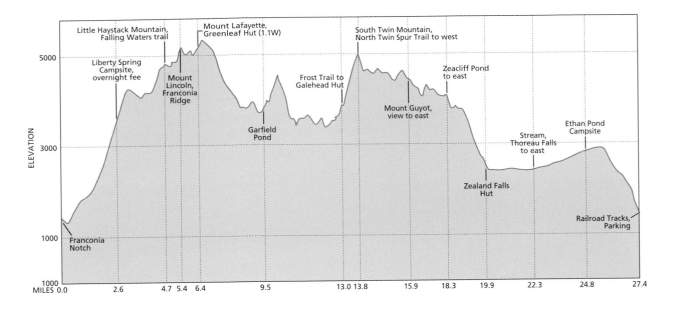

THE HIKE

For this hike, we will travel northbound on the AT, beginning at Franconia Notch, where the Liberty Springs Trailhead is located. Hike roughly 2.5 miles, gaining in elevation, to the Liberty Spring Campsite. If you want to stay here your first night, there is a small overnight fee. From the campsite, make your way to the 4,729-foot summit of Little Haystack Mountain. The trail is above tree line for the next 2 miles, so be prepared and research weather conditions. Mount Lincoln is less than 1 mile from Haystack, sitting at 5,089 feet, with incredible views overlooking Franconia Notch. The third peak you will come to is beautiful Mount Lafayette, at 5,246 feet. Greenleaf Hut, visible from the summit, is located 1.1 miles down a steep side trail marked with blue blazes. Remember, camping is not allowed near the huts, and you shouldn't count on staying in one of them unless you have a reservation.

From the peak of Mount Lafayette, the AT descends steeply to Garfield Pond and carries on to Mount Garfield. Then it passes a short side trail that leads to Garfield Ridge Shelter and Campsite. Half a mile from there is the junction with the Franconia Brook Trail, which leads steeply down 2.2 miles to the Thirteen Falls Campsite. Finally, a few miles and a short elevation gain away, the trail roams past Galehead Hut before ascending South Twin Mountain, the last big climb of the hike.

The Bondcliff Trail leads to Guyot Shelter; the shelter is 1 mile off the AT but has water if you need it. Otherwise, the trail goes across Mount Guyot and down to Zeacliff Pond, with views along the way. Continue to descend to the bottom of Zealand Falls. Zealand Falls Hut sits next to the falls and is an excellent spot to take a rest while enjoying the cascading water. The trail mellows out for a good 5 miles, crossing two footbridges before reaching a spur trail to the Ethan Pond Campsite. From the campsite, the parking area is approximately 2.5 miles away. Continue following the white blazes as the trail descends to Crawford Notch.

Sign at Little Haystack Mountain, Mile 1824.7 northbound; 2013 thru-hike

View from Mount Lafayette, Mile 1826.4 northbound; 2013 thru-hike

View from Mount Lafayette, Mile 1826.4 northbound; 2013 thru-hike

Trail sign at Mount Lafayette, Mile 1826.4 northbound; 2013 thru-hike

Mount Garfield, Mile 1829.9 northbound; 2013 thru-hike

Ryan "Samba" Underwood; 2013 thru-hike

South Twin Mountain, Mile 1833.8 northbound; 2013 thru-hike

Zealand Falls Hut, Mile 1839.9 northbound; 2013 thru-hike

Zealand Falls Hut, Mile 1839.9 northbound; 2013 thru-hike

Thoreau Falls, Mile: 1842.3 northbound; 2013 thru-hike

TALES FROM THE TRAIL: SUNNY DAYS DON'T LAST LONG ON FRANCONIA RIDGE

By Amber Adams Niven ("Dandelion")

Let me set the scene.

Imagine being on top of a mountain that you had never been on, in a dark freezing hailstorm, far away from shelter with thoughts of your life flashing before your mind's eye as you start to wonder if this is the end.

I had some lingering anxiety as we crossed the Presidential Range above tree line. I was nervous about getting caught in a storm. After all, Mount Washington is said to be the most dangerous place in the United States. Passage through "the Whites" can be perilous, with the weather changing on a whim. However, we were fortunate enough to have clear skies and sunny days the entire way through. After climbing Mount Madison, we enjoyed a long nap, an epic sunset from Lake of the Clouds Hut, and a clear view from Mount Washington.

One of my favorite nights was camping near Webster Cliffs, located just South of Mizpah Spring Hut and north of Crawford Notch. It was a clear night, and I still had some vegan marshmallows left from Gorham. So we made a fire and enjoyed toasting marshmallows while watching the stars come out. Unfortunately, a few days later, our good weather streak ended rather abruptly as we were crossing Franconia Ridge. If you are an avid hiker, chances are you've experienced some form of inclement weather. I think every hiker has a story of inclement weather. Well, here's mine.

The storm clouds started rolling in just as we began to hike up Mount Lafayette. It was a steep ascent and required us to climb more than 1,300 feet in elevation before we reached the top. We planned to camp after Little Haystack Mountain, but as the dark, ominous clouds kept moving in, we started thinking we needed to find shelter before Haystack. It was a grueling hike, and the higher we climbed, the thicker the fog was. We could barely see 2 feet in front of us. My dad was somewhere behind us. I wasn't sure how far, and we had no way of communicating with him.

By the time we finally reached Mount Lafayette, the rain had started and the wind had picked up. We covered our packs and put on our rain gear. We had a decision to make: We could take

Tucker Adams and Amber Niven enjoying a sunset on Webster Cliffs, Mile 1850.1 northbound; 2014 thru-hike

a side trail down to Greenleaf Hut or continue toward Haystack. We knew we had to take shelter soon. Our rain gear was not holding up, and the temperature was dropping, turning the rain to hail.

We decided to change plans and find shelter at Greenleaf Hut; now, we just had to tell Dad. We huddled together near a stone wall and waited for him to reach the peak in hopes that he wasn't far behind. But as time passed, we started to wonder if he had found alternative shelter elsewhere. The storm was only getting worse, and we desperately wanted to be in the trees, dry and safe.

Stacey, Tucker, and I spent half an hour figuring out how to get a message to Badweather (Dad) that we were cutting our day short. Stacey pulled out the duct tape, and I attempted to write a note, but the marker was smearing all over the paper and the duct tape wasn't holding up. So we were forced to get creative. Tucker gathered some loose rocks that Stacey and I used to spell out "DAD," with an arrow pointing to the side trail. We said a prayer, crossed our fingers, and made a run for the trees, hoping he could decipher our message. Little did we know that side trail would continue above tree line for another mile.

After hours of being annihilated by the storm, we finally reached Greenleaf Hut. We walked into the place drenched to the bone (rain pants and jackets can only take so much), praying they would allow us to do work-for-stay. There was still the chance that those staffing the hut would turn us away. But they didn't.

Instead, the crew welcomed us with open arms and treated us like family. Kimble, the hut master at the time, fed us warm soup and coffee cake as soon as we dried off. He even offered us one of his beers.

Not long after we finished our soup, Badweather walked through the door, and I could breathe easy, knowing he was safe. How he managed to see our message still baffles me. As for our "work" duties, Stacey and Badweather had to give a thru-hiker storytelling presentation to the guests, while Tucker and I had to accompany the crew on a short walk to watch the sunset (*best work-for-stay ever*). Our stormy hike ended up being a pretty great day. One I will never forget.

Tucker Adams and Amber Niven huddled atop Mount Lafayette during a hailstorm, Mile 1826.4 northbound; 2014 thru-hike

26

PRESIDENTIAL RANGE

PINKHAM NOTCH TO CRAWFORD NOTCH

The Presidential Range is the crown jewel of New Hampshire's White Mountain National Forest—and some of the finest hiking on the Appalachian Trail. This multi-day hike will take you across several prominent mountains, including Mounts Madison, Jefferson, and Washington, the highest peak in the northeastern United States. Traversing the Presidential Range is a rite of passage. If you're a northbound thru-hiker, the Presidentials will prepare you for the mighty mountains of Maine that lie ahead. Plan enough time to enjoy long lunches—the landscape will undoubtedly enchant and enthrall you!

DISTANCE: 26.0 miles one way
DIFFICULTY: Strenuous due to steep, technical terrain and alpine conditions
TRAILHEAD GPS: 44.2569 / -71.2531
NEARBY TOWN: Gorham, New Hampshire
HIGHLIGHTS: Alpine hiking over multiple summits with endless views, scenic Lake of the Clouds

Lakes of the Clouds Hut, Mile 1858.7 northbound; 2013 thru-hike

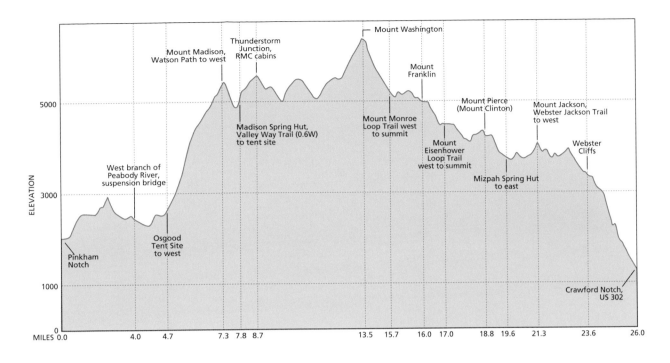

TIPS

- Contact the Appalachian Mountain Club if you are interested in staying in a hut. The AMC also has a hiker shuttle that you can schedule by calling (603) 466-2727. If you are thru-hiking, ask about the AMC Thru-hiker Pass program for discounts on campsites and other perks.
- Camp in designated sites or at least 200 feet from water, trails, and facilities.
- Do not camp above tree line (where trees are 8 feet tall or less) or within a Forest Protection Area (FPA).
- Fires are not permitted above tree line.
- Hiking the Presidential Range is great any time of year; however, you will likely have the best weather in the summer. Unfortunately, the weather can turn on an instant and can become extremely hazardous. The highest peak, Mount Washington, rising 6,288 feet, once held the world record for the highest recorded wind gusts. As always, it's best to be prepared for any sort of weather while hiking, but take special precautions while traversing the exposed ridgelines of the Whites.

MILEAGE MARKERS (NORTH TO SOUTH)

SECTION	MILES FROM SPRINGER MOUNTAIN	LANDMARK	ELEVATION (IN FEET)
0.0	1873.7	Pinkham Notch	2,050
0.7	1873.0	Peabody River	2,268
2.0	1871.7	Mount Washington Auto Road	2,747
4.0	1869.7	West Branch Peabody River; suspension bridge	2,300
4.7	1869.0	Osgood tent site to the west	2,545
7.3	1866.4	Mount Madison; Watson Path to the west	5,366
7.8	1865.9	Madison Spring Hut; Valley Way Trail (0.6 mile west) to tent site	4,800
8.7	1865.0	Thunderstorm Junction; RMC cabins	5,500
9.2	1864.5	Israel Ridge Path to RMC Perch Shelter (0.9 mile west; fee)	5,261
10.3	1863.4	Six Husband Trail (0.4 mile west) to Jefferson	5,356
10.7	1863.0	Mount Jefferson Loop Trail (0.3 mile west) to summit	5,402
11.5	1862.2	Mount Clay Loop to the east; Sphinx Trail to the east	5,021
13.5	1860.2	Mount Washington	6,288
15.7	1858.0	Mount Monroe Loop Trail west to summit	5,039
16.0	1857.7	Mount Franklin	5,004
17.0	1856.7	Mount Eisenhower Loop Trail west to summit	4,477
18.8	1854.9	Mount Pierce (Mount Clinton)	4,312
19.6	1854.1	Mizpah Spring Hut to the east, Nauman Campsite (fee)	3,800
21.3	1852.4	Mount Jackson; Webster Jackson Trail to the west	4,052
22.7	1851.0	Mount Webster (AT goes east and Webster Jackson Trail goes west.)	3,910
23.6	1850.1	Webster Cliffs	3,381
25.9	1847.8	Saco River; Saco River Trail to the east, Sam Wiley Trail to the west	1,270
26.0	1847.7	Crawford Notch; US 302	1,277

THE HIKE

Begin at Pinkham Notch, where you will find the AMC Visitor Center and Joe Dodge Lodge. From here, the trail gradually ascends while crossing several streams and side trails before climbing up to Mount Madison, the first presidential peak. Standing at 5,366 feet, Mount Madison boasts incredible views of what lies ahead. It is a grueling hike to the summit, so be sure to fill up on water at the stream near the mountain's base. At roughly 7 miles from the start, Mount Madison is a great place to rest your legs and grab a bite to eat before continuing to search for a place to pitch a tent. Madison Spring Hut is 0.5 mile from the summit, but don't count on staying there unless you have a reservation. The 3 miles between here and Mount Jefferson afford the best opportunity to find shelter for the night. A short distance off the AT, two shelters and two cabins maintained by the Randolph Mountain Club (RMC) are nestled within the woods. Each is an affordable overnight option and also dog-friendly.

The trail continues onward to Mount Jefferson (5,336 feet) and upward to the central peak within the presidential range, Mount Washington.

On your way to the 6,288-foot summit of Mount Washington, you will be richly rewarded the whole way with endless views on clear days. You will most likely see large crowds of people scattered about from a distance, all making their way up the highly prominent mountain peak. You will pass the cog railroad, or perhaps it will pass you, as it chugs its way up the

Madison Spring Hut, Mile 1858.7 northbound; 2013 thru-hike

Ryan "Samba" Underwood looking out at the Presidentials; 2013 thru-hike

Crossing the Mount Washington cog railroad, Mile 1860.6 northbound; 2013 thru-hike

side of the mountain. Don't be surprised if you see hikers baring their bottoms to passengers. Mooning the cog has been a longtime thru-hiking tradition. Some say it's to protest the noisy train; others say it's all for fun.

Once you reach the top, you will find more than exceptional views—and crowds of people. There is a weather station, observatory, museum, gift shop, eatery, and vehicles. Yes, cars, shuttles, and buses—oh, my! You just climbed this mighty beast while others took the auto road option. Try not to be sour while standing in line behind the well-rested non-hikers as you wait to get your photo with the sign.

Mount Washington summit, Mile 1860.2 northbound; 2013 thru-hike

Bad weather sign; 2013 thru-hike

Lakes of the Clouds Hut, Mile 1858.7 northbound; 2013 thru-hike

Lakes of the Clouds Hut, Mile 1858.7 northbound; 2013 thru-hike

You might feel a sense of entitlement wash over you, but remember that the auto road and the cog railway provide incredible opportunities of accessibility for many people who aren't able to hike.

Take your time taking in the views from an Adirondack chair while charging your devices. Then leave the bustle to enjoy more of what the Whites have to offer. Just south of here, you will come to a dreamy little spot called Lakes of the Clouds. Perched between Mounts Washington and Monroe is Lakes of the Clouds Hut, a popular lodging spot. You can often see beautiful alpine flowers growing around the lake.

From the hut, keep walking southbound across the top of Mount Franklin, bypassing a trail to Mount Eisenhower's summit. The trail gently descends to Mizpah Spring Hut as it passes over Mount Pierce. You will climb a short distance to Mount Jackson and roughly 1.5 miles to Mount Webster from the hut. Next, you will find yourself at Webster Cliffs. For the next 0.5 mile there are many incredible views overlooking Crawford Notch. The route is downhill from here. Crawford Notch is approximately 3 miles from the cliffs and where our hike concludes. End your adventure by catching a ride to the AMC Highland Center for a post-hike meal.

Lakes of the Clouds Hut, Mile 1858.7 northbound; 2013 thru-hike

Nick Browne, Ryan "Samba" Underwood, and Mellow Johnny leaving Mount Jackson; 2013 thru-hike

Wildcat Mountain Peak D, Mile 1876.7 northbound; 2013 thru-hike

Carter Notch Hut; 2013 thru-hike

Carter Dome, Mile 1880.08 northbound; 2013 thru-hike

TALES FROM THE TRAIL: LAKES OF THE CLOUDS*

By Gary Sizer ("Green Giant"), author and AT thru-hiker

The trail resumed at the other side of the clearing, and I walked into the tight tunnel of thick small pines. Rocky and too narrow for switchbacks, it went straight to the top. The rocks were mostly granite, light gray slabs that sparkled from the drizzle. Hiking through the pine boughs was like going through a car wash; my raincoat was saturated and my legs were soaked.

Thanks to all the effort I was exerting, at least I was warming up from the inside. Whenever I came to a brief break in the trees, my hood would slap my face on the windward side. A few times the white blazes were difficult to locate, often at the top of vertical scrambles.

The higher I climbed, the stronger the wind. I left the tree line for good somewhere near the peak called Mount Eisenhower. According to a sign, the actual summit was at the end of a loop trail. But I couldn't tell which way, because the wind had knocked the sign free of the pile of rocks that served as its base.

The gusts were coming from behind, so I had to lean backward while I walked forward. My poles kept slipping on the wet rocks and were only useful when they kept me from falling. I leaned back more and held them in front of me, scurrying along like some giant praying mantis.

Extreme weather on the AT PHOTO BY GARY SIZER

Then the trail switched back and the wind was in my face, blowing back my hood and filling my eyes and nose with water. I turned my head, and my ear filled too. I crouched, and tightened my hood. Then I squinted and leaned into the wind. Four more miles and another 1,000 feet up. This was insane. It was already getting dark.

Suddenly someone—or something—tackled me. That was the first explanation my brain could conjure when confronted with the question, *Why am I lying on my stomach and sliding toward that ledge?*

I rolled onto my back, and my pack snagged momentarily on a withered stump, slowing my slide somewhat. I grabbed another stump and stopped completely. I turned back to the trail, and again my hood flew back and my face was splashed by spray. Crouching again, I turned just in time to see my pack cover sail off into the abyss, a flapping green sacrifice. But not offered by me. Something the storm had just taken.

It's going to take me next, I thought. This is beyond insane—this is stupid. I have to get down, not up.

I crawled back to the trail and turned back the way I thought I'd come, hunching and crouching and clutching at my hood for half a mile before realizing I was still going up. Dejected but determined, I turned back again, for real this time. This time when I reached the point where I'd fallen, I was braced for the crosswind. Even so, it still almost took me.

Despite my steady exertion, I was no longer warming up from the inside. Even walking as fast as I could without slipping on the wet rocks, I was still shivering. The tree line brought moderate relief, but I knew I would have to repeat the steepest part of the day, only in reverse this time. Hand over hand in a freezing, sideways rain.

I did it.

When I stumbled back in through the front door of the Mizpah Spring Hut, the guy in charge, with his long beard and bald head, was there to greet me. "Wow! You're lucky to be here. Lakes of the Clouds just radioed down: They've got 70-mile-per-hour winds up there! You're not heading north, are you?"

He didn't recognize me. Of course he didn't. He saw dozens of hikers every day, and I hadn't looked like a drowned rat the first time we met.

"I am."

"Well, you're in luck," he said. "We have room for exactly one more work-for-stay. You should probably go put on dry clothes and eat some turkey first." He led me to the kitchen. "Here, eat this." He handed me some hot meat and a cup of tea.

I took it and thanked him as I stood dripping all over the kitchen floor. In a blink, Breakfast Club was on it with a mop. The guy in charge asked me my name and I told him. He introduced me: "Guys, this is Green Giant."

Two Pack was washing dishes with his back to us. He didn't turn around. "Never heard of him."

Ninja Mike handed me a towel. "You look like hell, brother."

*This story is an excerpt from Gary's book, *Where's the Next Shelter?*

by Amber Adams Niven ("Dandelion")

Just hike until ya get tired then pull over. . . . Take your time and enjoy everything.
—Birdman

White Mountain National Forest, better known as "the Whites," was an experience I will never forget. I can't wait to take my kids and watch their faces light up in wonder at the vast scenery. I hope they meet someone like Birdman.

Birdman was a plump 60-year-old man with stark white hair, a tall wooden walking stick, and a sort of kindness that radiated past his physical body. As I sat atop the grassy bald with Stacey and my brother, eating a lunch of peanut butter–and–honey tortilla, I could see him coming from a mile away in his bright red shirt.

He meandered along like he had nowhere to be at any certain time. It was a nice changeup, since most of the hikers we encountered were in a hurry. There is a fast-paced energy and a sense of competitiveness in the thru-hiker community that exhausts me. Many hikers are in a hurry, whether it's to get to the shelter before the day hikers take it over or to get to Katahdin before it closes for the winter. The clock seems to always be ticking for a thru-hiker. But as I watched Birdman get closer to us, I felt a shift within myself. He was clearly not worried about his pace or getting his miles in. He was in the moment, enjoying every step of the way.

Birdman was going north and bestowed some simple elderly wisdom upon us before we parted ways, continuing on our own journeys. But one thing he said stuck with me throughout my entire time on the Appalachian Trail: "Just hike until ya get tired, then pull over. . . . Take your time and enjoy everything."

The Whites had me love-swooned. I wanted to linger. I wanted to daydream with them. I wanted more time but felt the pressure to get the miles in. So when Birdman came along and reminded me that I was hiking to experience nature, I decided to do something radical. I planned a humble pace of 6 to 8 miles a day while traversing the Whites.

People talk about Trail Magic as these planned events of dropping a cooler of sodas in the stream for us hikers or setting up an extravagant cookout at a road crossing. These types of Trail Magic get the most attention and praise, but I'm here to say that there are more subtle and auspicious forms of Trail Magic that are just as good, if not better. Birdman was one of them. Birdman had no clue how much I needed to hear someone say, "Take your time and enjoy everything." He favored simplicity and spontaneity, which is something I was needing at that time in my hike. Here's to Birdman and taking it easy on the Appalachian Trail.

CREATURE FEATURE: GROUSE

Grouse are common in deciduous, mixed, and coniferous forests along the entire route of the AT. Hearing or seeing one of these chicken-like birds can be a startling event. The drumming of a male grouse as he beats his wings on his chest in an attempt to attract a mate sounds like a lawnmower starting up in the nearby woods. Grouse often crash out of the trees, making noises while running in a frenzy as if they have a broken wing. The hysteric flapping display is a tactic used to divert predators from the grouse's chicks.

Spruce grouse; 2013 thru-hike

FLORA FEATURE: PINK LADY'S SLIPPER

The pink lady's slipper has been New Hampshire's state wildflower since 1991. It can be seen growing in moist wooded areas of pine-oak forest. A member of the Orchid family, the enchanting, showy flower typically blooms late April through July, depending on elevation. It can be spotted along the entire Appalachian Trail, from Georgia to Maine. The soil conditions have to be just right for the pink lady's slipper to thrive. Like many orchids, the plant needs to have certain fungi present in the soil in order to survive and reproduce.

Pink lady's slipper; 2021

FEATURED SHELTER: LAKE OF THE CLOUDS HUT

Lake of the Clouds Hut is one of the most loved shelters on the entire AT. It's nestled between Mount Washington and Mount Monroe, with its namesake lake nearby. Perched high in the clouds on a rocky edge at 5,000 feet, the views are spectacular in every direction. The hut accommodates up to ninety people on a first-come, first-served basis. It closes for the spring and winter; however, a small basement room called "the Dungeon" stays open year-round for emergencies. Lake of the Clouds Hut is maintained by the Appalachian Mountain Club.

Lake of the Clouds Hut, Mile 1858.7 northbound; 2013 thru-hike

TRAILBLAZER SPOTLIGHT: MYRON AVERY

by Ricky J. Adams ("Chief Badweather")

To those who would see the Maine wilderness, tramp day by day through a succession of ever delightful forest, past lake and stream, and over mountains, we would say: Follow the Appalachian Trail across Maine. It cannot be followed on horse or a wheel. Remote for detachment, narrow for chosen company, winding for leisure, lonely for contemplation, it beckons not merely north and south but upward to the body, mind and soul of man.

—Myron Avery, *In the Maine Woods*, 1934

Benton MacKaye's revolutionary idea to connect the Appalachian Mountain range by trail could not have been done alone. It took an army of volunteers to create the Appalachian Trail and a very special person to form and manage all the trail clubs and organizations these volunteers would belong to. Myron Avery, born in Maine, had just the right credentials for the job—a strong work ethic, glowing education, and numerous contacts. He was the person most responsible for the completion of the Appalachian Trail in the 1930s and was also the strongest defender of the trail from the time he assumed chairmanship of the Appalachian Trail Conference in 1931 until his death in 1952.

In addition, he cofounded the Potomac Appalachian Trail Club in 1927 and helped birth a number of other trail maintaining clubs along sections of the trail south of the PATC territory in northern Virginia, Maryland, and southern Pennsylvania. He became the first person to hike the entire length of the trail, one section at a time. He is a legend with the Appalachian Trail community as the person who completed another dream for the good people of America.

Myron Avery FROM THE ATC ARCHIVES

On the AT in Maine; 2013 thru-hike

Maine

WELCOME TO MAINE!

Maine is home to majestic moose, ancient boulders, wild blueberries, old forests, steep mountains with amazing views, and pristine swimming ponds. Lakes and swampy bogs mingle with craggy mountains and isolated woodland paths. The trail is rugged and, at times, disappears; you have to be very careful not to lose sight of the white blazes. There are many famous "bucket-list" sections to experience in Maine, such as the state's tallest peak, Mount Katahdin, the Hundred Mile Wilderness, Avery Peak, Mahoosuc Notch, and crossing the Kennebec River by canoe ferry.

Maine has something for everyone, but beckons loudly for those who hunger for a deep, primal connection with nature. Hikers flock to Maine for its raw wildness. The remoteness and overall sense of serenity this section of the country emanates is what keeps hikers coming back. It's why Myron Avery worked so hard to make sure that Maine would be included in the Appalachian Trail. It's why Henry David Thoreau retreated to the state and chose to hike Katahdin multiple times.

The untouched wilderness, the way the moss grows on the fallen trees, the peaceful, pristine ponds, the songbirds, the damp boulders beneath your hands—everything in Maine invites a sense of wonder and stillness into your life unlike any other section of the trail. Although Maine is remote, you will find you are never truly alone. Foxes and porcupines roam campsites after dark. Chipmunks and squirrels scurry throughout the forest floor. Moose ramble around looking for twigs to munch on. There is much activity going on; even though you may not see it, you can feel the presence of life within the Maine woods.

Thru-hikers tend to move slower in Maine. Northbounders are soaking in the last of their journey, while Southbounders are practicing patience and self-compassion with themselves as their hiker legs develop.

> Maine is beautiful but slippery, rugged and wet. It's like someone waters it before you get there every day.
> —Carl Miller, *From War to the A.T.: Finding the Best of Humanity* (appalachiantrail.org)

New Hampshire–Maine border sign, Mile 1911.3 northbound; 2013 thru-hike

Goose Eye Mountain; 2013 thru-hike

I personally found that there is something special about how these woods awaken the naturalist within. Whether it's the challenging terrain or simply Maine's natural beauty, something invites us to linger, to stay a little bit longer, and look a little bit deeper. Maine has us crouched down on our hands and knees, studying the translucent, candy cane–like Indian pipe and savoring every bite of wild blueberries. She inspires us to observe the behavior of river otters and how beavers construct their dams. She has us scrutinizing every foot- and handhold as we make our way through Mahoosuc Notch. Maine shakes us up and enlivens us to become curious, alert, and focused hikers. Maine brings us back to the purpose of hiking the Appalachian Trail, as Benton MacKaye ever so transcendentally once said, "to walk, to see, and to see what you see."

27

MAHOOSUC NOTCH: MAINE'S NATURAL JUNGLE GYM

GRAFTON NOTCH, ME 26 TO GORHAM, NEW HAMPSHIRE

Here is your chance to get off your feet and onto all fours! Mahoosuc Notch presents the most challenging and time-consuming section of the Appalachian Trail. The boulder-filled obstacle course creates a one-of-kind hiking experience that many call a "hiker's jungle gym." If you embrace the terrain, you could find yourself having a blast—getting in touch with your inner kid as you slide on your backside down rocks and squeeze through tight stone crevices. Many narrow passageways require you to remove your pack and crawl through on your hands and knees. It takes most hikers longer than expected to finish this section. A calm and relaxed spirit is needed to get you through "the Notch." But don't worry, the trail will help keep you cool with cold misty vapors that rise from below. It's so shaded in some areas that you can find pockets of ice lingering in the Notch, even in the middle of summer.

DISTANCE: 30.4 miles one way on AT plus a short walk to parking area (0.25 mile west)
DIFFICULTY: Strenuous due to technical terrain and quick elevation changes
TRAILHEAD GPS: 44.5897 / -709467
NEARBY TOWN: Gorham, New Hampshire
HIGHLIGHTS: Natural jungle gym—enough said!

Mahoosuc Notch south end, Mile 1917.8 northbound; 2013 thru-hike

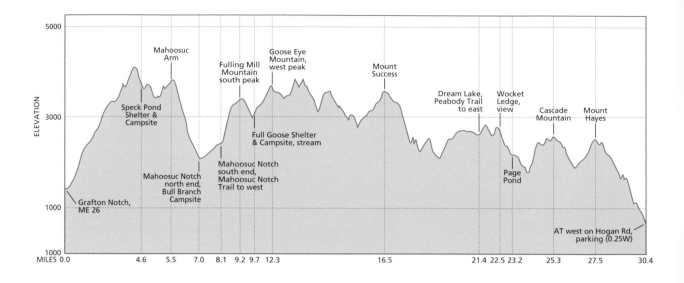

ELEVATION

5000

3000

1000

1000

MILES 0.0   4.6   5.5   7.0   8.1   9.2 9.7   12.3   16.5   21.4 22.5 23.2   25.3   27.5   30.4

Grafton Notch, ME 26

Speck Pond Shelter & Campsite

Mahoosuc Arm

Mahoosuc Notch north end, Bull Branch Campsite

Mahoosuc Notch south end, Mahoosuc Notch Trail to west

Fulling Mill Mountain south peak

Full Goose Shelter & Campsite, stream

Goose Eye Mountain, west peak

Mount Success

Dream Lake, Peabody Trail to east

Wocket Ledge, view

Page Pond

Cascade Mountain

Mount Hayes

AT west on Hogan Rd, parking (0.25W)

TIPS

- Although the hike through Mahoosuc Notch is only about 1 mile, allow at least 3 hours one way.
- The best times to hike are generally June through October—Mahoosuc Notch can be especially hazardous in snow or ice.
- Be sure to carry adequate water, warm clothing and rain gear, high-energy food, a first-aid kit, and your whistle.
- Day hikers can reach Mahoosuc Notch by several side trails; one is the Notch Trail, which starts on a spur road off Success Pond Road and climbs 2.5 miles upward to meet the AT. Continuing northbound will bring hikers through Mahoosuc Notch.
- Fires are illegal outside of designated overnight sites.

Nick Browne and Ryan "Samba" Underwood traversing Mahoosuc Notch; 2013 thru-hike

MILEAGE MARKERS (NORTH TO SOUTH)

SECTION	MILES FROM SPRINGER MOUNTAIN	LANDMARK	ELEVATION (IN FEET)
0.0	1925.9	Grafton Notch; ME 26	1,495
0.9	1925.0	Stream	2,392
1.2	1924.7	Eyebrow Trail to the west	2,507
3.5	1922.4	Trail intersection; side trail (0.3 mile easl) to Old Speck summit and observation tower	4,066
4.6	1921.3	Speck Pond Shelter and Campsite; water at caretaker's yurt	3,429
4.8	1921.1	Speck Pond Brook	3,420
5.5	1920.4	Mahoosuc Arm	3,770
6.0	1919.9	Spring	3,265
7.0	1918.9	Mahoosuc Notch north end; Bull Branch Campsite	2,116
8.1	1917.8	Mahoosuc Notch south end; Mahoosuc Notch Trail to the west	2,447
9.2	1916.7	Fulling Mill Mountain south peak	3,395
9.7	1916.2	Full Goose Shelter and Campsite; stream	2,999
10.7	1915.2	Goose Eye Mountain, north peak	3,678
11.9	1914.0	Goose Eye Mountain, east peak	3,790
12.3	1913.6	Goose Eye Mountain, west peak	3,823
13.7	1912.2	Mount Carlo	3,565
14.1	1911.8	Carlo Col Shelter and Campsite (0.3 mile west); water	3,210
16.5	1909.4	Mount Success	3,565
19.3	1906.6	Gentian Pond Shelter and Campsite (0.2 mile east); water	2,164
21.4	1904.5	Dream Lake; Peabody Trail to the east	2,633
22.5	1903.4	Wocket Ledge; view	2,697
23.2	1902.7	Page Pond	2,233
24.2	1901.7	Trident Col Campsite (0.2 mile west); spring on side trail	2,020
25.3	1900.6	Cascade Mountain	2,631
27.5	1898.4	Mount Hayes	2,555
29.5	1896.4	Brook	1,217
30.4	1895.5	AT west on Hogan Road; parking (0.25 mile west)	769

Taking a break inside a tunnel; 2013 thru-hike

Nick Browne traversing Mahoosuc Notch; 2013 thru-hike

Ryan "Samba" Underwood traversing "the Notch"; 2013 thru-hike

THE HIKE

Begin at the trailhead at Grafton Notch and trek southbound on the AT. Starting in the south allows you to complete the more-challenging terrain with fresh legs. Next, start the long climb up Old Speck Mountains, gaining 2,850 feet in roughly 3.5 miles. A short spur trail leads to an observation tower at the summit. Descend to Speck Pond, where there is a shelter and campsite. See the caretaker to pay the overnight fee if you want to camp here. Continue hiking upward along the Mahoosuc Arm and then downward for about 1 mile to the north end of Mahoosuc Notch.

OK, you made it! Welcome to "the Notch." It's time to slide on your backside, shimmy through the narrow openings, and make the best of nature's playground. The terrain stays challenging for the next mile. Be careful, as the rocks are often wet and slippery. Remember, you can still find ice here in summer!

Once you reach the south end of the Notch, push onward to Full Goose Shelter and Campsite. It's just under 2 miles from the Notch, but it's no walk in the park. Pace yourself through the jungle gym, because the final push to the shelter is a 1,000-foot climb up the south peak of Fulling Mill Mountain. Once you reach the top, the shelter is 0.5 mile away. From there, the trail climbs across the north and east peaks of Goose Eye Mountain before reaching its 3,823-foot summit. Views are spectacular in this stretch, so be sure to take your time and enjoy the scenery. Next, the trail dives down and climbs rapidly back up to Mount Carlo, where a shelter and campsite are just beyond. Push on another 0.5 mile to cross the border into New Hampshire. Mount Success is roughly 2 miles away and a great spot to enjoy lunch with a view. Finally, descend the mountain and hike a couple more miles to Gentian Pond Shelter, an excellent place to camp (although it sits a bit off the AT) before heading into Gorham the next day.

The AT travels up to Dream Lake and over Wocket Ledge, where you can catch a view before descending to Page Pond. Next is a climb up and down Cascade Mountain, then another climb up and over Mount Hayes. Mount Hayes rises more than 2,500 feet and offers a nice view of the surrounding mountains. Enjoy some trail mix and rest a while before your final descent of roughly 3 miles.

When you are ready to depart, follow the white blazes until you reach Hogan Road; walk 0.25 mile west to the parking area.

Nick Browne passing his pack through a hole at "the Notch"; 2013 thru-hike

AT blaze in Maine; 2013 thru-hike

The AT in Maine; 2013 thru-hike

TALES FROM THE TRAIL: BECOMING "DANDELION"

By Amber Adams Niven ("Dandelion")

It was a clear sunny day in southern Maine. Three weeks into our thru-hike, and I still didn't have a trail name. My entire crew had theirs. Stacey was dubbed FireSquirrel for his obsession with the flame and his squirrel-like nature of constantly moving. Tucker was given the name Tall-Milk during our first meal after the 100-mile wilderness. Luke was named Tree Frog for no apparent reason, and Dad was Chief Badweather because he was a newly retired police chief, and every time he went into the woods, well, the bad weather followed.

I wanted to be in the club. Receiving a trail name is a sacred rite of passage. Some people don't like using trail names; others love them. I was one of those people who looked forward to the day that I received my trail name. Since we were traveling south, we had fewer interactions with other hikers, thus giving people fewer opportunities to provide us with a name. I thought long and hard about this new name I would take on. I wanted it to feel original and meaningful. But mostly, it just needed to feel right. You can't force a good trail name.

We had just topped out on Baldpate Mountain, four weeks into our thru-hike, when I suddenly lost my balance and fell backward to the ground as a great gust of wind came sweeping through. Dad laughingly joked about how I looked like a wildflower blowing in the wind. It was rather strange.

After my graceful topple, we hiked down into a valley and came to a clearing where there had to have been a million white, feathery dandelions swaying in the breeze. It was a sight that stopped you in your tracks. I met Dad's eyes, and we both knew it—I was to be called "Dandelion." Watching the weedy flowers dancing in the wind was like Earth celebrating my newfound trail name with me. That night, I signed the trail register as "Dandelion" and later wrote in my journal: "Happy to be living on the trail and bending in the wind."

28

BIGELOW MOUNTAIN RANGE

STRATTON POND ROAD TO EAST FLAGSTAFF ROAD

Want to get out of the woods and up above tree line? We recommend hiking in the Bigelow Range to summit multiple peaks with spectacular views in just one day. The Bigelow Mountain Range, located in the 36,000-acre Bigelow Preserve, comprises a compact group of seven summits, including Avery Peak, West Peak, The Horns, Cranberry Peak, and Little Bigelow Mountain. This hike is challenging, with steep inclines, but you will enjoy incredible views of Flagstaff Lake and other surrounding mountains such as Sugarloaf and Croker Mountain on good-weather days. In addition, there are several places to camp, including Horns Pond Lean-to, Avery Memorial Campsite, Safford Notch Campsite, and Little Bigelow Lean-to.

DISTANCE: 16.7 miles one way
DIFFICULTY: Difficult due to heavy elevation gain and some steep spots
TRAILHEAD GPS: 45.1034 / -70.3569
NEARBY TOWN: Stratton, Maine
HIGHLIGHTS: Incredible scenery from multiple peaks and amazing camping spots

Horns Pond; 2013 thru-hike

TIPS

- Fires are illegal outside of designated overnight sites.
- Alpine vegetation is fragile. Please stay on-trail, especially above tree line.
- Camping is not permitted above tree line in the Bigelow Preserve.
- Be aware of the weather. Carry equipment and gear for cold temperatures year-round.

DID YOU KNOW?

The AT crosses the Kennebec River in Caratunk, just 40 miles from the South end of the 100 Mile Wilderness. At 400 feet wide, the Kennebec River is the most formidable unbridged crossing along the entire Appalachian Trail. Use the ferry service to cross. Don't try to ford this swiftly flowing river without it!

MILEAGE MARKERS (SOUTH TO NORTH)

SECTION	MILES FROM SPRINGER MOUNTAIN	LANDMARK	ELEVATION (IN FEET)
0.0	2004.9	ME 27	1,391
0.8	2005.7	Stratton Brook Pond Road	1,250
0.9	2005.8	Stratton Brook; footbridge	1,206
1.8	2006.7	Cranberry Stream Campsite	1,350
3.2	2008.1	Bigelow Range Trail (0.2 west) to Cranberry Pond	2,400
5.1	2010.0	Horns Pond Lean-to; water	3,158
5.6	2010.5	South Horn	3,831
7.7	2012.6	Bigelow Mountain west peak	4,145
8.1	2013.0	Avery Memorial Campsite; spring (0.2 mile n) on AT, Fire Wardens Trail to the east	3,838
8.4	2013.3	Avery Peak	4,090
9.6	2014.5	View	2,851
10.4	2015.3	Safford Notch Campsite (0.3 mile east)	2,254
12.6	2017.5	View	2,941
13.6	2018.5	Little Bigelow Mountain	3,010
15.3	2020.2	Little Bigelow Lean-to; water	1,795
16.7	2021.6	East Flagstaff Road	1,200

Back of Horns Pond; 2013 thru-hike

THE HIKE

Begin at the trailhead on ME 27 and begin hiking north on the AT. The terrain gently traverses through a forest, over streams, and past the Cranberry Stream Campsite before gaining in elevation. Follow the white blazes as you climb steadily to the Horns Pond Lean-to at 3,158 feet. There is a spring located here, as well as tent sites. It's an excellent spot to camp before the strenuous terrain ahead. From the shelter, the trail shoots up to the tip of South Horn. It's a steep climb, gaining elevation quickly in less than 0.5 mile. From South Horn, the trail travels down and back up to reach the west peak of Bigelow Mountain at 4,145 feet. Views abound as you make your way to Avery Peak, less than 1 mile away, with vistas equally as good.

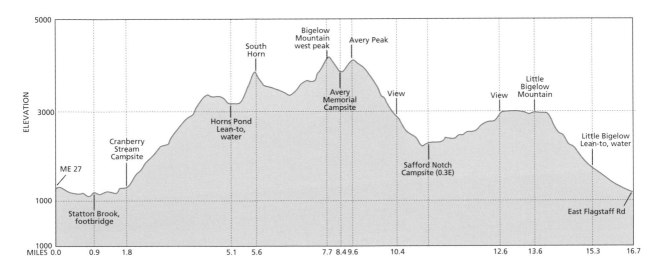

Once you reach Avery Peak, at 4,090 feet, you will start to descend for 2 miles until you come to a side trail for the Safford Notch Campsite at 2,254 feet. Although it's a bit off the AT, the campsite is a nice place to stay before continuing to Little Bigelow Mountain. Next, hike uphill from the Safford Notch Campsite for roughly 3 miles to views atop Little Bigelow Mountain. As you descend, a shelter about half-way down makes a beautiful spot to rest and eat lunch. Swimming spots are nearby. East Flagstaff Road, where this hike ends, is roughly 1.5 miles away.

View from Bigelow Mountain west peak, Mile 2012.6 northbound; 2013 thru-hike

Avery Peak trail sign, Mile 2013.3 northbound; 2013 thru-hike

Avery Peak memorial to Myron H. Avery, Mile 2013.3 northbound; 2013 thru-hike

View of Avery Peak from Little Bigelow Mountain; 2013 thru-hike

Trail blaze toward end of Bigelow Range hike; 2013 thru-hike

Kennebec River ferry service, the only moving blaze on the AT, Mile 2041.5 northbound;
2013 thru-hike

29

THE 100 MILE WILDERNESS

MONSON, MAINE, TO ABOL BRIDGE

The 100 Mile Wilderness is the most isolated and inaccessible section of the Appalachian Trail, stretching from the village of Monson to the edge of Baxter State Park. The name alone, "100 Mile Wilderness," creates a sense of hesitation; it seems to illuminate a journey that is not easy, convenient, or comfortable. If you do a quick internet search, you might find such descriptions as "one of the most remote trails in the United States," "uninhabited," "seldom traveled," "harsh contrasts," and "unforgiving to the ill-prepared."

A walk through the 100 Mile Wilderness may evoke feelings of fear and anxiety for some. However, for others, the idea of a trek through the Maine woods is music to their ears. It's a sort of homecoming that our backcountry roots long for—a vast stretch of forests, waters, and mountain peaks that seem to beckon to those who want to reconnect with the wild and with the self. However, don't expect to be alone for too long. You are bound to see others retreating to the wilderness, as this has become a popular section of the trail.

Welcome sign, southern end of the 100 Mile Wilderness, Mile 2078.6 northbound; 2013 thru-hike

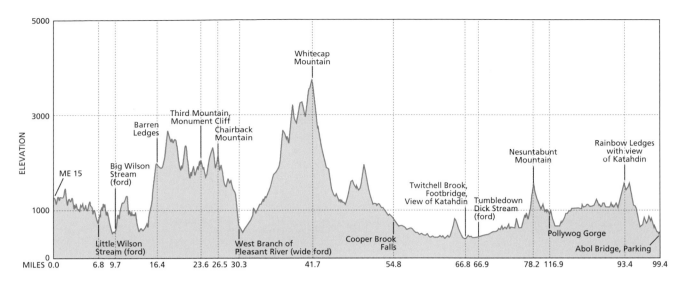

DISTANCE: 99.4 miles one way

DIFFICULTY: Strenuous; not for the faint of heart due to the isolation and length of the trip. Please be well conditioned and have experience before attempting this hike.

TRAILHEAD GPS: 45.3311 / -69.5355

NEAREST TOWN: Monson, Maine

FEATURES: Remote wilderness with incredible views and swimming ponds; chances for solitude

TIPS

- Most backpackers complete this stretch in a week; however, it's encouraged to carry ten days' worth of supplies. Some hikers complete it quicker, especially northbound thru-hikers, who have developed their robust and capable hiker legs. It's strongly encouraged to be prepared with an adequate food supply and proper equipment.
- There are plenty of water sources.
- Fires are illegal outside of designated overnight sites.
- Alpine vegetation is fragile. Please stay on-trail, especially above tree line.
- With this section being at the doorstep of Baxter State Park, you can easily extend your trip to include climbing Maine's tallest peak, Mount Katahdin. Please be aware of the special regulations within Baxter Park if you choose to visit. More information on regulations and current conditions are available at the ATC visitor center in Monson, Maine, open June to early October (207-573-0163; email: monsonvisitorcenter@appalachiantrail.org).

MILEAGE MARKERS FOR LEAN-TOS AND CAMPSITES (SOUTH TO NORTH)

SECTION	MILES FROM SPRINGER MOUNTAIN	LANDMARK	ELEVATION (IN FEET)
3.0	2081.6	Leeman Brook Lean-to	1,060
10.4	2089.0	Wilson Valley Lean-to	963
15.1	2093.7	Long Pond Stream Lean-to	909
19.1	2097.7	Cloud Pond Lean-to	2,467
26.0	2104.6	Chairback Gap Lean-to	1,982
35.9	2114.5	Carl A. Newman Lean-to	1,906
37.7	2116.3	Sidney Tappan Campsite	2,436
43.1	2121.7	Logan Brook Lean-to	2,399
46.7	2125.3	East Branch Lean-to	1,254
54.8	2133.4	Cooper Brook Falls Lean-to	940
62.7	2141.3	Antlers Campsite	500
66.2	2144.8	Potaywadjo Spring Lean-to	636
70.5	2149.1	Nahmakanta Stream Lean-to	533
76.3	2154.9	Wadleigh Stream Lean-to	674
84.4	2163.0	Rainbow Stream Lean-to	1,001
88.2	2166.8	Rainbow Spring Campsite	1,100
95.9	2174.5	Hurd Brook Lean-to	703

THE HIKE

Begin at the trailhead in Monson, Maine, and start hiking north on the AT. (If you prefer to end your trip in town, you can start at the Abol Bridge on Golden Road near Baxter State Park [45.8352 / -68.9693] and hike southbound.) Your first day in the wilderness is a nice walk with little elevation change and plenty of opportunities to get water as you pass multiple streams. Wilson Valley Lean-to is roughly 10 miles away and is a great first stop. The trail climbs from there to the Barren Ledges and then another 1.8 miles to the top of Barren Mountain. The views are outstanding, even from the ledges, which are shy of 2,000 feet. Keep the white blazes in sight; many are painted on the rocks below. Next, the trail descends steeply across Fourth Mountain Bog and then travels up and over Fourth Mountain. Onward lies Chairback Gap Lean-to, a nice spot to camp before climbing the mountain in the morning.

DID YOU KNOW?

This remote section was colorfully labeled "the 100 Mile Wilderness" in the 1980s by Stephen Clark, longtime editor of the *Appalachian Trail Guide to Maine*, to alert hikers to be well prepared due to the fact that no resupply points exist along this remote stretch of trail.

Stephen "Animal" Whipple at Little Wilson Falls, Mile 2085.1 northbound; 2013 thru-hike

Creek crossing; 2013 thru-hike

Fourth Mountain Bog, Mile 2099.2 northbound; 2013 thru-hike

Hiker fording the West Branch Pleasant River, Mile 2108.9 northbound; 2013 thru-hike

Make your way across Gulf Hagas Mountain to Sidney Tappan Campsite. Enjoy a night here before tackling White Cap Mountain the next day. The next 4 miles are strenuous as you hike up and down West Peak and Hay Mountain before summiting White Cap, your last significant climb of the trip. As you descend the mountain, you will be rewarded with views of Mount Katahdin in the distance. Logan Brook Lean-to is located on the way down and offers a picturesque setting with tumbling cascades—a lovely spot for lunch. From the shelter, continue your downhill stride to

View of Katahdin from Pemadumcook Lake, Mile 2145.4 northbound; 2013 thru-hike

View of Katahdin from Nesuntabunt Mountain, 16 miles as a bird flies to the summit, Mile 2156.8 northbound; 2013 thru-hike

View of Katahdin from Nesuntabunt Mountain, Mile 2156.8 northbound; 2013 thru-hike

the East Branch of Pleasant River. Here is your opportunity to rinse off before you wade across and continue onward. From here, hike to Cooper Brook Falls Lean-to—and be glad you are halfway through the wilderness. The remainder of the hike stays at low elevation and on reasonably gentle terrain. If it rains, however, be prepared to hike through mud and water. Antlers Campsite is roughly 8 miles from the shelter. It sits along the shores of Jo-Mary Lake and is a serene place to camp. If you decide to push on, there are two more lean-tos ahead: Potaywadjo Spring and Nahmakanta Stream.

Farther north, the trail passes Nahmakanta Lake and Wadleigh Stream Lean-to before you grab another view of Mount Katahdin from the top of Nesuntabunt Mountain. Enjoy more scenic walking as you pass ponds and streams. Keep your eyes peeled for beavers playing in the water. Rainbow Stream Lean-to is a fantastic spot to spend your last night in the wilderness. You may recognize the iconic log footbridge in front of the shelter. Hike 9 miles to enjoy a lunch on Rainbow Ledges, with incredible views of Maine. Soak in the last of your wilderness journey before hiking 6 miles to the Abol Bridge parking area. This point is the northern border of the 100 Mile Wilderness and where the adventure ends unless you feel like trekking to Mount Katahdin. In that case, hike on!

Rainbow Stream Lean-to, Mile 2163.0 northbound; 2013 thru-hike

View of Katahdin from Rainbow Ledges, Mile 2172.0 northbound; 2013 thru-hike

Little Niagara Falls, Baxter State Park, Mile 2184.4 northbound; 2013 thru-hike

by Amber Adams Niven ("Dandelion")

I woke up to the sound of my dad's voice carrying off in the distance. "See y'all up the trail," he said so calmly, like it was just another day in our lives. It wasn't, though, because today was the day we would officially start our southbound journey. At the moment, I had no idea how many times I would wake up to those exact words throughout our adventure. It's how every morning began.

I watched with squinty eyes as he walked off and disappeared into the foggy wilderness. The sun was starting to peek through the trees. "What time is it?" I asked as I peeled my bandana off my face. I slept with it over my mouth for fear of spiders crawling down my throat. "It's 4:15," Stacey answered as he began to crawl out of his sleeping bag.

I sat up and took a look around the shelter. My younger brother, Tucker, and cousin, Luke, were on my left, still sleeping. The coals in the fire pit in front of us were still

Katahdin Falls; 2014 thru-hike PHOTO BY AMBER NIVEN

warm. I watched the faintest line of smoke drift into the sky as my thoughts shifted into a daydream, fantasizing about all the mornings I would wake up and watch dancing embers from last night's fire. *This is it; today we summit Katahdin.*

The click of Stacey's hip belt snapped me out of my morning daze. I quickly shimmied out of my sleeping bag and began to lace up my boots. We both adjusted our trekking poles and set foot on the trail. "We're heading out," I called out to the boys. Luke raised his head slightly with his eyes half-open. He couldn't get any words out, but I was glad to know that he heard us leaving. Stacey and I hit the privy and met back up at the trail register. It marked when hikers left for Katahdin and when they returned. We signed in at 4:25 a.m. Dad was just 10 minutes ahead of us. I was glad he got a bit of a head start. He likes to meander. "Are you ready for this?" Stacey asked. Without hesitation, I answered, "I am." So we took off into the Maine woods with a hunger for adventure. That's why I was hiking, for the experience of a lifetime and to commune with nature. People hike the Appalachian Trail for myriad different reasons. I was out to have a good time in the woods with my family.

I knew hiking the Appalachian Trail would change me—you know, kind of like how a nice long vacation does. But I didn't think it would be a transformative experience that could change the core of my being or shift my steps in life the way it did. I thought I would return home refreshed, renewed, and inspired. I would go back to work with stories to tell and maybe even new tips to share with my hiking friends. However true that was, the trail had more in store for me, and I was about to get a taste of it during the strenuous hike up Katahdin.

That early morning in June marked a new beginning of a whole new phase of life for me. As I huffed and puffed up the trail, I grew tired and discouraged. My face became pale and my breathing shallow. I was quick to doubt if I could make the journey. *Can I keep up with my manly hiking family? Am I out of my element?* Finally, I stopped to catch my breath, and the mist of Katahdin Falls landed on my face like a kiss from my ancient ancestors. A sign. My first, of what ended up being many personal messages from the natural world I would receive throughout my hike, reminding me that I belong here. That the trail is in me. Just like John Muir says in his essay "Mountain Thoughts": *"The sun shines not on us but in us. The rivers flow not past but through us."* I felt connected to nature. I felt the kind of connection I did when I was a child, carrying around a big chunk of rose quartz that I considered a best friend. I felt a sense of home even though I was more than a thousand miles away from Tennessee. If the trail is a part of me, just as I am a part of it, then, indeed, I have what it takes to make the journey. No matter how slow or fast or what direction I decide to travel, I belong out here in these woods.

So with the misty kiss from the falls, I continued onward. Just like that, I was changed. I walked past Thoreau Spring and got a rush of energy as I felt the presence of one of my favorite writers and naturalists. I couldn't help but think about the many feet that had traveled across the same rocky path searching for something—adventure, solitude, answers. I was part of them now—the seekers. So not only did I learn that I had a place in the wilderness, I also realized that I was part of a community—a vast web of hikers, ridge walkers, explorers, trailblazers, and soul seekers that stretched out far and wide. I wondered how many of them got the same message of belonging that I had received at the falls.

I reached the crest of Mount Katahdin on a cool, clear day. Unfortunately, some people are not so lucky. The mountain often gets surrounded by clouds, making any sort of view impossible. Feeling a sense of gratitude, humility, and personal accomplishment, I outstretched my arms and gave Maine the biggest air hug. I bathed in the sensation with a full heart. I felt my spirit expanding, making room for all the memories, friends, and life lessons I would gather on my journey. I welcomed the new beginning as a sacred rite of passage, a milestone marking my reconnection with nature and with myself.

Amber Niven feeling on top of the world at Mount Katahdin; 2014 thru-hike

30

MOUNT KATAHDIN

KATAHDIN STREAM CAMPGROUND TO MOUNT KATAHDIN, BAXTER PEAK

Soaring to a grand height of 5,268 feet, Mount Katahdin, the highest peak in Maine, truly lives up to its name. "Katahdin," named by the local Penobscot Indians, means "the Greatest Mountain" in Algonquian.

It marks the northern terminus of the Appalachian Trail and is the crown jewel of Baxter State Park. This short but strenuous hike packs a lot of punch with picturesque views of Katahdin Stream Falls, life-size granite boulders, and a rewarding finish with 2.4 miles of hiking above tree line. The trail is hardly on a smooth path—it's mostly rocks, roots, and mud. Expect to use your hands and some upper body strength to pull yourself over boulders.

Much of this hike is above tree line, so be prepared for all types of weather. However, don't worry so much about hiking on a perfect weather day. Whether it's cloudy, windy, too hot, or brilliant blue skies, most hikers will agree that simply standing atop the summit makes the effort worthwhile.

DISTANCE: 10.4 miles out and back
DIFFICULTY: Strenuous due to challenging, technical terrain and steep elevation gain
TRAILHEAD GPS: 45.8872678, -68.9967133
NEARBY TOWN: Millinocket, Maine
HIGHLIGHTS: Unforgettable views, rock scrambling, beautiful waterfall, photo ops

Ascending Katahdin; 2013 thru-hike

TIPS

- Trails to Katahdin close in October and don't open again until the snow has melted (typically late May–June).
- Blackflies swarm in the summer. Consider bringing a bug net.
- Hand-over-hand climbing and scrambling are required.
- Fires are illegal outside of designated overnight sites.
- Alpine vegetation is fragile. Please stay on-trail, especially above tree line.
- Baxter State Park requires all hikers to obtain an AT Hiker Permit card at the Katahdin Stream Campground ranger station before hiking to Katahdin. Hikers must also sign in and out at the trailhead register before and after their hike. For park information and reservations, call (207) 723-5140 May–October. Making reservations in advance is strongly recommended.
- Inclement weather may prompt trail closures. Weather reports along with "trail status and alerts" are posted at the ranger station daily at 7 a.m.

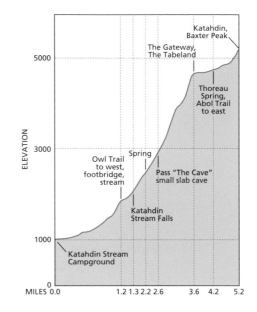

Ascending Katahdin; 2013 thru-hike

MILEAGE MARKERS (SOUTH TO NORTH)

SECTION	MILES FROM SPRINGER MOUNTAIN	LANDMARK	ELEVATION (IN FEET)
0.0	2187.9	Katahdin Stream Campground	1,087
1.2	2189.1	Owl Trail to the west; footbridge, stream	1,532
1.3	2189.2	Katahdin Stream Falls	1,610
2.2	2190.1	Spring	2,383
2.6	2190.5	"The Cave," small slab cave	2,859
3.6	2191.5	The Gateway, the Tableland	4,531
4.2	2192.1	Thoreau Spring; Abol Trail to the east	4,620
5.2	2193.1	Mount Katahdin, Baxter Peak	5,268

THE HIKE

Begin at the trailhead, located at Katahdin Stream Campground. Hike on the AT for roughly 1 mile as the trail gradually ascends through the forest and presents a view of picturesque Katahdin Falls. This is a great place to snap a photo while you catch your breath.

Pass the slab cave formed by two large rocks as you begin to steadily gain in elevation. Continue the upward climb along a rocky spine to the "Gateway" as it transitions into the "Tableland," a flat, vast expanse with amazing views. The hike is strenuous, and you will have to use hand-rungs to pull yourself up and over the massive boulders. From the Tableland you are at roughly 4,500 feet, with nearly 700 feet left to climb to reach Katahdin. The views are endless on clear days and make for a nice distraction from all the effort. Take your time and enjoy the rock scrambling.

Thoreau Spring, at 4,620 feet, is the last landmark before you begin your final

View from summit of Baxter Peak on the trail, Katahdin's shadow across the landscape with the full moon behind, Mile 2193.1 northbound; 2013 thru-hike

View of Katahdin's shadow and full moon from the summit, Mile 2193.1 northbound; 2013 thru-hike

push to Baxter Peak, the northern terminus of the Appalachian Trail. Finally at the top of Mount Katahdin, drink in the incredible scenery. From the 5,268-foot summit, you can see the Knife Edge ridge, views of the surrounding mountains, and lakes in the valley below. There is a lot to take in on Katahdin, especially if you just walked more than 2,000 miles to get there.

"Hikers remember their emotions on the mountain more than its unique geographical features," says Jennifer Pharr Davis in her memoir, *Becoming Odyssa*. "It is a peak that has launched dreams and fulfilled goals. It is a summit that will change your life."

Be sure to take a photo at the iconic wooden sign before descending, following the white blazes to Katahdin Stream Campground.

Katahdin trail sign, Mile 2193.1 northbound; 2013 thru-hike

The blue-blazed Knife Edge Trail, a secondary route off the summit, Mile 2193.1 northbound; 2013 thru-hike

View descending Mount Katahdin; 2013 thru-hike

View descending Mount Katahdin; 2013 thru-hike

TALES FROM THE TRAIL: COMPLETING A LIFELONG DREAM

by Joshua Niven

On September 19, 2013, around 5:30 in the morning, I reached the summit of Katahdin, accompanied by Nick "Brownie" Browne, Jonathon "Mellow Johnny" Harvey, and Ryan "Samba" Underwood.

We woke up at the long-distance hiker shelter known as "The Birches," located at the mountain base in Baxter State Park. It was 2 a.m., still dark outside. My goal was to photograph the full moon and some stars before the early sun lit up the sky, making them all disappear. I knew trying to reach the summit before the sun broke the horizon would be a race against time, but we were determined.

We hit the trail and used our head-lamps to light the way. Once we reached the alpine zone, the full moon lit up all the rocks about 2 miles into the hike, and we turned off our headlamps. As we climbed up the steep, vertical shelf of boulders, the whipping winds were nearly strong enough to throw you off the mountain. About 0.5 mile from the summit, I noticed the sun was starting to breach the horizon with its orange and pink intensity. Realizing that I might not make it to the sign before the stars disappeared, I asked Samba to let me pass and proceeded to run ahead.

At the time, running seemed like a good idea. Although, about twenty steps into my sprint, I got thrown to the ground on all fours. I turned around and saw Samba laughing. Running is not something I rec-ommend anyone do on Mount Katahdin, especially at night. However, if I wanted to get my pictures, it was necessary, so I got myself together and continued to run. I recall screaming "Come on" over and over,

Joshua signing in at the trailhead in Baxter State Park before hiking to Mount Katahdin; 2013 thru-hike

Katahdin trail sign at Baxter Peak (shadow of Katahdin across the landscape caused by the sun to my back and the full moon on the horizon in front), Mile 2193.1 northbound; 2013 thru-hike

frustrated at the rate at which the sun was rising. Finally, I reached the summit, threw my bag down, pulled out all my equipment, and began to take my photos.

After 20 minutes of shooting, I took a break to breathe life back into my hands. The cold weather had made them lock up. As I continued to warm up, I saw the guys approaching the summit; it finally hit me: The journey was over. We did it! The view of the Katahdin summit sign as the sun was shooting across the land on my right at the same time the full moon was blasting on my left, with Katahdin's shadow draped across the landscape pointing at the full moon, was among one of the greatest views I have ever seen. The feeling of accomplishment and being lucky enough to be here on this mountain at a full-moon sunrise will remain embedded in my brain for the rest of my days.

Almost a decade later, reviewing my account of my summit on that morning in 2013, I had no idea what the trail had done to me. The decision to embark on this adventure shaped the next ten years of my life. It led to my meeting the love of my life, moving to the woods, and starting my family. Deciding to thru-hike the Appalachian Trail is the best decision I have ever made, and I am eternally grateful for everything it has done for me and my family.

Self-portrait at the Katahdin summit, Mile 2193.1 northbound; 2013 thru-hike

Nick Browne, Ryan "Samba" Underwood, Mellow Johnny, and myself minutes after finishing our journey across the entire Appalachian Trail, Mile 2193.1 northbound; 2013 thru-hike

What is most striking in the Maine wilderness is the consciousness of the forest, with fewer open intervals or glades than you had imagined. Except the few burnt lands, the narrow intervals on the rivers, the bare tops of the high mountains, and the lakes and streams, the forest is uninterrupted.
—Henry David Thoreau, *The Maine Woods*

Henry David Thoreau PUBLIC DOMAIN

Henry David Thoreau was an American naturalist and writer best known for his book *Walden*, in which he shares his reflections from his two years living alone in a cabin by the shore of Walden Pond. Thoreau was one of the first environmental writers in American culture. As a major figure in the transcendentalist movement, along with his close friend Ralph Waldo Emerson, Thoreau inspired others to get back to nature and to value the wilderness in the American landscape.

In 1846 he set out to climb Mount Katahdin in order to "come face-to-face with the raw soul of nature." Although he never reached the top of the mountain due to poor weather, he helped popularize the hike. Thoreau Spring, located 1 mile from Baxter Peak, is named in his honor. Before his ascent of Katahdin, Thoreau had climbed other peaks such as Mounts Washington, Greylock, and Lafayette.

DID YOU KNOW?

Moose are herbivores. The word "moose" comes from an Algonquian term meaning "eater of twigs." Moose prefer to feed on leaves, bark, and twigs from trees and shrubs because their massive size makes it difficult for them to bend down to eat grasses.

The wilderness is a place of rest—not in the sense of being motionless, for the lure, after all, is to move, to round the next bend. The rest comes in the isolation from distractions, in the slowing of the daily centrifugal forces that keep us off balance.
—David Douglas, *Wilderness Sojourn*

Perhaps Maine's greatest gift is that of intimacy—a sort of intimacy where we can seek and find a real kinship with nature.

The section of the Appalachian Trail that winds through the luscious Maine woods allows us to get up close and personal with untouched lands, elusive species, and even ourselves. Some places demand moments of solitude and reflection, like the many glistening ponds or monumental mountain tops, encouraging us to meet our true nature as we set our gaze outward and contemplate our place in such a marvelous world. Maine gives us the space to unearth parts of ourselves we might not have ever discovered had we not bravely set foot in the wild. The pieces of

View of Katahdin from Nesuntabunt Mountain, Mile 2156.8 northbound; 2013 thru-hike

ourselves we hide in fear of being separated from society. Or the pieces that feel like they don't belong at all.

Most of us share a fear of loneliness that can be traced back to our deep human ancestry. In today's modern world, we are hyper-connected, yet we are still starving for meaningful relationships. Even when people surround us, we feel alone. Little devices in our pocket promise connection to friends and family, but we often feel anything but true companionship when engaging with technology. Could this mean "our senses need to be put back in order"? This sort of faux connection is confusing.

While in nature, we often find that our senses are all out of sorts due to living in a modern world where the natural pace is far too busy and the stress is far too high. Our priorities are quickly turned around by just trying to make ends meet. Many times, work comes before family, and convenience comes before health, even though we would like to have it the other way around. Indeed, this is what American naturalist and writer John Burroughs is referring to when he proclaimed, "I go to nature to be soothed and healed, and to have my senses put in order."

The wilderness in Maine is a personal and ecological sanctuary that makes way for such profound insight into our daily lives. We can think, see, hear, and even sense more clearly when free of modern distractions and noises. Isn't that why so many of us retreat to nature? For it is when we are in the remote wilderness that moments of clarity wash over us and, to our amazement, we realize that although we are, by definition, "isolated," we are never truly alone.

Life is buzzing and blooming all around us. Yet we have to slow down and get quiet to notice just how much we are a part of the larger picture. Standing atop Maine's Mount Katahdin, looking out at the valley, one can only feel grateful for such a beautiful, thriving piece of the world. A place to remember that we are a part of nature. A place to have our "senses put in order."

Mary Oliver says it best in her book *Upstream*:

I would say that there exist a thousand unbreakable links between each of us and everything else and that our dignity and chances are one. The farthest star and the mud at our feet are a family; and there is no sense in honoring one thing, or a few things, and then closing the list. . . . We are at risk together, or we are on our way to a sustainable world together. We are each other's destiny.

CREATURE FEATURE: THE MAINE MOOSE

Catching a glimpse of the massive and majestic Maine moose is a cherished experience. An icon of the Maine woods, this creature can best be spotted during dusk or dawn, often found swimming in lakes to cool off or feeding in boggy areas. The largest of the deer family, a moose can stand up to 7 feet tall and run up to 35 miles per hour. Moose have poor eyesight but excellent hearing and a keen sense of smell. Both males and females make calling sounds during mating season. Moose typically live alone.

Maine moose, Baxter State Park; 2015 PHOTO BY MICHAEL "EAGLERUNNER" BEGANSKY

FLORA FEATURE: PITCHER PLANT

Maine's boggy areas are home to the visually striking pitcher plant. The red-veined leaves form a perfectly shaped container designed to hold water and enzymes, giving the plant its name. Enticing nectar lures insects into the "pitcher," and bristles help trap them inside, allowing bacteria and enzymes to break down their bodies for the plant to absorb. You may also encounter pitcher plants at Ethan Pond in New Hampshire.

Pitcher plant in Maine; 2013 thru-hike

FEATURED SHELTER: COOPER BROOK FALLS LEAN-TO

Cooper Brook Falls is an incredible place to camp while trekking through the 100 Mile Wilderness, especially if you are hiking in summer. Named for the falls located in front of it, this lean-to is perfect for those in search of a swimming hole. There is room for six people in the lean-to, and a tent site is nearby. Cooper Brook Falls Lean-to is maintained by the Maine Appalachian Trail Club.

Cooper Brook Falls Lean-to, Mile 2133.4 northbound; 2013 thru-hike

By Ricky J. Adams ("Chief Badweather")

Dear Maine,

You have my respect for being a true "wilderness." Your mucky bogs (some knee-deep) have slowed our pace. Your blackflies and mosquitoes have fed off us for days. Your many river crossings are cold and deep. Your trails are wet, rocky, full of roots, and some are straight up and straight down.

Our equipment has suffered from breaks, rips, tears, and smells just plain ol' plumb nasty. Our bodies are swollen, bruised, bit, scraped, cut, and blistered, and smell just plain ol' plumb nasty.

Ricky J. Adams on the AT in Maine; 2014

After 281 miles, we are leaving so that you can greet the next bunch of hikers. We will remember the days of hiking through you for the rest of our lives. Seeing equipment from hikers that went before us scattered all over the first 25 to 50 miles made us nervous. What was the rest of the trail going to do to us? The clothes, tents, tarps, packs, sleeping bags, pots, pans, cups, bowls, axes, machetes, food, water bottles, rain gear, cold-weather gear, and more were lying everywhere on the side of the trail. It looked like the dark forest just chewed up the lone hikers and spit them out on different parts of the path. I had given a name to these "lone hikers". . . "Divorced Hikers". . . since the trail had taken everything.

Our memories will be of the days we topped out on mountains like White Cap; The Bigelows; Old Blue; Old Speck; The Baldpates; The Horn; the granddaddy, Katahdin; and my favorite, Avery Peak. Sleeping at Antlers Campsite and the other big ponds and lakes while watching the beavers play and hearing the loons at night will never be forgotten.

The people of Maine have treated us very well. May God bless those on and around the Appalachian Trail.

Ricky J. Adams crossing the Maine–New Hampshire border with his son Tucker, daughter Amber, and Stacey McDermid

Glossary of Trail Terms

Aqua-blaze: To bypass a section of the AT by watercraft (e.g., canoe, kayak, raft).

AT: Appalachian National Scenic Trail.

ATC: Appalachian Trail Conservancy, the organization that oversees the maintenance of, conservation on, and advocacy for the preservation of the AT. Their headquarters is in Harpers Ferry, West Virginia.

CCC: Civilian Conservation Corps, a voluntary public work relief program that operated from 1933 to 1942. The CCC helped build the AT and many shelters.

Chostle: A hostel housed in a church.

Flip-flop: To thru-hike the entire AT but in a noncontiguous manner.

GAME: Acronym used by northbound thru-hikers meaning "Georgia to Maine"; often written as "GA→ME."

Gorp: Nickname for "trail mix."

Hiker legs: Strong legs capable of climbing mountains and long walks.

HYOH: "Hike your own hike."

NOBO: "Northbounder"; someone traveling north on the AT.

Purist: Someone who hikes every tiny inch of the AT, careful not to miss a single blaze.

Section hikers: Those who hike the AT in pieces, often over the course of several years.

Shakedown: Combing through your gear, determining what is absolutely necessary for your hike. Often done by an expert hiker.

Slackpacking: Hiking without a full pack during a multiday trip. Generally, "slackpackers" hand off their pack to someone while they complete a section of the AT unencumbered by their backpack.

SOBO: "Southbounder"; someone traveling south on the AT.

The bubble: A large group of hikers traveling in the same direction. Commonly used when talking about "NOBO and SOBO thru-hiker bubbles."

"The trail provides": A phrase meaning that in emergencies or difficult situations, a hiker's needs somehow will be met.

Thru-hiker: Someone who hikes the entire AT in one season.

Trail Angel: Someone who shows kindness to hikers, often by giving rides into town or gifting food or cold drinks without asking anything in return (see Trail Magic).

Trail Magic: Any act of kindness or gift bestowed on hikers, including water, meals, transportation, lodging, even money.

Trail maintainer: Someone, usually a volunteer, who cares for a section of the AT.

Trail name: A special nickname adopted by long-distance backpackers; a tradition on the AT and many other trails.

Trailblazer: Someone who hikes. Someone who sets their own path or makes way for others.

Tramily: Short for "Trail family," referring to those you spend a significant amount of time hiking with.

Triple Crown: Achievement of thru-hiking the Appalachian Trail (AT), Pacific Crest Trail (PCT), and Continental Divide Trail (CDT).

Yellow-blazing: Using the highway to bypass a section of trail, either by walking, hitchhiking, or driving. "Yellow blaze" is a reference to the yellow dashes on the road.

Zero Day: A day when 0 miles are hiked. Generally used when thru-hikers take a "day off" in town.

From the beginning, the trail's existence and success were dependent upon the goodwill of countless individuals—notably volunteer workers and cooperative landowners.

—Benton MacKaye

Appalachian Trail Maintaining Clubs

CONTACT YOUR LOCAL CLUB FOR VOLUNTEER OPPORTUNITIES.

Appalachian Mountain Club
outdoors.org

Georgia
Georgia Appalachian Trail Club
georgia-atclub.org

North Carolina
Carolina Mountain Club
carolinamountainclub.org

Nantahala Hiking Club
nantahalahikingclub.org

Tennessee
Smoky Mountains Hiking Club
smhclub.org

Tennessee Eastman Hiking & Canoeing Club
tehcc.org

Virginia
Mount Rogers Appalachian Trail Club
mratc.pbworks.com

Natural Bridge Appalachian Trail Club
nbatc.org

Old Dominion Appalachian Trail Club
olddominiontrailclub.onefireplace.org

Outdoor Club at Virginia Tech
ocvt.club

Piedmont Appalachian Trail Hikers
path-at.org

Potomac Appalachian Trail Club
patc.net

Roanoke Appalachian Trail Club
ratc.org

Tidewater Appalachian Trail Club
tidewateratc.com

Maryland
Mountain Club of Maryland
mcomd.org

Pennsylvania
AMC—Delaware Valley Chapter
amcdv.org

Allentown Hiking Club
allentownhikingclub.org

Batona Hiking Club
batona.wildapricot.org

Blue Mountain Eagle Climbing Club
bmecc.org

Cumberland Valley Appalachian Trail Club
cvatclub.org

Keystone Trails Association
kta-hike.org

Susquehanna Appalachian Trail Club
satc-hike.org

York Hiking Club
yorkhikingclub.com

Delaware
Wilmington Trail Club
wilmingtontrailclub.org

New York / New Jersey
New York–New Jersey Trail Conference
nynjtc.org

Connecticut
AMC—Connecticut Chapter
ct-amc.org

Massachusetts
AMC Western Massachusetts
amcberkshire.org/at

Vermont
Green Mountain Club
greenmountainclub.org

New Hampshire
Dartmouth Outing Club
outdoors.dartmouth.edu

Randolph Mountain Club
randolphmountainclub.org

Maine
Maine Appalachian Trail Club
matc.org

Appalachian Trail Communities

Explore beyond the trail by visiting the hiker-friendly towns that surround the AT. The following towns are currently recognized as an "A.T. Community" by the Appalachian Trail Conservancy for their devotion to protecting and promoting the AT.

Georgia
Blairsville—Union County
Dahlonega
Gilmer County
Helen—White County
Hiawassee—Towns County

North Carolina
Fontana Dam
Franklin
Hot Springs

Tennessee
Roan Mountain
Unicoi County

Virginia
Abingdon
Berryville—Clarke County
Bland County
Buena Vista
Damascus
Front Royal—Warren County
Glasgow
Harrisonburg
Luray—Page County
Marion—Smyth County
Narrows
Nelson County
Round Hill

Troutville
Pearisburg
Waynesboro

West Virginia
Harpers Ferry and Bolivar

Pennsylvania
Boiling Springs
Delaware Water Gap
Duncannon
Greater Waynesboro area
Wind Gap

New Jersey
Blairstown Area—Warren County

New York
Harlem Valley (Dover & Pawling)
Warwick

Massachusetts
Cheshire
Dalton
Great Barrington
North Adams

Vermont
Manchester
Norwich

New Hampshire
Gorham
Hanover

Maine
Kingfield
Millinocket
Monson
Rangeley

Sources

Adkins, Leonard M. *Nature of the Appalachian Trail: Your Guide to Wildlife, Plants, and Geology*, second edition. Menasha Ridge Press, 1998.

Anderson, Larry. *Peculiar Work: Writing about Benton MacKaye, Conservation, Community.* Quicksand Chronicles, 2012; revised 2013.

Appalachian Trail Conservancy. "ATC History." Appalachian Trail Conservancy, 2021. appalachiantrail.org/our-work/about-us/atc-history/. Accessed August 5, 2021.

Cark, Sandra H. B. *Birth of the Mountains: The Geological Story of the Southern Appalachian Mountains*. CreateSpace Independent Publishing Platform, 2014.

Earl Shaffer Foundation. *Walking with Spring*. Appalachian Trail Conference, 2004.

Foster, Steven, and James A. Duke. *Peterson Field Guide to Medicinal Plants and Herbs of Eastern Central North America*, third edition. Houghton Mifflin Harcourt, 2014.

Friends of Peace Pilgrim. *Peace Pilgrim: Her Life and Work in Her Own Words*. Ocean Tree Books, 1982.

Johnson, Thomas R. *From Dream to Reality: History of The Appalachian Trail*. The Appalachian Trail Conservancy, 2021.

Jones Decker, Sarah. *The Appalachian Trail: Backcountry Shelters, Lean-tos, and Huts*. Rizzoli, 2020.

MacKaye, Benton. "An Appalachian Trail: A Project in Regional Planning." *Journal of the American Institute of Architects*, 1921.

Miller, David. *The A.T. Guide*. Wilmington, NC: AntiGravityGear, LLC, 2021.

Montgomery, Ben. *Grandma Gatewood's Walk: The Inspiring Story of the Woman Who Saved the Appalachian Trail*. Chicago Review Press Incorporated, 2014.

National Geographic Society. *The Appalachian Trail*. The National Geographic Society, 1972.

Opler, Paul A. *Peterson First Guide to Butterflies and Moths of North America*. Houghton Mifflin Harcourt Publishing Company, 1994.

Pittsburgh Post-Gazette. "It's All Downhill From Here." *Appalachian Trail Adventure: From Georgia to Maine, A Spectacular Journey on the Great American Trail*. Longstreet Press, Inc., 1995.

Roosevelt, Franklin D. *The public papers and addresses of Franklin D. Roosevelt. 1940 volume, War-and aid to democracies: with a special introduction and explanatory notes by President Roosevelt.* Macmillan, 1941.

Underwood, Paula. *Franklin Listens When I Speak.* San Anselmo: A Tribe of Two Press, 1997.

Weidensaul, Scott. *Mountains of the Heart: A Natural History of the Appalachians,* twentieth anniversary edition. Fulcrum Publishing, 2016.

About the Authors

Joshua Niven was born in Germany and raised in the hills surrounding Charlotte, North Carolina. He graduated from the Savannah College of Art and Design with a degree in photography in 2012. He completed the Appalachian Trail on foot in 2013 and self-published a photography book with more than 150 images he made during his thru-hike. In addition to creating artwork, Joshua owns and operates Asheville Fine Art Printing, where he helps reproduce and facilitate other artists' work. He lives in Madison County, North Carolina, with his wife and children.

Amber, Joshua, River, Indie, and Mundo at the ATC in Harpers Ferry; 2021

Amber Adams Niven grew up in the heart of the Great Smoky Mountains, where she developed a deep love for nature and hiking at an early age. At 26, she backpacked more than 1,400 miles of the Appalachian Trail from Maine to Virginia with her family. Amber's journey on the AT resulted in a move to western North Carolina, a few years of soul-searching, and a venture in creative entrepreneurship. Amber is a lifelong journal keeper, certified yoga teacher, and mother of two children. This is her first book.

The End

Well, folks, we made it to the end. If you experienced the book from cover to cover, then congratulations on your literary thru-hike. We hope you had a blast. Putting this together has been an adventure in itself. In the words of Jerry Garcia, "What a long, strange trip it's been."

We hope to see you on the AT someday. Until then, hike on!